THE NEW GROVE GUIDE TO
Verdi and His Operas

THE NEW GROVE GUIDE TO

VERDI

and His Operas

Roger Parker

OXFORD
UNIVERSITY PRESS

OXFORD
UNIVERSITY PRESS

Oxford University Press, Inc., publishes works that
further Oxford University's objective of excellence
in research, scholarship, and education.

Oxford   New York
Auckland   Cape Town   Dar es Salaam   Hong Kong   Karachi
Kuala Lumpur   Madrid   Melbourne   Mexico City   Nairobi
New Delhi   Shanghai   Taipei   Toronto

With offices in
Argentina   Austria   Brazil   Chile   Czech Republic   France   Greece
Guatemala   Hungary   Italy   Japan   Poland   Portugal   Singapore
South Korea   Switzerland   Thailand   Turkey   Ukraine   Vietnam

Copyright © 2007 by Oxford University Press

Published by Oxford University Press, Inc.
198 Madison Avenue, New York, NY 10016
www.oup.com

Oxford is a registered trademark of Oxford University Press

Library of Congress Cataloging-in-Publication Data
Parker, Roger, 1951–
The New Grove guide to Verdi and his operas / Roger Parker.
    p. cm.—(New Grove operas)
Includes bibliographical references and index.
ISBN 978-0-19-531313-0
ISBN 978-0-19-531314-7 (pbk.)
1. Verdi, Giuseppe, 1813–1901. Operas.   2. Opera—Italy—19th century.   I. Title.
ML410.V4P156   2007
782.1092—dc22
[B]   2006034980

9   8   7   6   5   4   3   2   1
Printed in the United States of America
on acid-free paper

Contents

PREFACE   vii

LIST OF ILLUSTRATIONS   xi

Chronology of Verdi's Life and Operas   3
Life and Works   9

{ The Operas

Oberto, conte di San Bonifacio   57
Un giorno di regno   59
Nabucco   61
I Lombardi alla prima crociata   67
Ernani   72
I due Foscari   79
Giovanna d'Arco   84
Alzira   88
Attila   93
Macbeth   98
I masnadieri   105
Jérusalem   110
Il corsaro   115
La battaglia di Legnano   119
Luisa Miller   124
Stiffelio   130
Rigoletto   136
Il trovatore   144
La traviata   152
Les Vêpres siciliennes   159
Simon Boccanegra   165
Aroldo   173
Un ballo in maschera   177
La forza del destino   185
Don Carlos   195
Aida   206

Otello   214
Falstaff   223

GLOSSARY   231
INDEX OF ROLE NAMES   237
SUGGESTED LISTENING GUIDE   243
SUGGESTED FURTHER READING   251

Preface

In 2001 we reached the centenary of Verdi's death; all around the world people competed with each other to mark the event. In most countries Verdi's operas already form the bedrock of the operatic repertory, but 2001 saw still more revivals. It is likely that virtually all of his twenty-seven operas were staged somewhere during the year (indeed, during any other recent year). Yet this was just one side of the industry. As if not content with the deluge of performance activity (and the deluge of trivia 'branding' the centennial that came in its wake), the Italian government set up a National Committee to oversee the centenary celebrations. Among many other events, there was a huge exhibition in Milan's Palazzo Reale, and a week-long international academic conference devoted exclusively to the composer—the first phase in Verdi's home town of Parma, the second in New York City and New Haven. Publications rained down from all sides, and show no signs of stopping. As this book demonstrates, the Verdi show must, it seems, go on and on.

It is well to recall that the composer has not always enjoyed such attention. In the years immediately following his death, only about eight of his most popular operas kept their places in the repertory. All the early works, and quite a few of the later ones, had fallen out of fashion, at least in the most prestigious houses of Western Europe and North America. The enthusiasm for Wagner (and for Meyerbeer before that) encouraged many to pronounce Verdi's dramatic language somehow too naïve. Particularly as the elite values of musical modernism began to take hold, he was also damaged by being far too popular with the masses ('barrel-organ music' was a favourite epithet). But this cultural tide gradually turned, as so often happens. Verdi began to make new headway in Germany during the 1920s and 1930s, where a reaction against Wagner, together with a vogue for resurrecting old operas, developed into a full-scale 'Verdi renaissance'. From then on, his operas have marched on ever more triumphantly. The global expansion of opera in the 1980s and 1990s (the age of 'Pav' and the Three Tenors, when even Michael Bolton had a try at 'Celeste Aida') was spearheaded by Verdi, and more of his operas are now in the standard repertory than at any time in the past. We live, in other words, in an ever-enlarging Verdi museum.

In this sense of a constantly expanding universe, it is interesting to look at how ideas about the composer are still changing. Those old clichés about Verdi urging revolutionaries to the barricades in 1848 still have some currency; but for the most part they are now being laid to rest— understood as the legacy of the later nineteenth century in Italy, when nostalgia for past heroic deeds prevailed and a need to create national monuments in a new and fragile nation state was pressing. What has come in place of these easy equations, though, are a collection of harder ques- tions: questions about the precise meaning of Verdi's operas for nineteenth- century audiences, whether in Italy or (increasingly) almost everywhere else. Evidence here is hard to come by, and of its nature fragmentary. But there is now an emerging understanding that opera was indeed a powerful social force, not so much because of any politically coded messages it might contain but through its ability to expose in emotionally arresting ways some important changes taking place along the fault lines of contem- porary human society: in the new strains on family relationships brought about by urbanization, for example; or in new negotiations between the power of the state and the rights of the individual. These issues are doubly hard to discuss, of course, because inevitably they seem also to impinge on *us*: they make us think about how we now learn from opera, and why the uncompromising directness of Verdi's musical language seems to appeal to us so powerfully.

The topic of Verdi and *us*, though, probably brings to mind for many the continuing debate about contemporary staging practice: the tendency of many modern producers aggressively to update and otherwise 'interfere' with the opera in order, they claim, to make it more relevant to our present condition. There is much to be said on both sides of this debate, of course, but an interesting new perspective comes from thinking of the issue in his- torical terms. Verdi, at least in later life, was a staunch conservative when it came to staging. He wanted all productions of his operas, everywhere, to conform to a fixed conception: particularly about how performers should move around on stage but also about visual and other details. To this end, he encouraged his publisher, Ricordi, to imitate the French practice of re- leasing production books (in Italy called *disposizioni sceniche*) that went into considerable detail about the 'correct' performance. Such books exist for most of the later operas (from *Les Vêpres siciliennes* on), and could of course become part of our text for the operas.

Would we want this? Studying the *disposizioni sceniche* at our historical distance suggests that the answer would not be simple—few of us today would be happy to see (for example) the chorus move all in step, with regimental discipline about the stage; or for singers to make a series of elaborate (and, to us, melodramatic) gestures as they sing. But there's a more basic issue here; even in Verdi's time there was clearly a tension between modern theatrical practice (what would be acceptable in spoken theatre productions) and what was expected on the operatic stage. By the time of *Otello*, for instance, Verdi voiced concerns about the new fashion for 'realistic' acting in the spoken theatre; and, true to his prejudices, the *disposizione scenica* for *Otello* presents in many ways a rearguard action in the debate—an attempt to turn the theatrical clock back several decades. But what Verdi thought of as 'modern' would seem to us today hopelessly old-fashioned; so what should we do to be true to his conception? He wanted the clock put back 30 or so years; but if we followed him precisely, we would now put it back 150 years. Perhaps a more sensible option would be to regard an *authentic* staging as one that engaged with the production books not by slavishly aping their every pronouncement but by following their lead in constructing a *dialogue* between today's visual culture and the composer's musical text: by engaging, in other words, in a continual process of redefinition, as today becomes tomorrow and the next day.

But what about the next one hundred years? Will the vast Verdi caravan, with its expanding museum and its continuing debates about staging and other performance practices, roll serenely on during the twenty-first century? Will there be another spate of revivals, another National Committee and another transcontinental conference in 2101? None of us will be around to find out, alas; but there are reasons to think that, at the least, the caravan's course will change and its primary colours will adapt to new circumstances. For one thing the public image of Verdi, the picture that was constructed (with his help) during the latter half of his long life, and that retained such remarkable currency during the twentieth century, is at last showing some cracks. I have already mentioned Verdi's changing reputation as a political force within nineteenth-century Italian nationalism; but there is also that more personal image—endlessly recycled in the 2001 celebrations—of the genial old man with the white beard, the flowing artist's cravat, and the farmer's battered felt hat. We are now beginning to construct a more complex, and perhaps rather darker, picture: a composer who was far from naïve in his intellectual attitudes and who could, particularly in later life, be uncompromising, even cruel, to those closest to him. Again, how this new understanding will impact on our perception of the operas is hard to say; at the least, though, it is unlikely to make them less alive to modern sensibilities, to the mass of us who now wish to gain new meanings from these works created so long in the past.

A more serious obstacle to the caravan, though, is the fact that the Verdi renaissance has now been followed by further operatic rebirths: of Rossini, Donizetti, and—in particularly full flood today—of Handel. These movements have made the repertory more crowded than it used to be; but, even more important, they have brought in their wake new types of star singers, ones whose techniques are honed on the demands made of them by Handel or by Rossini, and thus—almost by definition—unable to sustain the rigours of Verdian vocal writing. Certain Verdi operas—*Il trovatore* is a classic case—now seem almost impossible to cast at the highest international level; if the vogue for lighter, more flexible voices continues, then more and more his operas will become virtually unperformable.

So it may be that 2001, when Verdi and his operas were performed and celebrated wherever we looked, marked a high point in the composer's fortunes. In a vocal world where countertenor David Daniels enjoys the position once occupied by, say, tenor Franco Corelli, the writing would seem to be on the wall. But one shouldn't exaggerate. Verdi's most hardy operas, those that have never left the repertory since the day of their first performance, have somehow survived many passing fashions. They will continue to pose questions that each generation will learn to answer in its own fashion. And there is no doubt that some of the early works have now forged, or rather re-forged, their repertory status: they have now become obligatory ports of call for every operatic pilgrim. If this is true, then the present book will inevitably be superseded in the years to come; and that circumstance, at least, should for all of us (the present author included) be a cause for celebration.

List of Illustrations

PLATE 1   Wolfgang Gussmann's stark but dramatic set for the Netherlands Opera's production of *Don Carlos*, 2004. Courtesy of The Netherlands Opera.

PLATE 2   Title-page of the first edition of the vocal score *Rigoletto* (Milan: Ricordi, 1851), with a vignette showing the opening scene of Act 3; the costumes are identical to Ricordi's published *figurini* for the opera. The Eda Kuhn Loeb Music Library of the Harvard College Library.

PLATE 3   Michael Levine's strikingly modern set for the Netherlands Opera's production of *Rigoletto*, 2004. Courtesy of The Netherlands Opera.

PLATE 4   Franco Zeffirelli's opulent set and Raimonda Gaetani's costumes for the Metropolitan Opera's production of *La traviata*, 2006. (Jonas Kaufmann as Alfredo and Angela Gheorghiu as Violetta) Photo: Ken Howard/Metropolitan Opera.

PLATE 5   Gianni Quaranta's large-scale set for the Metropolitan Opera's production of *Aida*, 2005. Photo: Marty Sohl/Metropolitan Opera.

PLATE 6   A photograph of Act 2 scene iii, of an early-twentieth-century production of *Aida*. Mary Evans Picture Library.

PLATE 7   This engraving of the opening scene of *Otello*, first performed 1887, depicts a set that follows Verdi's set directions almost exactly. Mary Evans Picture Library.

PLATE 8   This 1994 production of *Otello* at the Verona Arena, Italy, also closely follows Verdi's original set directions and uses the space of an outdoor set. Credit: Gianfranco Fianello/ArenaPAL.

PLATE 9   This 2005 production of *Otello* at the Glyndebourne Festival, with sets designed by Peter Hall, breaks with Verdi's set directions for a more modern look. Credit: Clive Barda/ArenaPAL.

PLATE 10   Photograph of Giuseppe Verdi by Nadar, 1860s. Biblioteca e Archivio del Museo Teatrale alla Scala.

THE NEW GROVE GUIDE TO

Verdi and His Operas

Chronology of Verdi's Life and Operas

{ 1813

9/10 OCT   Born at Roncole, near Busseto, in the Duchy of Parma, northern Italy, to Carlo and Luigia Uttini Verdi

11 OCT   Baptized Giuseppe Fortunino Francesco

{ 1818

Begins musical studies in Busseto

{ 1822

Becomes organist at the church at Roncole

{ 1825

Sponsored by the merchant Antonio Barezzi; begins studies with Ferdinando Provesi, director of the municipal music school in Busseto

{ 1832

Moves to Milan, initially applying to attend the Milan Conservatory; when he is rejected, enrols for private study with Vincenzo Lavigna, *maestro concertatore* at La Scala

{ 1835

Returns to Busseto, having completed his lessons with Lavigna

{ 1836

Becomes *maestro di musica* in Busseto; writes an opera called

Rocester (later revised as *Oberto*) that he hopes to have performed in Milan

4 MAY   Marries Margherita Barezzi

{ 1838

Resigns his post in Busseto

{ 1839

Moves to Milan

17 NOV   *Oberto, conte di San Bonifacio*, Milan, La Scala

{ 1840

18 JUN   Death of Margherita Barezzi

5 SEP   *Un giorno di regno*, Milan, La Scala

{ 1842

9 MAR   *Nabucco*, Milan, La Scala

Giuseppina Strepponi (1815–97) creates the role of Abigaille and, some years later, becomes Verdi's lifelong companion

{ 1843

11 FEB   *I Lombardi alla prima crociata*, Milan, La Scala

{ 1844

9 MAR   *Ernani*, Venice, La Fenice

3 NOV   *I due Foscari*, Rome, Argentina

{ 1845

15 FEB   *Giovanna d'Arco*, Milan, La Scala

12 AUG   *Alzira*, Naples, San Carlo

{ 1846

17 MAR   *Attila*, Venice, La Fenice

{ 1847

14 MAR   *Macbeth*, Florence, Pergola

22 JUL   *I masnadieri*, London, Her Majesty's

AUG   Takes up residence in Paris, which become the base of his operations until mid-1849

26 NOV   *Jérusalem*, Paris, Opéra

{ 1848
APR   Returns briefly to Milan during the revolutions, which, for a few months, drive the Austrians from the city

25 OCT   *Il corsaro*, Trieste, Grande

{ 1849
27 JAN   *La battaglia di Legnano*, Rome, Argentina

AUG   Returns from Paris to live in Busseto

8 DEC   *Luisa Miller*, Naples, San Carlo

{ 1850
16 NOV   *Stiffelio*, Trieste, Grande

{ 1851
11 MAR   *Rigoletto*, Venice, La Fenice

MAY   Establishes a permanent home with Strepponi at Sant'Agata, near Busseto

{ 1853
19 JAN   *Il trovatore*, Rome, Apollo

6 MAR   *La traviata*, Venice, La Fenice

OCT   Takes up residence in Paris, where he will largely base himself for the next two years

{ 1855
13 JUN   *Les Vêpres siciliennes*, Paris, Opéra

DEC   Returns to Sant'Agata

{ 1857
12 MAR   *Simon Boccanegra*, Venice, La Fenice

16 AUG   *Aroldo*, Rimini, Nuovo

{ 1859
17 FEB   *Un ballo in maschera*, Rome, Apollo

29 AUG   Verdi and Giuseppina Strepponi marry at Collonges-sous-Salève in Savoy

{ 1861
MAR   Proclamation of the Kingdom of Italy. At the invitation of the Prime Minister, Camillo Cavour, Verdi becomes a member of the first parliament

NOV   Departs for St Petersburg

{ 1862
FEB   Leaves St Petersburg, travels to Paris and London
AUG   Departs again for St Petersburg
10 NOV   *La forza del destino*, St Petersburg, Imperial

{ 1863
         During the first part of the year, travels extensively, spending
         time in Madrid and Paris.

{ 1865
21 APR   *Macbeth* (revised version), Paris, Lyrique

{ 1866
JUL   Takes up residence again in Paris.

{ 1867
11 MAR   *Don Carlos*, Paris, Opéra; leaves immediately afterward to re-
         turn to Italy

{ 1868
JUN   Verdi returns to Milan after a twenty-year absence; on the
         death of Rossini, proposes to Ricordi a *Messa per Rossini* to
         be written by leading Italian composers of the day; composes
         the 'Libera me' movement

{ 1870
NOV   The Papal States finally become part of united Italy

{ 1871
24 DEC   *Aida*, Cairo, Opera

{ 1873
         In Naples for a revival of *Aida*; writes the String Quartet in
         E minor

{ 1874
22 MAY   *Messa da Requiem* in honour of Alessandro Manzoni, Milan,
         San Marco

{ 1875
APR   Begins European tour with the *Messa da Requiem*, directing performances in Paris, London, Vienna, Venice, and Florence during the next five months

{ 1879
JUN   First references to the *Otello* project

{ 1880

First performance at La Scala, Milan, of the *Pater noster* and the *Ave Maria*

{ 1881
24 MAR   *Simon Boccanegra* (revised version), Milan, La Scala

{ 1884
10 JAN   *Don Carlo* (revised, four-act version of *Don Carlos*), Milan, La Scala

{ 1887
5 FEB   *Otello*, Milan, La Scala

{ 1888
5 NOV   The hospital at Villanova d'Arda is inaugurated

{ 1889
MAR   Composes an *Ave Maria* based on an 'enigmatic scale'
JUN   First discussions of *Falstaff* with Boito

{ 1893
9 FEB   *Falstaff*, Milan, La Scala

{ 1897
14 NOV   Death of Giuseppina Strepponi

{ 1898
7 APR   First performance of the *Tre pezzi sacri* (*Stabat mater*, *Laudi alla Vergine Maria*, *Te Deum*), Paris, Conservatoire; they are later published, together with the 1889 *Ave Maria*, as *Quattro pezzi sacri*

{ 1899

16 DEC   Signs the documents that mark the official founding of the
          Casa di Riposo in Milan, a home for retired musicians

{ 1901

27 JAN   Dies in Milan, age eighty-seven; he is buried in Milan's
          Cimitero Monumentale

27 FEB   His and Strepponi's remains are transferred to the Casa di
          Riposo in a grand official ceremony

Life and Works

Introduction

A month after Verdi's death, a solemn procession through Milan accompanied by hundreds of thousands of mourners assisted the transfer of his remains to their final resting place. The procession was sent on its way by a rendition of 'Va pensiero', the chorus of Hebrew slaves from one of Verdi's earliest operas, *Nabucco*.

It is easy to see why this event has captured the imagination and assumed significance. By the time of his death, Verdi had established a unique position among his fellow countrymen: although many of his operas had disappeared from the repertory, he had nevertheless become a profound artistic symbol of the nation's achievement of statehood. Parts of his operatic legacy had entered into a kind of empyrean, divorced from the passing fashions of operatic taste. The fact that 'Va pensiero', written some sixty years earlier, could express contemporary Italians' feelings for their departed hero demonstrated the extent to which Verdi's music had been assimilated into the national consciousness.

We are now more than one hundred years after Verdi's death; an event such as the Milan burial ceremony is likely to take on other meanings, and it can serve as a cautionary note on which to introduce this story of the life and the works. To begin at the end of Verdi's long career is to remind ourselves of our inevitably present perspective. Verdi's story has continually been written backwards; the early events and achievements have accrued narrative force and meaning through the powerful attraction of our sense of their ending. This is, of course, true of all biography, but the extent to which it has influenced our perceptions of Verdi nevertheless makes his an exceptional case. In an attempt to revalue (rather than evade) that perspective, this account of Verdi's life and achievements will follow much recent scholarship in attempting to place his operas more firmly in the context of their time; perhaps more important, it will treat their reception as a separate historical phenomenon, so far as is possible disentangled from present-day views of the composer.

After an outline of Verdi's early years, his career will be broken into three unequal periods. The dividing lines are not those usually followed, but are as defensible as any other; they are, though, made primarily for practical reasons and should not be thought to imply the hierarchies of value traditionally signalled by subheadings such as 'youth' or 'maturity'. The first period takes in the nineteen operas from *Oberto* (1839) to *La traviata* (1853). This involves the bulk of Verdi's operas, and perhaps for this reason claims are often made for a qualitative leap within it: to a 'second period', beginning some time in the late 1840s or early 1850s, with *Macbeth*, *Luisa Miller* or *Rigoletto* as the watershed; but the entire period is probably best seen as a gradual unfolding within the Italian operatic tradition. A second period, during which the influence of French opera is much more overt (it was certainly not lacking earlier), includes the operas from *Les Vêpres siciliennes* (1855) to *Aida* (1871). After the *Messa da Requiem* and the compositional hiatus of the 1870s, a final period, that of Verdi's last style, includes the revisions to *Simon Boccanegra* and *Don Carlos*, the operas *Otello* (1887) and *Falstaff* (1893), and the final religious works.

Life and works, 1813–39

Verdi was born in Roncole, a small village near Busseto in the Duchy of Parma. His exact birth date is uncertain. The baptismal register of 11 October records him as 'born yesterday', but as days were sometimes counted as beginning at sunset, that could mean either 9 or 10 October. The birth register describes his father Carlo (1785–1867) as an 'innkeeper', his mother Luigia Uttini (1787–1851) as a 'spinner': both belonged to families of small landowners and traders, certainly not the illiterate peasants from whom Verdi later liked to present himself as having emerged.

Carlo Verdi was anxious for upward social mobility, and thus energetic in furthering his son's education. Before he was four, Verdi began instruction with the local priests, probably in music as well as other subjects; his father bought him an old spinet when he was seven, and he was soon substituting as organist at the local church of San Michele, taking the position permanently at the age of nine. In 1823 he moved to Busseto, and at the age of eleven he entered the *ginnasio* there, receiving training in Italian, Latin, humanities, and rhetoric. In 1825 he began lessons with Ferdinando Provesi, *maestro di cappella* at San Bartolomeo, Busseto, and director of the municipal music school and local Philharmonic Society. The picture emerges of youthful precocity eagerly nurtured by an ambitious father and of a sustained, sophisticated, and elaborate formal education—again something Verdi tended to hide in later life, giving the impression of a largely selftaught and obscure youth.

In 1829 Verdi applied unsuccessfully for the post of organist at nearby Soragna. He was becoming increasingly involved in Busseto's musical life, both as a composer and as a performer. As he recalled much later in life:

> From the ages of thirteen to eighteen I wrote a motley assortment of pieces: marches for band by the hundred, perhaps as many little *sinfonie* that were used in church, in the theatre and at concerts, five or six concertos and sets of variations for pianoforte, which I played myself at concerts, many serenades, cantatas (arias, duets, very many trios), and various pieces of church music, of which I remember only a *Stabat mater*.

In May 1831 he moved into the house of Antonio Barezzi, a prominent merchant in Busseto and a keen amateur musician. Verdi gave singing and piano lessons to Barezzi's daughter Margherita (b. 4 May 1814; d. 18 June 1840) and the young couple became unofficially engaged.

At about the same time, it became clear to Verdi's circle of promoters that the musical world of Busseto was too small for their young protégé. Carlo Verdi applied to a Bussetan charitable institution (the Monte di Pietà e d'Abbondanza) for a scholarship to allow his son to study in Milan, then the cultural capital of northern Italy. The application, bolstered by glowing references from Provesi and others, was successful; but no scholarship was available until late 1833. Barezzi guaranteed financial support for the first year and in May 1832, at the age of eighteen, Verdi travelled to Milan and applied for permission to study at the conservatory. He was refused entry, partly for bureaucratic reasons (he was four years above the usual entering age and was not a resident of Lombardy-Venetia), partly on account of his unorthodox piano technique; it was an 'official' rejection that Verdi remembered, and perhaps still felt keenly, until the end of his life. Barezzi agreed to the added expense of private study in Milan, and Verdi became a pupil of Vincenzo Lavigna, who had for many years been *maestro concertatore* at La Scala.

According to Verdi's recollections in old age, his lessons with Lavigna involved little but strict counterpoint: 'in the three years spent with him I did nothing but canons and fugues, fugues and canons of all sorts. No one taught me orchestration or how to treat dramatic music'. This account is (to put it gently) one-sided, and was part of Verdi's attempt in later life to fashion himself as a 'self-taught' composer, someone not influenced by contemporary fashion. Evidence from the period suggests that Lavigna encouraged Verdi to attend the theatre regularly, and his letters of recommendation specify study in *composizione ideale* (free composition) as well as in counterpoint. Lavigna also helped his pupil into Milanese musical society; in 1834 Verdi assisted at the keyboard in performances of Haydn's *Creation* given by a Milanese Philharmonic Society directed by Pietro Massini, and a year later co-directed with Massini performances of Rossini's *La Cenerentola*.

By the time Verdi had completed his studies with Lavigna, in mid-1835, Busseto again claimed his attention. Provesi had died in 1833, leaving open the post of musical director there; by June 1834 one Giovanni Ferrari had been appointed organist at San Bartolomeo but, encouraged by Barezzi, Verdi was eventually appointed *maestro di musica* (that is, to the secular portion of Provesi's post) in March 1836, although not before a prolonged struggle between rival factions in the town. On 4 May 1836 Verdi married Margherita Barezzi and settled in Busseto, directing and composing for the local Philharmonic Society and giving private lessons. He held the post for nearly three years, during which time he and Margherita had two children to whom they gave unmistakably 'republican' names, Virginia (b. 26 March 1837; d. 12 Aug 1838) and Icilio Romano (b. 11 July 1838; d. 22 Oct 1839).

Verdi's provincial existence from 1835 to 1838 is likely to have been frustrating to him professionally, and he used the time actively to pursue more ambitious plans. In April 1836 he renewed contact with Massini's Milanese society by composing for them a cantata, to words by Count Renato Borromeo, in honour of the Austrian emperor Ferdinand I. A series of letters to Massini informs us that during 1836 Verdi composed an opera called *Rocester*, to a libretto by the Milanese journalist and man of letters Antonio Piazza. During 1837 he tried unsuccessfully to have this work staged at the Teatro Ducale in Parma. Eventually, again with Massini's help, Verdi arranged for a revised version of *Rocester*, now called *Oberto, conte di San Bonifacio*, to be performed at La Scala. This was a considerable coup for an unknown composer. In October 1838 he resigned as *maestro di musica* of Busseto and in February 1839 left for Milan. Nine months later his first opera received its première in the Lombard capital's most famous theatre, where it was received positively.

Little remains of Verdi's music from this period in Busseto, although some of the pieces he wrote there were perhaps recycled in his early operas. What has come down to us are mostly *pièces d'occasion*, written either for the church or for the Bussetan Philharmonic Society and other local groups. The influences are predictable, with Rossini much in evidence in the pieces that approach the operatic. A collection of songs, called *Sei romanze*, was published by the Milanese house of Giovanni Canti in 1838.

Life, 1839–53

From the première of *Oberto* until at least the midpoint of his long career, the outward progress of Verdi's life is inseparable from that of his professional activities: a continual round of negotiations with theatres and librettists, of intense periods of composition, arduous travel, and exhausting preparations for and direction of premières and revivals.

The success of *Oberto* apparently encouraged Bartolomeo Merelli, impresario at La Scala, to offer Verdi a contract for three more operas, to be composed over the next two years. The first of these was the comic opera *Un giorno di regno*, which failed disastrously on its first night in September 1840. Verdi's later autobiographical glosses on this period are notoriously unreliable. They state that his professional failure, together with the loss of his young family (his wife Margherita died in June 1840; they had lost their two children in the previous two years), caused him to renounce composition. There may indeed have been a period of retrenchment after the debacle of *Un giorno di regno*: his next opera, *Nabucco*, appeared some eighteen months later, an unusually long delay. But Verdi continued a level of professional activity by supervising, and writing new music for, several revivals of *Oberto*.

After *Nabucco*, the public success of which in Milan was unprecedented, the round of new operas was virtually unremitting: in the eleven years from March 1842 (the première of *Nabucco*) to March 1853 (the première of *La traviata*), Verdi produced sixteen operas, an average of one every nine months. He also supervised numerous revivals, on occasion writing new music to accommodate a star performer or a new venue. Although this rate of production was torpid by the standards of a Pacini or a Donizetti (the latter produced around seventy operas in twenty-five years), Verdi nonetheless found himself constantly moving from one operatic centre to another, dividing what time remained between Milan and Busseto. The years 1844–47 were particularly arduous (eight operas appearing in less than four years); his health broke down frequently, and more than once he vowed to renounce operatic composition once he had achieved financial security and fulfilled outstanding contracts. His gathering fame did, though, have its advantages. He was soon able to charge theatres unprecedentedly high fees for each new opera, and even though copyright protection was not fully established, he would supplement this income with rental fees and sales of printed materials. As early as 1844 he began to acquire property and land in and around Busseto. The success of *Nabucco* also opened doors in Milanese society, and Verdi soon made some long-standing friendships, notably with Countess Clara Maffei, whose salon he frequently attended. It is likely that during these early years of success he formed a lasting attachment to the soprano Giuseppina Strepponi, who was to become his lifelong companion.

Apart from a brief visit to Vienna in 1843, Verdi remained within the Italian peninsula until March 1847 when he undertook a long foreign expedition, initially to supervise the premières of *I masnadieri* in London and *Jérusalem* in Paris (his first operas to be commissioned from outside Italy). He set up house with Strepponi in Paris, staying there about two years, although with a visit to Milan during the 1848 uprisings, and a trip to the short-lived Roman Republic to supervise the première of *La battaglia di Legnano* in early 1849. Verdi returned with Strepponi to Busseto in mid-1849, still unmarried and causing a local scandal; in 1851 they moved to a permanent home in the nearby farm of Sant'Agata, land once owned by Verdi's ancestors.

Oberto (1839) to *La traviata* (1853)

Composition

The genesis of a typical Verdi opera in this period follows a predictable pattern, one that can teach us much about the composer's creative priorities and aims. The first step almost always involved negotiations with a theatre, an agreement of terms (the theatre would typically buy the rights to the first performance) and deadlines. Unlike most of his Italian predecessors, Verdi was reluctant to deal through theatrical agents, preferring to negotiate fees for the première directly with the theatre management. As his career progressed, Verdi's publisher (almost always the Milan firm of Ricordi) took an active part in commissioning new works. The eventual contract with the theatre often included stipulations about the cast of the première, and Verdi chose operatic subjects with a direct eye to the available performers.

The subject itself was decided upon either by Verdi or his librettist, although—as success brought new levels of artistic freedom—Verdi became increasingly likely to reserve for himself this crucial decision. He favoured works that had proved their worth as spoken dramas, and he had a fondness for foreign subjects, in particular Romantic melodramas set in the Middle Ages, by Byron, Schiller, and Hugo, or by their more obscure contemporaries. In searching for new subjects he constantly stressed the need for unusual, gripping characters, and for what he called 'strong' situations: scenes in which these characters could be placed in violent confrontation.

The first stage in fashioning an opera from the source text would typically involve a parcelling of the action into musical 'numbers' such as arias, duets, and ensembles, the location of a convincing central finale (the so-called *concertato*) often proving a crucial first step in deciding on the overall structure. This transformation into numbers was often done by annotating a prose summary of the source, and would typically be a collaborative effort between Verdi and his librettist. Once the work's formal outlines had been fixed, the librettist would prepare a poetic text in which the configuration of verse forms would reflect in detail the various musical forms agreed upon, and in which the individual dispositions of characters would often be inflected by the personalities and capabilities of the singers engaged as their 'creators'.

Verdi's relationships with his librettists varied considerably. In the early operas written in collaboration with Temistocle Solera (*Nabucco, I Lombardi, Giovanna d'Arco*), he tended by his own admission to alter the text very little, possibly because Solera was himself a powerful personality and had as much theatrical experience as Verdi. With other figures he respected, such as Salvadore Cammarano (*Alzira, La battaglia di Legnano, Luisa Miller, Il trovatore*), who was the author of some of Donizetti's most famous librettos, he sometimes negotiated for changes and was usually—not always—accommodated. But with his favoured collaborator in this period, Francesco Maria Piave, he became ever more dictatorial and exigent, so much so that the dramatic shape of the operas they created together was sometimes more the work of the composer than his 'poet'. More than this, Verdi might require certain sections to be cut down (he was in general anxious to avoid long passages of recitative), might ask for changes of poetic metre in fixed forms, and even for line-by-line rewording to clarify the dramatic effect.

Finally came composition of the score, which typically occurred in stages. After miscellaneous jottings, with or without words, Verdi drafted the opera in short score, usually on just two or three staves (only a couple of these so-called continuity drafts—those for *Rigoletto* and *La traviata*—are currently available, although we can infer from the structure of Verdi's autographs that similar documents existed at least from the time of *Nabucco*). Although the libretto was almost always complete before this stage began, we know that on several occasions Verdi rejected the words he had before him and composed arias (and even passages of recitative) without text, relying on his librettist to supply suitable verses after the event. In writing this short-score draft, Verdi differed from predecessors such as Rossini and Donizetti, who typically moved from the 'jotting' phase straight to the autograph; his more slow-moving practice perhaps gives an indication of the care and time he was willing to spend on each new work. The second stage of composition involved transferring the short-score draft to the autograph (a loose gathering of fascicles of orchestral-score manuscript paper), adding essential instrumental lines (usually the first violin and bass) to create what has been termed a 'skeleton score'. From this skeleton score, vocal parts would be extracted by copyists and given to the singers of the première. Pressure of time often dictated that only when Verdi arrived at the venue of the first performance, and had heard his singers in the theatre, would he complete (often in extreme haste) the orchestration. Verdi's contracts often stipulated that he would 'direct' the first three performances: at this period 'direct' rarely meant conduct in the modern sense (the task of bringing the musical forces together was shared between the principal violin and the *maestro al cembalo*); but he would certainly be near at hand, ready to appear before the audience and accept their applause after successful numbers.

Dramatic forms

It is clear from the summary above that various fixed forms were at the basis of Verdian musical drama during this period. These forms, geared as they mostly were to the individual expression or patterned confrontation of the major characters, arose from an awareness of the overwhelming importance of the principal performers in the success of an operatic event. The basic forms, inherited by Verdi from his Italian predecessors, are fairly simple to outline. The normative structure was the solo aria, called *cavatina* if it marked the first appearance of a character, and typically made up of an orchestral prelude and recitative followed by three 'movements': a lyrical first movement, usually slow in tempo, called *cantabile*, *primo tempo*, or named after its tempo designation; a connecting passage, often stimulated by some stage event—the entrance of new characters or the revelation of new information—and called the *tempo di mezzo*; and a concluding, two-verse cabaletta, usually faster than the first movement and requiring agility on the part of the singer. The grand duet was identically structured, although with an opening block before the cantabile, commonly employing formal exchanges between the characters and called by Abramo Basevi, one of Verdi's earliest commentators, the *tempo d'attacco*. Large-scale internal finales followed the pattern of the grand duet, though often with a more elaborate *tempo d'attacco;* the *primo tempo* in ensembles was often called the 'Largo' or 'Largo concertato', and the final movement was called a 'stretta'. Ranged around these large, multisectional units were shorter, connecting pieces, notably various choral movements and shorter, one-movement arias, often called 'Romanza'. There is a close parallel between musical and poetic forms, each 'movement' tending to be in a different type of *versi lirici* (rhyming stanzas of fixed line length and internal stress) while recitative is almost always in *versi sciolti* (unrhymed successions of seven- and eleven-syllable lines). Given the nature of the opera's genesis, this parallel is of course unremarkable; the fact that it has occasioned so much detailed discussion in the recent Verdi literature is as much due to the possibilities it furnishes for formal abstraction as to the insights it occasionally offers.

The demands of principal singers ensured that, at the start of this period, the overall structure of an opera had many essential formal ingredients. If there were three principals (increasingly the norm), each would require a multimovement entrance aria; and each would expect to appear in at least two grand duets. Particularly important singers would expect a further solo (often a one-movement piece such as a Romanza) later in the action. The rest of the numbers (there were usually between ten and fourteen in all) would comprise the inevitable central concertato, one or two choruses (sometimes front-of-the-curtain numbers to allow changes of scene), and perhaps a brief solo for a secondary character. The action was preceded by an instrumental movement: sometimes a full-scale overture (either of the 'potpourri' type or of more 'symphonic' construction), but more frequently an atmospheric prelude.

In discussing Verdi's approach to these fixed forms, commentators both ancient and modern have tended to paint a Romantic picture, one that equates release from formal 'constraints' with progress, and that celebrates the composer's gradual emancipation. According to this interpretation Verdi is a formal revolutionary, constantly striving towards a more naturalistic mode of musical drama. A few of Verdi's letters, in particular some often-quoted ones to Salvadore Cammarano about the libretto of *Il trovatore*, seem to support this view. Verdi sometimes showed a fondness for 'revolutionary' rhetoric when urging librettists to avoid the ordinary:

> If in the opera there were no cavatinas, duets, trios, choruses, finales, etc., and if the whole work consisted . . . of a single number I should find that all the more right and proper.

There is some truth in this image: as the nineteenth century progressed, opera in all countries turned to looser, less predictable musical forms. But Verdi is better seen as a conservative influence within this broad trend, especially when compared to his immediate predecessors in Italy. The operas up to *La traviata*, while they show a progressive trend away from formal predictability, are for the most part easier to codify in formal terms than those, for example, of late Donizetti. As for statements such as the one quoted above, it is well to remember that, whatever his aesthetic pronouncements, Verdi declared himself well satisfied with the resolutely number-based libretto of *Il trovatore* that Cammarano eventually produced.

True, Verdi sometimes radically altered or ignored traditional forms. There are classic examples: the introduction of Macbeth by means of an understated duettino, 'Due vaticini', rather than a full-scale cavatina; the curious Act 1 duet between Rigoletto and Sparafucile, which is a kind of free conversation over an instrumental melody; the stretta-less grand finales of *Nabucco* Act 2, *I due Foscari* Act 2, *Attila* Act 1, *Luisa Miller* Act 1, and *Il trovatore* Act 2; the complete absence of a concertato finale in *I masnadieri* and *Rigoletto*. Other moments are equally striking but less often mentioned: the duets of *La battaglia di Legnano* Act 1 and *Stiffelio* Act 3 follow the fluctuations of character confrontation so minutely that they are extremely difficult to parcel out into the traditional four movements; the Act 1 duet in *Alzira* moves from *tempo d'attacco* straight to cabaletta, a process repeated in the Act 1 finale of *Il trovatore*.

Much more often, however, Verdi chose to manipulate forms from within, preserving their boundaries but expanding or condensing individual movements as the drama dictated. Famous examples include the Violetta-Germont duet in *La traviata* Act 2, which boasts a vastly expanded and lyrically enriched opening sequence, so much so that Basevi's term *tempo d'attacco* seems inadequate to encompass its complexity; or Leonora's aria in *Il trovatore* Act 4, in which the usually transitional *tempo di mezzo* expands to become the famous 'Miserere' scene. Equally important in this enrichment is Verdi's tendency to focus musical weight on ensemble numbers and to concentrate in these numbers on the opposition between characters. In this respect the rarity in his works of the so-called rondò finale (a favourite Donizettian form in which a soloist, usually the soprano, closes the opera with an elaborate, two-movement aria) is significant, as is its replacement by ensemble finales such as those of *Ernani* or *Il trovatore*. What is more, the lyrical movements of Verdi's ensembles, particularly of the grand duets, tend to establish at the outset a vivid sense of vocal difference and often retain that sense until the last possible moment. Those extended passages in parallel 3rds or 6ths so well known in Donizetti and Bellini are rare, such vocal 'reconciliation' being usually reserved for coda material.

Certain operas of this period, particularly those written in collaboration with Temistocle Solera, are notable for a dynamic new use of the chorus. While choruses in the earlier nineteenth century had typically served a neutral, scene-setting function, Verdi's chorus is frequently in the vocal forefront, offering not just sonic enrichment and a considerable affective presence in ensemble numbers but even intruding into the soloists' domain. *Nabucco* offers many early examples, from the dramatic incursion of the chorus in both the primo tempo and cabaletta of Zaccaria's Act 1 aria, their climactic appearance in the Act 2 canonic ensemble, 'S'appressan gl'istanti', and of course 'Va pensiero' in Act 3, where the chorus sings mostly in unison, with a directness and simplicity of emotional appeal that had traditionally been heard only from soloists.

Lyric prototype

In attempting to summarise the smaller-scale level of Verdi's lyrical movements, many critics have again appealed to a traditional norm, though one more abstractly analytical than the set-piece forms and one whose limitations need to be remembered. This is the 'lyric prototype', a four-phrase pattern usually represented by the scheme $AA'BA''$ or (its common variant) $AA'BC$. Such a model (which is found in Donizetti and Bellini, though less consistently) could also include subscript numbers to indicate phrase length — the normative phrase would be four bars; poetic lines could also be incorporated, as the usual consumption of text exactly parallels the musical periodicity, with two poetic lines matching one four-bar period. The prototype does, though, ignore harmonic movement, which can vary significantly within pieces that would have an identical phrase scheme. What is more, in its 'pure' form the scheme appears only rarely, usually as one character's solo statement in an ensemble movement: in solo arias, some level of expansion, typically in coda material, is clearly necessary to achieve

Ex. 1 *Oberto*, Act 2

['But you, proud youth, you will not exhaust me! For one of us, this day will be the last. From my corpse, a war-like cry will be heard: the dying Oberto cursing the Salinguerra!']

adequate length. These limitations notwithstanding, the prototype has proved the most reliable and flexible method of codifying Verdi's basic melodic shapes.

A very early example of the model, close to its basic form, comes in the cabaletta of the protagonist's aria in Act 2 of *Oberto* (ex.1). Even at this early stage, though, a Verdian novelty can be discerned in the restriction of the scheme. When approaching the music of Verdi's predecessors, the prototype tends to be less useful: many of Donizetti's or Bellini's arias start with 'open' declamatory phrases, finding a regular pattern only in the latter stages; and many others (particularly cabalettas) start periodically but dissolve after the *B* section into looser sequences of ornamental vocal writing and word repetition. Verdi did occasionally write arias of the latter type: for Riccardo in Act 1 of *Oberto*, or—significantly as the part was written for the 'old-fashioned' virtuosa Jenny Lind—for Amalia in both Acts 1 and 3 of *I masnadieri*. But his typical practice, even when writing a bravura aria, was to contain the ornamentation strictly within the periodic structure, even as an aria reached its final stages.

As with his conservatism in larger formal matters, this self-imposed restriction had the effect of channelling Verdi's invention into manipulations of the prototype from within, into small-scale expansions, contractions, and enrichments of the lyric form. Elvira's Andantino in Act 1 of *Ernani*, for example, sees a dramatic expansion of the *B* section that injects a new sense of dialectic tension into the aria. More than that: far from 'dissolving' into vocal virtuosity at the end, the aria continues to subordinate, or rather harness, the ornamentation, containing it within strictly controlled periods (ex.2). Such examples, which could easily be multiplied, demonstrate at least a part of how that energy so typical of Verdi's early operas is created: through a tightening of form coupled with an intensification of expressive content.

As the 1840s unfolded, Verdi's lyrical forms increasingly showed the influence of French models, especially after his prolonged stay in Paris in 1847–49. *Il corsaro*, for example, starts with two slow arias that, albeit in different ways, are both organized in two strophes. Later, more famous examples of this distinctly French formal type include the *couplets* form (so called because of the short refrain line that ends each stanza) found in Rodolfo's 'Quando le sere al placido' (*Luisa Miller* Act 2) and Germont's 'Di Provenza il mar, il suol' (*La traviata* Act 2). None of these examples entirely abandons the lyric prototype; indeed, in one sense it is more pervasive, tending to appear in miniature in each stanza. As Verdi moved into the early 1850s, the variety of internal structures

Ex. 2 *Ernani*, Act 1

Andantino piuttosto vivo

['Ernani!... Ernani, spirit me away from this horrible embrace. Let us fly... if love allows me to live with you, I will follow you through caves and barren lands. Those caves will be for me an Eden of delights.']

proliferated, giving rise to such startling experiments as Gilda's 'Caro nome' (*Rigoletto* Act 1), in which the second half of an initial *AA'BA"* form, remarkable for its simplicity, is subjected to an elaborate series of variations.

Harmony, tinta, local colour

Verdi's small-scale harmonic language is for the most part simple and direct, following patterns that can easily be summarised within the lyric prototype. The opening *A* sections tend to concentrate on tonic and dominant harmonies, sometimes ending with a modulation to a near-related key; the *B* section is comparatively unstable; the final *A* (or *C*) section returns to a stable tonic. Secondary modulations within an aria are frequently to keys a third apart, thus allowing new harmonic underpinning for important vocal sonorities. In large set pieces, notably in the Largo concertato, there is often a dramatic plunge into a distant key near the end, a gesture from which Verdi sometimes found difficulty in extricating himself. A few 'character' pieces show that Verdi was fully capable of an advanced, colouristic chromaticism—the 'Salve Maria' from *I Lombardi* Act 1 is an early example, the openings of the preludes to Acts 1 and 3 of *La traviata* a later, more persuasive one; but for the most part his liking for periodic structures made elaborate chromatic effects difficult to employ except at moments of high relief.

The extent to which tonal organization can be found at a larger level is still a matter of debate. Like most of his contemporaries and immediate predecessors, Verdi seemed indifferent to tonal closure at the level of the multimovement number (something that had been important only a few decades earlier): most multi movement arias, duets, and ensembles begin in one key and end in another; individual acts, let alone entire operas, rarely display any obvious tonal plan. It seems likely that Verdi chose the tonalities of movements within set pieces primarily with a view to the vocal tessituras he wished to exploit, and various last-minute transpositions he effected to accommodate individual singers would seem to support that supposition. There is, though, evidence in some operas of an association between certain keys or tonal regions and certain characters or groups of characters. *Il trovatore* is a good example: the flat keys are linked with the 'aristocratic' world of Leonora and Count di Luna, while sharp keys tend to accompany Manrico, Azucena, and the world of the gypsies. *Macbeth* shows a similar binary divide (Macbeth and Lady Macbeth on the flat side, the witches on the sharp side). Such associations may also attend other harmonic recurrences, such as the occasional repetition of large-scale tonal progressions (so-called double cycles). But these rather loose juxtapositions—by no means rigidly maintained—probably represent the ultimate point of tonal organization in Verdi of this period: there have as yet been no convincing demonstrations of 'directed tonal motion' across large spans of Verdian musical drama, nor evidence that the composer considered such motion a desirable aesthetic goal.

More important than harmony as a means of establishing what Verdi called the *tinta* or *tinte* (identifying colour or colours) of a given opera are various recurring melodic shapes. These should not be confused with recurring motifs, which Verdi occasionally used to great effect by association with an important element in the drama (the horn call in *Ernani* is a classic early example), and which gain their effect by means of a straightforward semantic identification and a sense of isolation from the basic musical fabric. Nor are they connected with the proto-Leitmotivic experiment of *I due Foscari*, in which the main entrances of certain characters or groups are marked by the repetition of a 'personal' instrumental theme. On the contrary, these recurring shapes tend to hover on the edge of obvious reminiscence, thus contributing to a general sense of musical cohesion without accruing semantic weight: their very vagueness is essential. The rising 6th that begins so many lyric pieces in *Ernani*, the 'bow shape' of *Attila*, perhaps even the stepwise rising line of *Oberto* are possible examples, ones that might cautiously be multiplied.

At least until the later part of this period, the fixing of an opera within a specific ambience, the use of what is often called 'local colour', was sporadic. The single gesture towards the exotic, 'eastern' ambience of *Nabucco* (the chorus that opens Act 3) is probably the opera's least inspired number; one reason why *Nabucco* is more successful than *I Lombardi* (Verdi's next opera, and a work that resembles *Nabucco* in many ways) is that the later opera's frequent changes of locale and ambience stimulate a larger amount of this rather pallid, 'colouristic' music. By the end of the 1840s, though, and in particular after his sojourn in Paris and prolonged exposure to the French stage, Verdi's attitude changed. In *Luisa Miller* the Alpine ambience is an important element of the opera's *tinta*, joining with certain recurring shapes (in this case as much rhythmic ideas as melodic ones) to give the work a pronounced individuality. This merging of local colour with other recurring elements is also clear in *Il trovatore*, where the 'Spanish' atmosphere is intimately bound to the musical sphere inhabited by Azucena. *Tinta* reaches a first pinnacle in *La traviata*, in which much of the opera moves in telling refractions of the waltz-laden social world so vividly depicted in the opening scene.

✓ **Influences**

When Verdi first began to make an operatic career, his main stylistic influences were those of his immediate Italian predecessors. Rossini, the inevitable point of reference a decade earlier, was now rather outdated in the field of serious opera (as *Un giorno di regno* shows, the 'code Rossini' remained sovereign in the declining genre of *opera buffa*). There are, though, echoes of Rossinian models in certain full-scale overtures (*Giovanna d'Arco* and *La battaglia di Legnano*); and the oratorio-like style of Verdi's first successes (*Nabucco* in particular) owes something to Rossini's *Mosè*. The influence of Bellini, who had died in 1835 but whose operas were by the early 1840s at the height of their fame, is sometimes heard, but his distinctive melodic style has a significant impact only in *Oberto* (in Riccardo's Act 1 cavatina and, especially, in the *Straniera*-like declamation of Leonora's rondò finale). Perhaps Bellini's trademark melodic style—close attention to melodic detail within arias that are often loosely structured at the individual phrase level, seemingly constructed out of declamatory fragments—was simply too caught up in nuances of sentiment: what Verdi was later to describe as Bellini's 'melodie lunghe, lunghe, lunghe' were thus unsuited to the younger composer's directness of approach and easily graspable periodic structures. Possibly more significant (though more research is needed) was the example of Mercadante, whose elaborate, rather academic manner left several traces in the earliest operas, not least in their occasional displays of contrapuntal expertise.

The most important of Verdi's first influences was undoubtedly Donizetti, by far the most successful composer then active in Italian opera. Charting the details of such influence is problematic, in particular because the relative fixity of Italian prosody and its relation to musical rhythm makes it inevitable that melodic profiles will recur across the repertory. Rather than leaning on such fugitive 'echoes', it is safer to locate moments of larger musical-dramatic similarity. One occurs in Act 1 of *Giovanna d'Arco*, in which the usual progression from lachrymose Andante to energetic cabaletta is reversed in Giacomo's cavatina, producing a moderate-paced, unusually touching, 'Donizettian' cabaletta, quite lacking in Verdi's usual rhythmic drive. Another, much grander example occurs in the Act 1 concertato finale of *Alzira*, 'Nella polve, genuflesso', which shows striking resemblances to the famous sextet in *Lucia di Lammermoor*, sharing the key of D♭ major and several melodic and harmonic ideas. However, the differences are also instructive. The *Lucia* sextet is a classic 'frozen moment' in which the principals, albeit at a moment of maximum conflict, join in a long, lyrical sweep that enwraps all their accumulated tension.

Verdi, on the other hand, is more fragmentary, highlighting that sense of vocal conflict so important to his operatic style. What is more, the *Alzira* ensemble is set in a far more dynamic harmonic context, as if the conflict, far from being encased in a lyrical idea, is developing before our ears.

As already mentioned, the late 1840s saw the gathering influence of French models on Verdi's aria forms. But this was not the only level on which the lure of Paris is felt. The remaking of *I Lombardi* into *Jérusalem* for the Paris Opéra (1847) put in the clearest context the effect that French grand opera was beginning to have, in particular in expanding Verdi's harmonic and orchestral imagination, and in broadening his conception of the uses of 'local colour'. However, the influence of Meyerbeerian dramaturgy was mostly a thing of the future. More important at this stage was the impact of non-operatic French theatre, in particular the *mélodrame* tradition Verdi was able to sample at firsthand during his long stay in Paris between 1847 and 1849. The final scene of *Stiffelio*, which is directly derived from a near-contemporary *mélodrame*, all but dispenses with sustained vocal expression in favour of the atmospheric orchestral background, tense declamation and telling visual images so typical of French boulevard theatre. This may be an extreme example, but melodramatic effects can be found in several other operas of the period, most famously at the start of the final scene of *La traviata*, in which Violetta reads Germont's letter to the sentimental strains of a solo violin reminiscence motif.

Singers and musical characterization

During his early career, Verdi was of his time in the care he took to mould individual roles to the skills of the singers who would create them. It was completely in his interest to do so, both because the success of a first performance often influenced the speed of a work's dissemination, and because singers were themselves influential in a theatre's choice of repertory. A good example is his treatment of the soprano Antonietta Ranieri Marini, who created the leading female roles in his first two operas: Leonora in *Oberto* and the Marchesa del Poggio in *Un giorno di regno*. In both cases Verdi took care to exploit the peculiarities of Ranieri Marini's voice—in particular to tailor the role to what we would now call her 'mezzo' range. Nothing could resuscitate *Un giorno di regno*, but with *Oberto* Verdi's efforts were rewarded—nearly all of its early revivals featured Ranieri Marini in the cast, and we can assume that she was instrumental in each decision to revive the work.

It is sometimes suggested that this attitude to performers changed once

Verdi's fame assured him a degree of artistic independence. In support come anecdotes about his refusal to write German soprano Sophie Loewe a rondò finale in *Ernani*; or his withering scorn when asked to accommodate another soprano with an additional aria for Gilda to *Rigoletto* ('Had you been persuaded that my talent is such that I could not have done better than I did in *Rigoletto*, you wouldn't have asked me for an *aria* in that opera'). But there is little evidence that Verdi's eagerness to suit roles to the skills of his interpreters diminished with time. Often his decision to set one subject rather than another was strongly inflected by the available cast. A typical example is his wavering between various operatic subjects in the summer of 1846 (he had a contract to fulfil with Florence's Teatro Pergola): he decided to tackle *Macbeth* only after he knew of the engagement of Felice Varesi, one of the finest actor-singer baritones of the day.

What is more, Verdi's knowledge of the strengths and limitations of his cast often profoundly affected the vocal character of a given opera. A case in point concerns the strongly contrasting roles he created for two very different early sopranos, Loewe (he probably wrote Abigaille with her in mind, and she created Elvira in *Ernani* and Odabella in *Attila*) and Erminia Frezzolini (Giselda in *I Lombardi* and Giovanna in *Giovanna d'Arco*). Loewe's voice had power rather than beauty, but it was extremely flexible and boasted an impressive chest register. Frezzolini, on the other hand, excelled in delicacy, beauty of tone, and ornamental passages; but she had little power below the staff. In some cases—Loewe as the sword-wielding Odabella, or Frezzolini as anxious Giselda—the singer-type seemed to suit the character-type very well. But in others—particularly the casting of Frezzolini as Joan of Arc—Verdi and his librettist used considerable skill to tailor the role to the 'creator', making sure that the gentler side of the character was emphasized whenever possible.

This sense of performer power, and of welcome accommodations on the part of composers, is the norm, and if it was occasionally resented by the latter, it much more often provided a creative stimulus. Within this framework, though, vocal style was changing, and in Italy the change was inevitably associated with Verdi. In all voice ranges robustness and sheer volume began to make inroads into vocal flexibility, and a new immediacy and 'realism' in acting style went hand-in-hand with a tendency to indulge ever more intensely in vehement declamato rather than seamless bel canto. We can see this most obviously in the emergence of the 'Verdian' baritone: a type characterized by high tessitura, intense declamatory skills, and a relative absence of ornamental writing; this was a very different animal from the mellifluous 'basso cantante' of twenty years earlier.

Verdi was in no important sense responsible for this pan-European shift in taste. Although he exploited it magnificently, he was merely one element in a complex symbiotic process involving changes in theatre architecture, in the socio-economic makeup of audiences, in ideas about 'realism', in the range of repertory that a singer would be required to tackle, in the power of orchestral instruments, and most importantly, changing views about what constituted human subjectivity and how it might be represented.

Although Verdi's close attention to singers' capabilities would continue throughout his long life, towards the end of this period we can locate a change of attitude, one that found him less willing to tailor his roles so specifically to individuals. Again this shift made practical sense—his fame now virtually assured his operas a wide dissemination—and it may also reflect his gathering sense of an international singing style, a levelling out of peculiarities among the leading singers brought on by the emergence of an Italian (and, later, an international) repertory. But we can see in Gilda (*Rigoletto*) and Violetta (*La traviata*) a new type of role, one in which important changes in the character's attitudes, brought on by developments in the plot, are articulated through important changes in the vocal persona. The pleasure-loving Violetta of Act 1 sings very differently from the passionately intense Violetta of Act 2, or again from the invalid of Act 3. This was a daring experiment: it was not much followed up in the later operas and has continued to present difficulties for performers. It suggests, though, something of the intensity of Verdi's relationship with the human voice, and the manner in which his vision of drama was always projected principally through such fragile vessels.

✓ Reception and politics

By the 1850s Verdi had become the most famous and frequently performed Italian opera composer in Europe, having wrested the former epithet from Rossini and the latter from Donizetti. He commanded unprecedented fees for new operas (although he lagged some way behind the most famous singers in earning potential), could choose more-or-less freely which theatres were to launch his latest works, and had begun to acquire substantial assets in farm lands and buildings. Admittedly, his 'noisy' orchestration (in particular his tendency to favour the middle to low register of the brass and woodwind, when compared to the Donizetti generation), his often extreme demands on singers, and his taste for extravagant melodramatic plots had on occasions brought him criticism in the press during the 1840s. Resistance was particularly intense (at least among critics) in the southern part of Italy. What is more, several of his operas failed to find a place in the repertory that was rapidly forming during this period. But by the early 1850s, and despite the occasional public failure such as that which initially greeted *La traviata*, opponents of Verdi (at least within Italy) were becoming an eccentric minority. Opposition was greater and more prolonged elsewhere: although France was largely won over by the early 1850s, neither England nor Germany would be wholeheartedly enthusiastic, even much later in the century.

The vast majority of Verdi's premières remained within the Italian peninsula, and on occasion it seemed that the composer's most serious opposition came from those elaborate and multifarious organs of state censorship that continued to police artistic expression. Librettos could be subject to modification on religious, moral, or political grounds; in Milan and Naples (probably elsewhere) the censor might also attend dress rehearsals, to ensure that the music and staging produced no improprieties. However, severity varied greatly from region to region, and because censorship in the northern states (in which Verdi concentrated his early career) was far more easygoing than that in Rome or Naples, the composer encountered few difficulties with his early operas. Religious scruples were most easily offended; at least until the eve of the 1848 revolutions 'political' matters were largely ignored. Zaccaria in *Nabucco*, for example, ended his Act 1 cabaletta with the words 'Che dia morte allo stranier' ('That gives death to the foreigner') without censorial interference in a huge number of early productions, and even the 'revolutionary' *Ernani* encountered only minor obstacles in the north. After 1848 the situation worsened, and it is significant that Verdi's most severe bouts with the censor occurred in the austere, counterrevolutionary atmosphere of the late 1840s and 1850s, over the religious subject matter of *Stiffelio* and over many aspects of both *Rigoletto* and *Un ballo in maschera*.

The business of government censorship inevitably leads to a consideration of Verdi's political status during this period and of the extent to which his operas served to heighten the Italian people's national consciousness. It is important to remind ourselves that Verdi's—or any one else's—operas were far from popular in the modern sense: only a tiny elite had the financial resources to attend such places as La Scala. But it is also true that the theatre fulfilled an important social function, being almost the only place in which large gatherings of people were permitted. There is no doubt that Verdi himself was a staunch patriot, as can be seen from many of his letters, particularly those surrounding his brief return to Milan during the 1848 uprisings. The 1848 revolutions also inspired him to attempt an opera in which the theme of patriotism would be overt: *La battaglia di Legnano* had its première in a beleaguered Roman republic in January 1849, by which time Milan and many other northern cities that had briefly liberated themselves were long back in Austrian hands.

Before 1846, however (when the wave of revolutionary feeling that culminated in the 1848 uprisings began to take shape), there is hardly any evidence that Verdi's operas were regarded as especially dangerous politically or that they excited patriotic enthusiasm in their audiences. In the period between the liberal reforms of Pius IX in 1846 and the revolutions of 1848, when the theatre sometimes became a focus of political demonstrations, Verdi's operas seem to have accompanied such outbursts no more often than those of other composers. It is also significant that during the months of mid-1848 when the Milanese governed their own city, neither the newly liberated theatrical press nor the public seemed especially interested in Verdi or his music. Furthermore, when the Austrians regained control of Milan, and instituted an extreme clamp-down on any expression that could lead to further civil unrest, the 1848–49 La Scala season staged revivals of *Ernani* and *I due Foscari*; *Attila* and *Nabucco* followed in the next full season. It seems inconceivable that any of these operas had been actively associated with the failed revolutions. This is not to deny the stirring force of Verdi's early music, in particular his treatment of the chorus (i.e., 'the people') as a dynamic new expressive power; but connections between his music and political events were largely made later in the century, some considerable time after the revolutionary atmosphere had cooled.

Life, 1853–71

After the première of *La traviata* in March 1853, the pace of Verdi's operatic production slowed considerably. The eleven years up to *La traviata* had produced sixteen operas; the eighteen years that followed saw only six new works: *Les Vêpres siciliennes*, *Simon Boccanegra*, *Un ballo in maschera*, *La forza del destino*, *Don Carlos*, and *Aida*. Admittedly, such a comparison paints a slightly exaggerated picture. Two of the new works (*Les Vêpres* and *Don Carlos*) were written for the Paris Opéra; they are thus both considerably longer than any other of Verdi's scores and required the composer's presence in Paris during extended rehearsal periods. Furthermore, Verdi devoted much time and creative energy to revising various works: there were relatively minor adjustments to

La traviata and *Simon Boccanegra* after unsuccessful first performances (the latter would undergo further and more important alterations later), and to *Il trovatore* for its Paris version; a thorough overhaul of *Macbeth*, again for Paris; the refashioning of *Stiffelio* as *Aroldo*; and substantial revisions to *La forza del destino* for a series of performances at La Scala. Such efforts notwithstanding, however, Verdi now spent an increasing amount of time away from the theatre, and on at least one occasion—in the more than three-year gap between finishing *Un ballo in maschera* (early 1858) and starting *La forza del destino* (mid-1861)—he seems to have decided to stop composing altogether.

His three most extensive foreign expeditions were all related to professional engagements: a two-year sojourn in Paris (1853–55) saw the completion and performance of *Les Vêpres siciliennes*; *La forza del destino* required two trips to Russia, with interim visits to Paris and London and Madrid (1862–63); and the production of *Don Carlos* kept him in Paris for nearly a year (1866–67). When not travelling, Verdi divided his life between periods of intense activity on his farmlands at Sant'Agata (he added substantially to his estate in 1857 and supervised extensive renovations in the 1860s) and visits to friends in other cities, notably Naples and Venice. In 1859, after more than ten years together, Verdi and Giuseppina Strepponi were secretly married in the village of Collonges-sous-Salève in Savoy. In 1866 they set up permanent winter quarters in Genoa.

Verdi entered briefly into public political life, becoming in 1861—after personal urging from none other than Cavour—deputy for Borgo San Donnino (now Fidenza) in the first Italian parliament, a post he retained until 1865, though attending sessions only sporadically after the first few months. For reasons that remain obscure, he lost touch with friends in Milan, his centre of professional operations and social milieu through most of the 1840s; after his dramatic return during the 1848 revolutions, he seems hardly to have visited the city for twenty years. (As early as 1845 he had quarrelled with the directors of La Scala over what he considered unacceptably low production standards; this may have contributed to his estrangement from the city, though it cannot have been the whole story.) But the late 1860s saw a rapprochement. In 1868 he returned to Milan to visit Clara Maffei, and to meet for the first time the great novelist Alessandro Manzoni, whom he had long revered. A year later he re-established contact with La Scala, supervising there the première of the revised *La forza del destino*. On hearing of the death of Rossini (in November 1868), Verdi suggested to his publisher Ricordi that a commemorative *Messa per Rossini* be written jointly by a team of the most prominent Italian composers of the day. The Mass was duly completed, Verdi supplying the final 'Libera me', but there was much wrangling over administrative problems, and the work was never performed.

Les Vêpres siciliennes (1855) to *Aida* (1871)

Expansion

If one had to encapsulate in a single word the key difference between Verdi's works of this period and those of the previous one, 'expansion' would be a strong contender. Almost all the operas are far longer than any up to *La traviata*, and added length routinely brought with it an expansion of the cast list (rather than the classic 'love triangle', further principals and secondary characters vie for attention) and a broadening of the geographical sweep of the plot, with more opportunities for (increasingly, obligations to provide) orchestral depiction of changed ambience and 'local colour'. The sheer volume of sound also increased: voices, particularly male voices, tended to be heavier and less agile, and so coloratura passages became an almost exclusively female domain; these vocal changes were linked to the increasing size of orchestras, and the extra power of individual instruments, in particular the lower brass. Generic boundaries also expanded, a mixture of comic and serious styles within the same work becoming common. With the advent of new technologies, particularly in lighting, staging practices became more elaborate; detailed *disposizioni sceniche* (production books, after the fashion of French *livrets de mise en scène*) began to appear, offering an exhaustive account of stage movement and scenic effect. In short, more and more performers crowded onto ever more elaborately bedecked stages; they sang louder and louder, at greater and greater length. Theatres expanded their auditoriums and stage space whenever possible, increasing the numbers of people that could attend a performance.

Of course, these changes echoed a general shift in Italian opera, indeed in European opera as a whole. The reasons behind such shifts will always be complex, but in the case of Italy, which became a modern nation state in 1861, one of the most powerful was an increasing desire, in both creators and audiences, to feel international, to enter the modern world. The most important musical model in attaining this desire was the type of grand opera associated with that most cosmopolitan of European cities, Paris. So Italian opera, for the first time in its history, began to fashion itself along 'foreign' lines. But there were other, equally important reasons. One was the development of an operatic repertory, a body of works that continued to be revived even after they became old-fashioned in style. Rather than having constantly to produce new works, composers could now invest greater time in each creation; what is more, increased copyright protection (particularly after 1865) ensured that they could earn substantial amounts from revivals of such repertory operas.

Verdi was actively involved in these fundamental changes; indeed, such was his primacy in Italian opera that he inevitably led the way. But he was also aware that progress came at a price. In a famous letter from the late 1860s, written to the Parisian librettist and opera director Camille Du Locle, he voiced serious doubts about the Parisian way:

> Everyone wants to express an opinion, to voice a doubt; and the composer who lives in that atmosphere of doubt for any length of time cannot help but be somewhat shaken in his convictions and end up revising, adjusting, or, to put it more precisely, ruining his work. In this way, one ultimately finds in one's hands not a unified opera but a *mosaic*; and, beautiful as it may be, it is still a *mosaic*. You will argue that the *Opéra* has produced a string of masterpieces in this manner. You may call them masterpieces all you want, but permit me to say that they would be much more perfect if the *patchwork* and the adjustments were not felt all the time.

This letter places the blame squarely on staging conditions in Paris, in particular the collaborative nature of the enterprise; Verdi went on to say that the situation in Italy was, at least for someone of his reputation, different: there the composer was assured absolute control. But the 'patchwork' problem was at least as much internal—within the very nature of modern opera—as it was to do with practical matters; opera had become too complex to be under any single person's jurisdiction. Verdi's works, whether created in Italy or elsewhere, were no exception.

Composition

The genesis, and thus to an extent the aesthetic premises, of a Verdi opera of this period had changed a little from those in the earlier period, the principal difference being that the composer's burgeoning reputation now allowed him greater creative freedom. He was besieged by offers from the major theatres of Italy, Europe, and beyond, and could choose the venue and subject of any new opera. He was also free to refuse commissions much more often than he had been in the hectic 1840s, as he could live from accumulated wealth for long periods. But when he did work, the old patterns remained. Although with the rise of the repertory system, singing style was becoming more homogenous, Verdi was still wary of committing himself to a subject until the principal singers had been engaged, refusing to sign a contract for *La forza del destino*, for example, before the company had been fixed. He still composed by way of a prose scenario to clarify the musical forms, a libretto that reflected those forms, a continuity draft and then a 'skeleton score', and finally an orchestration of that score, this last stage often completed near to the date of the première. He continued to compose with great facility and, allowing for the vastly increased length of several of these operas, probably took no longer in musical drafting than he had when writing his earlier works.

On the surface at least, the type of subject he chose was also unchanged: he remained loyal to Schiller and also to the greater and lesser lights of Romantic melodrama. Towards the end of the period, though, came a decisive move away from melodramatic extremes. In revising *Macbeth* in 1865, for example, he replaced the final, onstage death scene with a Victory Chorus; more telling still, in the 1869 revision of *La forza del destino* he replaced the bloody dénouement (in which the tenor curses God and flings himself from a precipice) with an ensemble of religious consolation. This move away from melodrama is part of a larger change in the dramatic and stylistic scope of his operas. Verdi now repeatedly called for more variety in his operatic subjects, and he criticized some of his earlier operas for being one-dimensional. He strove to blend or juxtapose comic and tragic scenes and genres (notably in *Un ballo in maschera* and *La forza del destino*) and to explore greater extremes of musical and dramatic ambience.

In his dealings with librettists Verdi became, if anything, more exigent. Even from French librettists he demanded important revisions (Scribe, his collaborator on *Les Vêpres siciliennes*, did not always comply). In his Italian operas he sometimes reduced the task of the librettist to that of a versifier. Piave set to work on *Simon Boccanegra* according to precise instructions: Verdi supplied a complete prose sketch of the action, one so detailed that he insisted that it (rather than a libretto draft) be submitted to the censors for approval. In the case of *Un ballo in maschera* and *Aida*, Antonio Somma and Antonio Ghislanzoni (both inexperienced in libretto-writing) received a constant stream of advice on every aspect of their task.

Dramatic forms

Were we to judge solely from Verdi's correspondence, it would seem that this period saw the composer seeking radical alternatives to the fixed dramatic forms that had characterized his early operas. In negotiations over a possible setting of *Re Lear*, for example, he more than once voiced his need for entirely new structures; in discussing *Un ballo in maschera*, he warned the Neapolitan impresario Torelli that Scribe's libretto (on which the opera would be loosely based) 'has the conventional modes of all operas, a thing that I have always disliked and now find insufferable'. However, these radical epistolary statements are better thought of as hortatory rather than prescriptive: a way of encouraging his librettists not to lapse into the merely routine. When it came to the discussion of concrete detail, Verdi often continued to think along traditional lines, and the eventual librettos for *Re Lear* and *Un ballo in maschera* are largely constructed in the conventional manner. As in the earlier period, the bulk of Verdi's operatic music remains definable within traditional formal types, although his tendency to manipulate these types according to the particular dramatic situation became ever more extreme.

The most fragile unit of the old, multimovement structure was the cabaletta (which, in its ensemble form as stretta, had already disappeared from certain finales in the 1840s). When Verdi revised *Macbeth* in 1865, one of the most prominent casualties was Lady Macbeth's Act 2 cabaletta, and a similar fate would greet Amelia's 'Il palpito deh frena' (*Simon Boccanegra* Act 1) when that opera was revised in the 1880s. Verdi was also inclined to shorten cabalettas (for example, in the Henri-Montfort duet of *Les Vêpres siciliennes* Act 3), making them nothing more than a fast coda section with no independent thematic ideas; or he omitted them entirely, ending the number with some prominent piece of stage action or with declamatory singing (as in the Boccanegra-Fiesco duet in the prologue of *Simon Boccanegra*), or with a final, climactic melody (as in Riccardo's aria in Act 3 of *Un ballo in maschera*). But, in particular with the earlier movements of set pieces, his usual practice was to continue those complex expansions and manipulations found in Leonora's aria-with-Miserere in Act 4 of *Il trovatore*, or the Violetta-Germont duet in *La traviata* Act 2; the multimovement form became extremely flexible and was thus able more powerfully to articulate important stages in the dramatic development. A fine example is the 'seduction' duet between Amelia and Riccardo in Act 2 of *Un ballo in maschera*, which charts the rising passion of the lovers in a succession of contrasting dialogue movements before closing with a cabaletta *a due*; and there are several classic illustrations of this internal renewal of form in the last opera of this period, *Aida*, which boasts an impressive series of grand duets, each traceable to traditional patterns but each offering an individual solution to the dramatic situation it underpins.

It is entirely in keeping with Verdi's ambivalent position towards formal conventions that, even as the various movements of set pieces became less and less predictable, he sought ever more vivid ways of using the moments of transition between one movement and the next to articulate dramatic turning points. One outward manifestation of this search was his coining of the term 'parola scenica', a 'scenic utterance' (typically a few short words) that would be declaimed immediately before a lyrical set piece, making verbally manifest the key issues of a dramatic situation (he described it to Ghislanzoni as a device that 'sculpts and renders clear and evident the situation'). Utterances such as Amonasro's 'Dei Faraoni tu sei la schiava!', in his Act 3 duet with Aida, signal with a violent injection of musical prose that a new stage of the dramatic conflict, and a new lyrical stage of the set piece, is to ensue. Although the technique clearly owes something to the aesthetics of melodrama, it also makes manifest the way in which Verdi's operatic style was becoming more dependent on isolated verbal effects to articulate an increasingly 'prosaic' musical drama.

Although traditional structures still constitute the main stylistic line, there are, especially in the French operas, passages where a new aesthetic emerges. Arias such as Philippe's 'Elle ne m'aime pas' (*Don Carlos* Act 4) show comparatively little tendency to formal partition, and are better regarded as descendants of the great ariosos of Verdi's youth, especially those for Macbeth and Rigoletto. Some duets go in the same direction: the Henri-Montfort confrontation in Act 3 of *Les Vêpres siciliennes* departs strikingly from Italian formal practice. In numbers such as the Elisabeth-Don Carlos duet in Act 2 of *Don Carlos* it may even be nugatory to search for remnants of traditional forms: the musical discourse follows in minute and constantly changing configuration the ebb and flow of the confrontation, creating a kind of 'musical prose' (or, as Verdi would call it, musical *Dramma*—the capital *D* was important) that was rapidly becoming the norm in European opera.

Lyric prototype

The proliferation of lyric types towards the end of the previous period continues into this one, with the influence of French operatic forms increasingly evident. While solo statements within duets and ensembles frequently retain the old *AA'BA''* form, full-scale aria movements often have a typically French ternary form, with larger *A* sections (themselves based on the old 'lyric prototype') flanking a looser, declamatory *B* section. Amelia's 'Come in quest'ora bruna' (*Simon Boccanegra* Act 1) shows this form at its most extended; the classic condensed example is Radames's 'Celeste Aida' (*Aida* Act 1), which brings back elements of the *B* material in a delicate coda. When Verdi chose to retain the old-fashioned Italian model, he usually did so for characters in old-fashioned melodramatic situations: Posa's 'C'est mon jour' in *Don Carlos* Act 4 is an obvious example. And frequently he made telling changes, ones indicative of a general shift in his lyric language. In Don Carlo's 'Urna fatal' (*La forza del destino* Act 3), the harmonic openness at the start of each lyric segment undermines the *AA'BC* form, encouraging us to hear the first two sections as one limb, and thus as the first part of a larger, ternary structure.

While the move towards longer, looser periods underlies much of Verdi's music during this period, he also continued to experiment in the opposite direction: following the example of 'Caro nome', he was occasionally encouraged by the dramatic situation to construct lyric movements of extreme formal simplicity. The final section of the Aida-Radames duet (*Aida* Act 4) is a telling example (ex.3). This passage, first sung by Aida, is repeated literally by Radames and then repeated again by both characters in unison. The energy is, as it were, turned inwards, the extreme angularity and sheer difficulty of the vocal line forming an uncanny complement to the well-nigh obsessive formal repetition.

Harmony, tinta, local colour

In comparison with his French and German contemporaries, Verdi remained for the most part within a firm diatonic framework. The musical surface of operas became, however, increasingly complex. Devices heard only exceptionally in the early operas—passages of rootless chromaticism, sudden shifts into remote keys (notably by way of unprepared six-four chords), a tendency to add surprising harmonic colour to much-used vocal sonorities—now become the norm. Nor are such devices so frequently subordinate to an uncomplicated diatonic melody. Even in conventional arias such as Posa's 'C'est mon jour', the vocal line may now be co-opted into a colouristic chromatic shift, creating a melody that makes little sense without its harmonic underpinning (ex.4). The effect, out of context, may sound wildly empirical; but unlike some parallel moments in the earlier operas, these daring harmonic shifts are usually prepared locally. In example 4, the slideslip onto a six-four chord of G major halfway through the third bar (G minor would have been conventionally lachrymose) is foreshadowed by a tonicization of G minor in the preceding *B* section.

Ex. 3 *Aida,* Act 4

['Farewell, earth; farewell valley of tears, dream of joy that vanished in sorrow. Heaven opens to us, and our wandering spirits to the beams of eternal day.']

The preparation for such daring chromatic moments may spread further still. In 'C'est mon jour' the shift up a semitone to an unexpected major-mode sonority can be traced back through the preceding recitative and, by means of motivic transformations there, ultimately linked to the solemn chanting of the monks that begins Act 2 ('Charles-Quint, l'auguste Empereur'), which is recalled orchestrally at the start of Act 5, and ends the entire drama. On a more local but more immediately perceptible level, the unusual harmonic span in the first limb of 'Celeste Aida', which moves from B♭ major to D major, only to shift back to B♭ at the start of the next

Ex. 4 *Don Carlos*, Act 4

['Death has its attractions, oh my Carlos, to one who dies for you.']

limb (ex.5), is anticipated by unmediated juxtapositions between and around these chords in the preceding scene, first in the recitative between Ramfis and Radames, then in Radames's recitative immediately before the aria.

These moments (and there are many more) contribute to the *tinta* of an opera, its overall sense of musical identity; but there remains little evidence of more purposeful and wide-ranging harmonic organization, still less of long-range goal direction. Indeed, the relative broadness of dramatic

Ex. 5 *Aida*, Act 1

['Heavenly Aida, beauty resplendent, mystical garland blooming and bright.']

Ex. 5 *Aida*, Act 1 *(continued)*

scope and looseness of construction among these operas (what Verdi might have called their 'mosaic' or 'patchwork' tendencies) works against even that loose juxtaposition of tonal regions or melodic types found in operas such as *Macbeth* or *Il trovatore*. Occasionally a key centre or progression may briefly shoulder the burden of semantic weight: the key of D♭ in *Un ballo in maschera*, for example, is persistently associated with the death of the protagonist, and the opera also makes much of alternations between the major and minor mode; but the continuing formal fixity of Verdi's musical language militates against programmatic use of such devices, and they never approach an important level of structural significance.

There is no doubt that recurring motifs become an increasingly vital aspect of Verdian *tinta*, although one should again be cautious in making extravagant claims for their centrality—nothing like a Wagnerian Leitmotif technique is ever attempted. A case in point is *La forza del destino*, in which the presence of recurring themes, in particular the main theme of the overture, frequently dubbed a 'destiny' or 'fate' motif, is sometimes said to exemplify the score's 'musical unity'. Perhaps this is so, but one could also see such elements as giving a degree of musical connectedness to a score that in other respects conspicuously lacks the cohesion Verdi so surely achieved in his middle-period works. The most thoroughgoing use of recurring themes is in *Aida*, but even there thematic reappearances sharply diminish towards the end of the opera. Far from emerging through developmental chains to become centrally expressive of the drama (as they can in Wagner's later operas), these themes have a fixity that tends to restrict them to the expository stages of the plot: they are points from which the musical drama develops and rarely become implicated in the great turning points of the plot.

The use of local colour becomes an ever more important connective device, perhaps as a necessary corrective to the expansion of dramatic scope and mood. The final act of *Les Vêpres siciliennes* begins with three 'atmospheric' numbers (the chorus 'Célébrons ensemble', Hélène's *sicilienne* 'Merci, jeunes amies', and Henri's *mélodie* 'La brise souffle au loin') in which the plot is barely advanced but local colour is richly explored; the last act of *Aroldo* seems as much concerned with its startling new ambience as with the dénouement of the plot. What is more, several of the operas take on a particular colour intimately associated with their setting—the sea images of *Simon Boccanegra* and the exotic Iberian character of *Don Carlos* are good examples. Again, the climax comes in the exoticism of *Aida*, arguably the first Italian opera in which depiction of geographical location becomes an essential aspect of the musical atmosphere. This added dimension is intimately bound up with Verdi's increasingly sophisticated use of the orchestra. The period saw the rise of more disciplined, conductor-led orchestras in Italy; particularly after his experience with the young Angelo Mariani at the première of *Aroldo*, Verdi was quick to exploit the opportunities this provided for more complex instrumental effects. By the time of *Aida*, he was capable of setting up a classic 'nature' scene such as the prelude to Act 3, in which the elements of harmony, melody, and rhythm are all subsumed under a mantle of evocative orchestral colour.

Influence

One might assume that the primary influences on the young Verdi, namely his Italian predecessors, would now have faded; and clearly his new musical style was very different from anything in Donizetti or Bellini. However, this period offers some striking 'reminiscences': the opening bars of the orchestral introduction to Ulrica's 'Re dell'abisso' (*Un ballo in maschera* Act 1) is virtually identical to that of Essex's prison scene in *Roberto Devereux* Act 2; *La favorite* and *La forza del destino* share several ecclesiastical effects; and the famous triumphal scene in *Aida* is anticipated by a similar moment in *Poliuto*. These similarities (and there are others) are probably less acts of deliberate homage than evidence that Verdi was still ready to draw on the lingua franca of Ottocento opera, in particular when (as in all these cases) 'characteristic' effects were called for. Rather different, though, is an aria such as Leonora's 'Pace, pace, mio Dio!' from *La forza del destino* Act 4, which sounds like a distant homage to Bellini, whose 'long, long, long melodies' Verdi had so admired but generally had found antithetical to his rhythmically direct early manner. He could now on occasions achieve Bellinian length and, more significantly, enrich the vocal line with those declamatory asides and harmonic shifts for which Bellini was famous.

The most important new influences, however, came from France, in particular from Meyerbeer, the acknowledged master of the grand Parisian manner. This debt is most obvious in *Les Vêpres siciliennes*, Verdi's explicit attempt to meet Meyerbeer on his own ground, which shows a tendency towards 'musical prose' in a lengthening and fragmenting of melodic lines. On the other hand, this fragmentation can also be seen in the Italian operas, *endecasillabi* and other lengthy verse lines becoming more common in lyrical numbers; and there the Meyerbeerian tone is harder to locate. Undoubtedly the new attention to orchestral detail was in part inspired by Parisian models, although even at his most elaborate Verdi never attempted those minute nuances of detail for which Meyerbeer was so famous. Nor was grand opera the only gesture towards Paris. *Un ballo in maschera* demonstrates that Verdi also took a lively interest in the *opéra comique* tradition and found ways of using this very different style as a foil for his more serious inspirations.

Reception and politics

As the 1850s unfolded, Verdi's pre-eminence in Italian music, and his international reputation, became ever more secure; although many of the early operas had been forgotten, *Rigoletto*, *Il trovatore*, and *La traviata* quickly became cornerstones of the newly emerging Italian operatic repertory. This did not, though, stop occasional clashes with the operatic censor; indeed, the revolution-shy 1850s created more obstacles than ever. *Les Vêpres siciliennes* caused continual difficulties in Italy and was often performed in a bowdlerized version (as *Giovanna de Guzman*). More problematic still was *Un ballo in maschera*, which caused trouble even as it was being composed. As soon as a synopsis reached the Neapolitan censors, it became clear that the assassination of a head of state would not be permitted, and even when this aspect was altered, there was still the issue of Amelia's adultery (the censor suggested she should become the sister rather than the wife of Riccardo). Negotiations broke down; the opera eventually had its première at Rome's Teatro Apollo, and even then with a change in locale (from regal Sweden to Ducal Boston) being enforced.

Despite these tribulations, each new Verdi opera generated enormous interest, both in Italy and in the international press. But by the mid 1860s it gradually became clear that Verdi's more recent works were not duplicating his successes of the early 1850s. Neither *Les Vêpres siciliennes* nor *Don Carlos* established themselves at the Opéra, and both had difficulties in transplanting to the Italian stage. *Simon Boccanegra* was poorly received, and *Un ballo in maschera* and *La forza del destino* made their way comparatively slowly. Part of the problem undoubtedly lay in the conservatism of Verdi's new creations. Although operas such as *Il trovatore* had quickly achieved 'classic' status, a new generation of Italians was emerging. Young artistic revolutionaries such as Arrigo Boito were now calling for an end to the insular, 'formulaic' musical dramas of the past; as early as 1864 Boito announced that Meyerbeer had 'caused Italian operas to collapse by the hundreds like the bricks of the walls of Jericho'. Italian intellectuals began to read Wagner's essays, and Italian theatres began to open their doors to French (and later to German) operas.

The paradox of this uncertain reaction to Verdi's 'new manner' was that it went hand in hand with his institution as a national figure beyond the operatic world. In 1858–59, his name was briefly taken up as an acrostic message of Italian nationalistic aspirations ('Viva VERDI' standing for 'Viva *V*ittorio *E*manuele *R*e *D'I*talia'), and by the late 1860s certain pieces of early Verdi had begun to be canonized through their supposed association with the revolutionary struggles of the 1840s. This was particularly true of the chorus 'Va pensiero', the rapidly achieved iconic status of which was encouraged by the composer, who reserved for it a central, revelatory role in the 'official' story of his early career he allowed to be disseminated. Such mythmaking was perhaps rendered more urgent by the economic collapses and social tensions of the newly formed Italian state, engendering as it did nostalgia for a past age in which Italians had been united against its 'foreign' enemies.

In the face of these momentous cultural and political developments, and despite periodic bursts of professional and social activity, Verdi chose strategic withdrawal: physically behind the walls of Sant'Agata; mentally into an image of himself as a rough, untutored man of the soil, the peasant from Roncole, the self-made man, an 'authentic' Italian willing to set himself against the tide of cosmopolitan sophistication he saw washing around him. It was overwhelmingly this image that he offered to those interviewers who now began to pester him for his pronouncements on cultural matters and for biographical tidbits; the resulting self-portrait was one he sedulously cultivated (along with his farmlands) for the rest of his long life.

Interregnum: The 1870s and the *Requiem* (1874)

After *Aida* in 1871, there was no Verdi operatic première for sixteen years. The creative stagnation was not quite so complete as this blunt statistic suggests. In 1873, while supervising performances of *Aida* at the Teatro San Carlo in Naples, Verdi wrote and had privately performed the String Quartet in E minor. And in 1874 came the *Messa da Requiem*, composed in honour of Alessandro Manzoni. But the fact remains that the 1870s and early 1880s, years in which Verdi might have been thought at the height of his creative powers, saw no new operas. The reasons for this silence are complex: his increasing financial security no longer made work a necessity; more of his energies went into the development of substantial land holdings, and—increasingly—into various charitable causes. He also spent much time supervising and directing performances of *Aida* and the *Requiem*, in 1875 undertaking a mini-European tour (Paris, London, Vienna) with the latter work. At the same time, his personal life underwent an upheaval: a continuing public scandal that caused much private anguish between him and his partner. The reason was his relationship with the soprano Teresa Stolz, who had been the first Leonora in the 1869 version of *La forza del destino*, the first Aida in the Milanese première of that opera (1872), and for whom Verdi wrote the soprano solo in the *Requiem*. Matters between her, Strepponi, and Verdi came to a crisis in 1876; but eventually they resolved with the status quo intact, Stolz remaining a close friend of Verdi, perhaps also of Strepponi, for the rest of their lives.

But surely the most serious obstacle to continued creative activity was his sense of disenchantment with the direction of newly cosmopolitan Italy. Early in the 1870s Verdi was asked for advice about a revised curriculum for the reformed Italian conservatories. His suggestions were austere in the extreme: students should submit to daily doses of fugue and should study only the old Italian masters; budding composers 'must attend *few performances* of modern operas, and avoid becoming fascinated either by their many beauties of harmony and orchestration or by the *diminished 7th* chord'. On many other occasions he voiced his discontent at the direction Italian music was taking, in particular its newest fascination for the Germanic and the 'symphonic'. It is easy to see how such a reaction further fuelled the reluctance to compose that Verdi had already shown in the 1860s. It would take all the ingenuity of his closest friends to coax him from this self-imposed retirement.

The 1870s did, though, produce the *Requiem*, and that is no small achievement. As already mentioned, the origins of the piece can be traced back to 1868 and Verdi's proposal for a composite *Requiem* in honour of Rossini, to be written by 'the most distinguished Italian composers'. This was duly completed, but plans to perform the piece came to nothing; in April 1873 Verdi's contribution, the 'Libera me' movement, was returned to him. It seems likely that about this time he decided to write an entire *Requiem* himself, a decision perhaps precipitated, perhaps strengthened, by the death in May of Alessandro Manzoni, to whom the work was dedicated.

In the circumstances, it is inevitable that the theatrical nature of the *Requiem* should be a principal matter for debate: even before its first performance, Hans von Bülow famously referred to it as an 'Oper in

Kirchengewande' (opera in ecclesiastical dress). Such sentiments can only be strengthened by the knowledge that a duet for Carlos and Philippe, discarded from *Don Carlos* during rehearsals in Paris, formed the basis of the 'Lacrymosa' section of the Dies irae. More operatic still is the manner in which the soloists occasionally take on what can only be called 'personalities'. This is most noticeable in the final 'Libera me', in which the soprano, isolated from the other soloists, seems in active dialogue with both the chorus and the orchestra, for all the world like a beleaguered heroine trying finally to make sense of the world into which she has been cast.

But we should not exaggerate. The main theme of the 'Lacrymosa' may have originated in an opera, but it develops in a markedly different fashion, without the vocal contrasts that typically fuel Verdian musical drama. None of the ensemble scenes or choruses (of which there is an unoperatic preponderance) resembles the texture of their operatic equivalents, in particular by their frequent use of contrapuntal writing and by the relative lack of differentiation between individuals. What is more, the levels of purely musical connection (particularly in motivic and harmonic gestures) are far greater than Verdi would have deemed appropriate in a drama, where contrast and tension between characters is so important a part of the effect.

The presence of that counterpoint may, though, chime with those partial reminiscences of his own student days: 'in the three years spent with [Lavigna] I did nothing but canons and fugues, fugues and canons of all sorts. No one taught me orchestration or how to treat dramatic music'. These reminiscences were made at a time when he was admonishing future conservatory students to study fugue rather than 'modern [i.e., foreign or foreign-influenced] operas'. We do well to recall that Verdi's original idea for a composite *Requiem* was as a celebration of Italian art and artists during what he thought of as a period of cultural crisis: as he said in his first letter about the project, 'I would like no foreign hand, no hand alien to art, no matter how powerful, to lend his assistance. In this case I would withdraw at once from the association'. In that sense, the decision to write a *Requiem*, and thus to celebrate through counterpoint a glorious era in Italy's musical past, makes the work as 'political' as any of the composer's operas.

Life, 1879–1901

In June 1879 Giulio Ricordi and Arrigo Boito mentioned to Verdi the possibility of his composing an opera based on *Othello*, surely a canny choice given Verdi's lifelong veneration for Shakespeare and his attempts after *Macbeth* to tackle further Shakespearean topics, notably *King Lear*. Verdi showed cautious enthusiasm for the new project, and by the end of the year Boito had produced a draft libretto, one full of ingenious new rhythmic devices but with a firm dramatic thread. After almost ten years without an operatic project, Verdi again started to create musical drama.

The project was long in the making. First came two other tasks: extensive revisions to *Simon Boccanegra* (effected with the help of Boito), and then to *Don Carlos*, both of which can be seen in retrospect as trial runs for the new type of opera Verdi felt he must create in Italy's new artistic climate. After many interruptions, *Otello* was finally premièred at La Scala in February 1887. Some two years later, Boito suggested another opera, largely based on Shakespeare's *The Merry Wives of Windsor*. Verdi was immediately enthusiastic about Boito's draft scenario, made relatively few structural suggestions, and by August 1889 announced that he was writing a comic fugue (quite possibly the fugue that ends *Falstaff*). Composer and librettist worked closely together during the winter of 1889–90, and by the spring of 1890 the libretto of *Falstaff* was complete. As with *Otello*, composing the opera took a considerable time, or rather involved short bursts of activity interspersed with long fallow periods. The opera was first performed, again at La Scala, in February 1893.

These years also saw the appearance of various sacred vocal pieces, some of which were later collected under the title *Quattro pezzi sacri*. It is certainly no accident that in these pieces Verdi made gestures to two figures from the Italian past whom he considered central to the cultural unity of the country. Most obviously there are texts by Dante. But in pieces such as the 'Laudi alla Vergine Maria', the musical gestures—both in contrapuntal treatment and word painting—are to Palestrina, the composer whose style should in Verdi's view have remained an essential point of departure for Italian musical art. This last, 'antique' style might well suggest an old man's retreat from the world; but on another level it speaks yet again of Verdi's passionate concern for the national traditions into which he had been born, and with which he had so constantly engaged.

Verdi continued to divide his life between Milan, Genoa, and Sant'Agata, where he oversaw his lands and added to his property. In his last years he devoted a considerable amount of money and energy to two philanthropic projects: the building of a hospital at Villanova sull'Arda Piacenza, and the founding of a home for retired musicians, the Casa di Riposo, in Milan.

In November 1897 Strepponi died at Sant'Agata. In December 1900 Verdi made arrangements for his youthful compositions (including, one assumes, those 'marches for band by the hundred') to be burnt after his death, and left Sant'Agata for Milan. On 21 January he suffered a stroke from which he died on 27 January. He was buried next to his wife in Milan's Cimitero Monumentale; a month later, amid national mourning, their bodies were moved to the Casa di Riposo. Before the procession left the Cimitero, Arturo Toscanini conducted a massed choir. They sang, of course, 'Va pensiero'.

The Last Style: *Otello* (1887) and *Falstaff* (1893)

An intangible divide

In spite of the chronological gap, critics have tended to see Verdi's last two operas as a logical continuation (and almost always as the 'culmination') of his previous work, thus stressing stylistic continuity across his entire career. There is much to be said for such an approach. Although Verdi was now firmly established as an international figure who could—and did—dictate his own terms, he continued to compose in the old manner: from sketches to continuity draft to 'skeleton score' to full orchestration. He also continued to pay careful attention to the singers at his disposal, and was willing to adjust passages to accommodate them: the Act 2 quartet in *Otello* was transposed down a half step in the passage from continuity draft to autograph, clearly to ease its tessitura; and the role of Quickly in *Falstaff* was amplified at a late stage after Verdi had heard (and approved of) the singer destined to create the role. Verdi also continued his unshakable allegiance to the grandest of the traditional Ottocento set pieces, the Largo concertato, examples of which occur in the revised *Boccanegra*, *Otello*, and *Falstaff*.

The strain and difficulty with which a suitable concertato was eventually accommodated into *Otello* indicates, however, a fundamental change in Verdian dramaturgy. At some time during the fallow period between *Aida* and *Otello*, we might hazard that Verdi crossed an intangible divide and now saw the basis of his musical drama residing in continuous 'action' rather than in a juxtaposition of 'action' and 'reflection'. (It was the difficulty of embedding comprehensible 'action' into the Act 3 concertato of *Otello* that continued to pose problems, even causing Verdi to revise the number for the opera's Parisian première in 1894.) The long Act 2 duet between Otello and Iago is a good example of how the new hierarchy worked. The duet itself cannot usefully be parsed as a set piece in contrasting 'movements'; the true set pieces—the Credo, Homage Chorus, Quartet, and Racconto—are embedded within the larger structure, acting as interruptions rather than points of arrival. The dynamics of this change, this crossing of the 'intangible divide', are intimately linked to Verdi's relationship with his last librettist.

Verdi and Boito

It seemed at first an unlikely collaboration, although it started smoothly enough in 1862, when Verdi and Boito worked together briefly on the *Inno delle nazioni* for the Great London Exhibition. But in the cultural context of the 1860s a more likely exchange occurred a year later. Boito, a leading figure in the *scapigliatura*, a nascent Italian branch of the Europe-wide bohemian movement, improvised an ode 'All'arte italiana' that described the present-day 'altar' of Italian art as 'defiled like the wall of a brothel'. Not surprisingly, Verdi took this personally. Perhaps, though, the acrimony Boito's comment generated holds a key, in that one of the most significant aspects of the Verdi-Boito collaboration was precisely that they came from different generations and thus had sharply divergent attitudes to the Italian operatic tradition. That the collaboration happened at all is in part thanks to the patient and sensitive manoeuvering of Verdi's publisher Giulio Ricordi; but it also reflects the fact that Boito had mellowed by the late 1870s. His magnum opus, the opera *Mefistofele*, had failed disastrously at La Scala in 1868, and when he restaged it seven years later, he toned down many of its most radical aspects, replacing them with more traditional operatic solutions. Here was rapprochement of a kind.

But the generation gap remained, and it is hardly surprising that the early days of work on *Otello* were punctuated by some remarkably basic differences of opinion about the structure of the opera. In Verdi's first letter commenting on Boito's draft libretto, the composer suggested that the 'dramatic element' was missing after the Act 3 concertato in which all on stage react to Otello's striking of Desdemona. Verdi's solution was a radical departure from Shakespeare in which, true to the theatrical conventions of his past, an external event (a resurgence of the warlike Turks) would lead the musical drama onwards. Boito strongly disagreed: for him *Otello* was above all a modern, claustrophobic, psychological drama, one that took place essentially within the psyche, in the realm Wagner liked to call that of the 'inner drama', a place of dense symbolic meaning in which characters are trapped, deprived of autonomy. To have Otello heroically rally his troops would have shattered the spell. But what is most striking about the difference of opinion is that Verdi—earlier a veritable tyrant in his dealings with librettists—gave way to Boito, trusting the younger man's perception of what modern drama needed. This trust obliged him to do nothing less than re-invent his operatic language, to find a newly flexible mode of musical expression.

Technical features

This need for the music to react minutely and spontaneously to the constant changes of mood and emphasis—typical of spoken dialogue—brought about a loosening of the traditional links between prosody and music. Boito was particularly adept at constructing verses that, although obeying the rules of Italian prosody, could be read simultaneously in a variety of verse metres, thus offering something like the flexibility of a prose libretto. There was also an inevitable decrease in periodic structures, and when aspects of the 'lyric prototype' can be found, they are usually placed in a dynamic harmonic context that obscures their origin in Verdi's earlier style. Vestiges of the old Ottocento forms are—with the exception of the Largo concertato, which continued even into Puccini's last works—equally hard to locate. Some have found shards of the old four-movement structure in the Act 1 love duet between Otello and Desdemona; but the divergences and anomalies are apt to make such demonstrations always smack of special pleading.

On rare occasions, Verdi may have sought to replace this absence of formally predictable units with purely musical structures: the sonata-form subtext of the opening scene in *Falstaff*, or its closing comic fugue, are likely examples, although both forms are, as it were, placed in inverted commas, ironically drawing attention to their structural difference from the norm. The necessary level of musical coherence was, though, often supplied by local increases in harmonic, motivic, and orchestral activity, all of which carried further the developments seen in the period between *Les Vêpres siciliennes* and *Aida*. Passages such as the Act 3 orchestral prelude to the revised *Don Carlos* (1884) show how a short motivic fragment could now be sufficient to construct large spans of music, so extensive was Verdi's control over orchestral nuance and chromatic detail.

Clearly, recurring motivic and harmonic aspects are sometimes found on a larger level. The famous 'bacio' theme in *Otello*, which first occurs near the end of the Act 1 love duet and then appears twice in the final scene of the opera, has a function difficult to compare with previous recurring themes: unlike those in *Aida*, which fade away as the drama reaches its climax, the final statement of the 'bacio' theme seems like a musical summing-up of the dénouement, thus having more in common with famous Puccinian endings, in spite of its restraint. More than this, the 'bacio' theme's harmonic character, with its typical late Verdian device of a predominant pause on a tonally distant six-four chord, also casts its influence over other confrontations between Otello and Desdemona. Further recurring motifs can approach a level of Wagnerian density over shorter spans: the Act 3 prelude to *Don Carlos* has already been mentioned; the 'jealousy' motif that winds through the prelude to *Otello* Act 3, and the 'dalle due alle tre' motif that underpins Ford's famous monologue in Act 2 of *Falstaff*, are further instances.

Verdi since 1901

By the time Verdi wrote his last operas, he had become a national monument: the premières of *Otello* and *Falstaff* were musical events of almost unprecedented importance, occasioning a flood of publicity all over Europe. Both works, inevitably in the circumstances, were heralded as brilliant successes, but—like so many of the operas after *La traviata*— neither established a place at the centre of the Italian repertory. The operatic times had changed and, in an era when Wagner and the Italian *veristi* were making the headlines, *Otello* and *Falstaff*, for all their 'modernity', were seen as *sui generis*, unsuitable for the common round of smaller theatres in particular. So far as performances and purely musical reputation were concerned, the years around the turn of the century represented a low point in Verdi's fortunes. In the increasingly sophisticated, cosmopolitan atmosphere of *fin-de-siècle* Italy, it became commonplace to find Verdi's musical personality too simple and direct. Although *Rigoletto*, *Il trovatore*, and *La traviata* remained the staple of smaller opera houses, they were rarely granted the prestige of important revivals. The situation was little different in other major European centres at the turn of the century. In both England and France, for example, a decisive shift away from Italian opera came in the wake of regular Wagner stagings in the 1880s and '90s. Nor did Verdi have much noticeable influence on younger generations of composers. The case of Puccini is instructive: although by his own admission an early experience of *Aida* was crucial to his development, Puccini's first operas show very few traces of the Verdian style, deriving predominantly from French models; the influence he struggled to overcome (we can see the struggle at its most intense in the second act of *Manon Lescaut*) was overwhelmingly that of Wagner.

Although there was some renewed attention to Verdi in his centenary year of 1913, the crucial change in his fortunes began in Weimar Republic Germany. This so-called Verdi renaissance is sometimes traced to the first production of Franz Werfel's version of *La forza del destino* (Dresden, 1926), or to the publication of Werfel's novel *Verdi: Roman der Oper* in 1924, but the movement was far too widespread to be attributed to just one event, and was marked by numerous restagings of forgotten operas, a considerable periodical literature and several important monographs. As was recognized at the time, the 'return' to Verdi had much to do with an awareness that opera was in crisis—that new works were not taking their place in the repertory—and also with a widespread reassessment (in some cases outright rejection) of the Wagnerian aesthetic. In the latter guise, as noble antithesis to Wagner, Verdi was even taken up by the avant-garde: some of the most innovative stagings of the period involved Verdi revivals, and an arch modernist such as Stravinsky could praise his achievement and even pay him veiled musical homage in works such as *Oedipus Rex*.

By the 1930s the 'renaissance' had spread, with revivals of forgotten works springing up all over Europe and America. Appropriated by fascists and antifascists alike, Verdi's music survived World War II relatively untarnished, as did his reputation as 'vate del risorgimento', the bard of Italy's achievement of statehood. In the 1950s and '60s his operas became the core repertory of the global opera industry. 'Forgotten' works continue to be revived, and today more Verdi operas are in the repertory than ever before, the centenary celebrations of 2001 stimulating huge interest both among performers and scholars. Even as these celebrations reverberate, though, there are hints that Verdi's operas have in the last decades hit some kind of peak, and may in relative terms be in decline. Certainly the explosion of Handel opera performances in the last twenty years must have caused losses elsewhere, as has the concomitant explosion in international voices that can sing Handel (and thus, almost by definition, not sing Verdi). But if some decline is to be expected, it is likely to be partial and slow-moving. Verdi continues to inspire performers and audiences to fresh interpretations and renewed energies. It is now hard to imagine an operatic world in which they will cease to do so.

{ *The Operas*

Oberto, conte di San Bonifacio

('*Oberto, Count of San Bonifacio*')

Dramma in two acts set to a libretto by Antonio Piazza and Temistocle Solera; first performed in Milan, Teatro alla Scala, on 17 November 1839.

The cast at the première included Antonietta Ranieri Marini (Leonora), Mary Shaw (Cuniza), Lorenzo Salvi (Riccardo), and Ignazio Marini (Oberto).

Cuniza, *sister of Ezzelino da Romano*	mezzo-soprano
Riccardo, *Count of Salinguerra*	tenor
Oberto, *Count of San Bonifacio*	bass
Leonora, *his daughter*	soprano
Imelda, *Cuniza's confidante*	soprano

Knights, ladies, vassals

Setting Bassano, in and around Ezzelino's castle, in 1228

Verdi's first opera has a chequered history. As we first hear of it in 1836, it was called *Rocester*, with a libretto by Antonio Piazza. After unsuccessful attempts to have the work put on in Milan and Parma, and after a lengthy hiatus during which the composer was employed in his home town of Busseto, Verdi—with the help of the librettist Temistocle Solera—revised and renamed the opera for its La Scala première. *Oberto* was moderately successful and was revived a number of times during the next three years, Verdi taking the opportunity to add various new numbers to the score. For Milan (1840) he supplied a new cavatina for Cuniza and a replacement duet for Cuniza and Riccardo, and adapted the role of Oberto for baritone; for

Genoa (1841) he wrote a replacement duet for Leonora and Oberto and new music for the chorus 'Fidanzata avventurosa'; and for Barcelona (1841–42) he supplied a new first-act aria for Oberto, the cabaletta of which ('Ma fin che un brando vindice') later became associated with *Ernani*.

*   *   *

Act 1 opens as Riccardo, Count of Salinguerra, is about to be married to Cuniza, the sister of Ezzelino da Romano. Riccardo has previously seduced Leonora, the daughter of Oberto, Count of San Bonifacio and Ezzelino's defeated enemy. Leonora and Oberto arrive in Bassano and enlist the sympathy of Cuniza. In a grand finale to the act, father and daughter confront Riccardo; Oberto challenges him to a duel.

The second act begins as Cuniza resolves to make Riccardo take back Leonora. Oberto, however, continues to swear revenge. After a further confrontation between the four principals, the men withdraw to fight their duel; Riccardo emerges victorious but, guilt-ridden at causing Oberto's death, he departs abroad. Leonora, desolate at her father's death, decides to enter a convent.

*   *   *

Although Verdi was twenty-six when *Oberto* was first produced, the opera is in some ways an apprentice work, not typical of his early manner. Some of the lyrical pieces have a formal looseness reminiscent of Bellini (clearly, with Rossini, the main stylistic influence), and connecting passages between the movements of set pieces are often curiously perfunctory or nonexistent. On the other hand, there are sometimes strong hints of the future: in powerful unison writing for the chorus, in some dramatically striking ensemble pieces, and perhaps most of all in the rhythmic vitality of many episodes. The slow movement of the Act 2 quartet, 'La vergogna', probably the last piece to be written, is in many ways the most impressive. Although, as elsewhere in the opera, the daring chromaticism of the opening is rather shakily deployed, the large-scale control of musical rhythm, in particular the dynamic use of triplet figures, offers compelling testimony to what was to be one of the young Verdi's great strengths. Such successes notwithstanding, it is unlikely that *Oberto* will become anything more than a curiosity in the operatic repertory.

Un giorno di regno

('*King for a Day*') [*Il finto Stanislao* ('*The False Stanislaus*')]

Melodramma giocoso in two acts set to a libretto by Felice Romani (probably revised by Temistocle Solera) after Alexandre Vincent Pineu-Duval's play *Le Faux Stanislas*; first performed in Milan, Teatro alla Scala, on 5 September 1840.

The cast at the première included Antonietta Ranieri Marini (Marchesa), Luigia Abbadia (Giulietta), Lorenzo Salvi (Edoardo), and Raffaele Ferlotti (Belfiore).

Cavaliere di Belfiore, *posing as Stanislaus, King of Poland*	baritone
Baron Kelbar	buffo bass
Marchesa del Poggio, *a young widow, the Baron's niece, in love with Belfiore*	soprano
Giulietta di Kelbar, *the Baron's daughter, in love with Edorado*	mezzo soprano
Edoardo di Sanval, *a young officer*	tenor
La Rocca, *Edoardo's uncle, the state treasurer*	buffo bass
Count Ivrea	tenor
Delmonte, *squire to the false Stanislaus*	tenor

Servants, chambermaids, vassals of the Baron

Setting Near Brest in the castle of Kelbar, 1733

Verdi's second opera, his only outright comic work until the end of his long career, was written at great speed. It is likely that Bartolomeo Merelli (impresario at La Scala) assigned him the libretto only in late June 1840; Romani's old *melodramma giocoso* (originally set by Adalbert Gyrowetz in 1818 under the title *Il finto Stanislao*) then had to be substantially revised to bring it some way up to date. (Although no direct evidence survives, the reviser was probably Temistocle Solera, who had helped with revisions of Verdi's first opera and seems then to have been something of a 'house poet' at La Scala during this period.) The opera was a fiasco, removed from the stage after only one performance. To judge from contemporary reviews, and from Verdi's later recollections, its failure had as much to do with the performance as with the music. *Un giorno di regno* (which in subsequent revivals occasionally reassumed the original title of *Il finto Stanislao*) enjoyed a few revivals in Verdi's lifetime, and has occasionally been staged in modern times.

*   *   *

Belfiore is an officer posing as King Stanislaus of Poland in order to protect the king from harm. But he is in love with a young widow, the Marchesa del Poggio, who is about to marry another. Secondary romantic interest comes from a pair of young lovers, Edoardo and Giulietta; comic scenes are supplied by a pair of *buffo* basses, Baron Kelbar (Giulietta's father) and La Rocca, the state treasurer (Edoardo's uncle), who wishes to marry Giulietta. After several farcical intrigues, Belfiore uses his disguise to effect the marriage of the young lovers and then reveals his true identity in time to claim the Marchesa as his own.

*   *   *

The opera is curiously uneven and, not surprisingly given the rushed circumstances of its creation, tends to peter out in the second act. It is heavily influenced by Rossini, but there are moments—particularly those passages that were altered from the old Romani libretto—in which we find a more up-to-date, Donizettian conception of sentimental comedy. The opera's most interesting vocal character is the Marchesa, whose role was written for Antonietta Ranieri-Marini, the singer who had earlier created Leonora in Verdi's first opera, *Oberto, conte di San Bonifacio*. The lovelorn tenor Edoardo shows early signs of Verdian robustness (particularly in his Act 1 duet with Belfiore), but later reverts to the lighter, higher style associated with the Rossinian tenor. *Un giorno di regno* must, by and large, be judged an unfortunate interlude in Verdi's progress; but even through the barrier of its alien style, there are glimpses of the vital individuality that was to emerge so decisively in his next opera, *Nabucco*.

Nabucco

[*Nabucodonosor*]

Dramma lirico in four acts set to a libretto by Temistocle Solera after Antonio Cortesi's ballet *Nabucodonosor* and Auguste Anicet-Bourgeois' and Francis Cornu's play *Nabuchodonosor*; first performed in Milan, Teatro alla Scala, on 9 March 1842.

The cast at the première included Prosper Dérivis (Zaccaria), Giuseppina Strepponi (Abigaille), Giorgio Ronconi (Nabucco), Corrado Miraglia (Ismaele), and Giovannina Bellinzaghi (Fenena).

Nabucodonosor [Nabucco; Nebuchadnezzar],	
King of Babylon	baritone
Ismaele, *nephew of Sedecia, King of Jerusalem*	tenor
Zaccaria, *High Priest of the Hebrews*	bass
Abigaille, *slave, presumed to be the first daughter*	
of Nabucodonosor	soprano
Fenena, *daughter of Nabucodonosor*	soprano
The High Priest of Baal	bass
Abdallo, *elderly officer of the King of Babylon*	tenor
Anna, *Zaccaria's sister*	soprano

Babylonian and Hebrew soldiers, Levites, Hebrew virgins, Babylonian women, magi, Lords of the Kingdom of Babylon, populace, etc.

Setting Jerusalem and Babylon, 587 BC

The story of *Nabucco* (or *Nabucodonosor* as it was originally called) began some eighteen months before its first performance, soon after the successful première of Verdi's first opera, *Oberto, conte di San Bonifacio*. A contract was drawn up between Verdi and Bartolomeo Merelli, impresario at La Scala, according to which Verdi would write three further operas. The first of these, the comic work *Un giorno di regno* (1840), was a disastrous failure and (at least according to Verdi's own later memories) the humiliation of public rejection caused the composer to give up his professional calling. However, in the winter of 1840–41, Merelli persuaded Verdi to take on Temistocle Solera's libretto of *Nabucco*, which had been turned down by the young Prussian composer Otto Nicolai.

The background of *Nabucco* derives from biblical sources, most extensively from *Jeremiah*; and although Nabucco (Nebuchadnezzar) is the only biblical character to appear, the part of the prophet Zaccaria has strong overtones of Jeremiah. Solera's main source was a French play, first performed in 1836, although some of his alterations can be traced to the scenario of a ballet also derived from the play, given at La Scala in 1838. The lack of documentation concerning the genesis of the opera can be put down to a number of factors: Verdi was relatively unknown at the time, and few of his letters were preserved; he and Solera were together in Milan and had little need of correspondence; and Solera—unlike some of Verdi's future librettists—was an experienced man of the theatre who apparently needed little help in constructing a dramatically convincing text.

After a number of delays, *Nabucco* was first performed at La Scala in March 1842. Strepponi, with whom Verdi probably formed a permanent attachment around this time, was in poor voice (and her final scene was cut after two performances), but the opera was nevertheless a great success. It was revived at La Scala for the autumn season of 1842 and ran for a record fifty-seven performances. For this revival Verdi made a number of small changes to suit the new Abigaille, Teresa De Giuli Borsi, and made some adjustments to the vocal line of Fenena's Preghiera in Act 4. For a Venice revival in the Carnival season 1842–43, he replaced this Preghiera with a Romanza for Fenena. It is likely that Verdi wrote ballet music for a revival of *Nabucco* in Brussels in 1848, although no trace of it has survived.

*   *   *

The overture, except for the chorale-like opening, is made up of themes from the opera: the main, recurring idea is from the 'Maledetto' chorus in Act 2; there is also a compound-time, pastoral version of 'Va pensiero' and several martial inspirations.

ACT 1 'JERUSALEM' Scene i *Inside the temple of Solomon* The Babylonian army has reached Jerusalem and is at the gates of the temple. The Israelites lament their fate, but the prophet Zaccaria rallies them: he has as a hostage Fenena, daughter of Nabucco, the Babylonian king, and God will assist them. The people follow Zaccaria into battle. The two numbers that encompass this action are linked and in many ways comprise a single unit. The opening chorus, 'Gli arredi festivi', is fashioned on a large scale and draws its effect from the juxtaposition of contrasting choral groups: a terrified populace, a group of praying Levites, another of supplicant virgins. Zaccaria's response is set in the usual cavatina form of a double aria. The first movement, 'D'Egitto là sui lidi', has an unusual two-stanza structure in which the opening of the second stanza is sustained by unison chorus. The cabaletta, 'Come notte al sol fulgente', also features a unison choral interruption.

The stage clears, leaving Fenena and Ismaele alone. We learn in recitative that the couple fell in love while Ismaele was imprisoned in Babylon, and that Fenena has helped him escape to Israel. They are interrupted by Abigaille, who has stolen into the temple at the head of a band of disguised Assyrian warriors. She had also fallen in love with Ismaele during his captivity and now taunts him with her victory. The accompanied recitative that introduces Abigaille immediately fixes her unusual vocal character, which requires power in the lower register, agility above the staff, and a forceful dramatic presence throughout. The ensuing Terzetto, 'Io t'amava', is a moment of lyrical relaxation graced with much vocal ornamentation, somewhat out of character with the rest of the score.

The finale of Act 1 begins with a pseudo-fugal chorus, 'Lo vedeste?', as the Israelites panic in defeat. Nabucco arrives on horseback to the triumphant strains of a *banda* march, but Zaccaria threatens to kill Fenena if Nabucco profanes the temple. This tableau precipitates the concertato, 'Tremin gl'insani', which is led off by Nabucco and which characterizes by turn the conflicting attitudes of the principals. When the stage action resumes Ismaele, fearful for Fenena, disarms Zaccaria. Nabucco is now free to act and, in a furious stretta, orders the destruction of the temple.

ACT 2 'THE IMPIOUS ONE' Scene i *The royal apartments in Babylon* While Nabucco has been away, Fenena has served as regent. The act opens with a full-scale double aria for Abigaille, who, it turns out, is the daughter of a slave, not the king. After an intense recitative her thoughts turn to Ismaele in the first movement of her double aria, 'Anch'io dischiuso un giorno'. The piece is highly ornamental, with each two-bar phrase rounded by a vocal flourish; but the ornaments, typically for Verdi, are strictly contained, giving their proliferation at the climax a compelling energy. The High Priest of Baal arrives with news that Fenena has freed the Israelites; urged on by a warlike chorus, Abigaille decides to assume power herself. Her cabaletta, 'Salgo già del trono aurato', returns to the forceful tone of the recitative and, although in a far more dynamic context, again succeeds in wedding ornamental gestures to a rigorously controlled structure.

Scene ii *A room in the palace, giving on to other rooms*   Zaccaria's Recitativo and Preghiera, 'Vieni o Levita', is an oasis of calm in this generally hectic opera: its accompaniment of six solo cellos is deployed with great variety of texture. As Zaccaria leaves by one door, Ismaele arrives by another, only to be shunned by the Levites in the chorus 'Il maledetto'. Then follows another grand concertato finale, similar in its opening sections to that of the first act. Abigaille is declared queen and is about to crown herself when Nabucco, whose death had been falsely reported, reappears to snatch the crown for himself. This precipitates the centrepiece of the finale, 'S'appressan gl'istanti', a quasi-canonic movement that gains its effect not from individual characterization (each of the principals sings the same melody) but from an inexorable increase in textural complexity and sonic power. Nabucco then faces the crowd and declares himself not only their king but their God. A thunderbolt strikes him down for this blasphemy, and the crowd murmurs in shocked response. Italian operatic convention would now suggest a fast concluding movement, but instead Solera and Verdi decided on a mad scene for Nabucco during which his discourse distractedly moves between fast and slow tempos before he rails at fate and then faints away. A triumphant cry from Abigaille brings down the curtain.

ACT 3 'THE PROPHECY' Scene i *The Hanging Gardens of Babylon*   The routinely cheerful opening chorus, complete with stage-band interpolations borrowed from Act 1 ('È l'Assiria una regina'), is in its orchestration perhaps an early Verdian effort at depicting local colour. It leads to one of the opera's most celebrated numbers: the Abigaille-Nabucco duet, in which Abigaille dupes her father into signing Fenena's death sentence. After an opening recitative, the duet unfolds in the traditional four-movement pattern. A fast-paced dialogue movement ('Donna, chi sei?'), in which repeated orchestral motifs supply the continuity, leads to a movement of lyrical repose in which the characters develop their opposing attitudes in greater detail ('Oh di qual'onta aggravasi'). The third movement reimposes the outside world, as offstage trumpets announce the death sentence; and then in the final cabaletta ('Deh perdona') Nabucco and Abigaille restate their fixed positions: he begging her to show mercy, she inflexibly maintaining her dominance.

Scene ii *The banks of the Euphrates* The closing scene of Act 3 is called 'Coro e Profezia'. The Hebrews' sighs for their lost homeland are violently countered by Zaccaria, who presents a vision of the future in which Babylon will be reduced to ruins. The Hebrews' choral lament ('Va pensiero') is the most famous piece in *Nabucco*, perhaps in all Verdi. It is deliberately simple, almost incantatory in its rhythmic tread, unvaried phrase pattern, and primarily unison texture; by these means it creates that powerful sense of nostalgia which, later in the century, gave the chorus its status as a symbol of Italian national aspirations. In the context of the drama, however, the chorus's attitude is cast aside by Zaccaria, whose two-part minor-major prophecy ('Del futuro nel buio') takes up rhythmic and melodic strands from 'Va pensiero' and places them in a freshly dynamic context.

ACT 4 'THE BROKEN IDOL' Scene i *The royal apartments* (as 2.i) The scene opens with Nabucco alone on stage, an orchestral prelude representing the king's distraction through scattered recollections of past themes. He hears a funeral march, sees Fenena on her way to execution, but is powerless to help her. As a last resort, he offers a prayer to the God of Israel; sanity returns and he marshals a band of followers to save his daughter. The scene is structured as a double aria for Nabucco, with his prayer ('Dio di Giuda') as the first movement. The ensuing cabaletta ('Cadran, cadranno i perfidi') is highly unusual in beginning with a choral statement of a subsidiary theme.

Scene ii *The Hanging Gardens* To an extended version of the funeral march heard fleetingly in the previous number, Fenena and the Israelites are led towards their deaths. Fenena offers a brief but touching Preghiera ('Oh dischiuso è il firmamento'), and then, just in time, Nabucco rushes on to save her. He announces his conversion and is restored as king; Abigaille (we learn) has taken poison. All now join in a triumphant hymn to their new God ('Immenso Jeovha'), a grandiose unaccompanied chorus with which, in most nineteenth-century performances, the opera came to a close. In the score, however, there is a far more restrained ending: the dying Abigaille enters to ask forgiveness, singing a fragmented melody ('Su me . . . morente') to the accompaniment of solo cello and English horn.

*   *   *

There are many ways in which *Nabucco*, as the composer himself said, is the true beginning of Verdi's artistic career, the true emergence of his distinctive voice. It is admittedly an uneven score, with some unsteady formal experiments that we shall rarely see in future works. But the essential ingredients of Verdi's early style are in place: a grandiose, oratorio-like vein, with a new and dynamic use of the chorus; an extraordinary rhythmic vitality and directness of vocal effect; and, above all, an acute sense of dramatic pacing. What is more, numbers such as the 'Coro e Profezia' in Act 3 show how Verdi could bind these elements into compelling scenic units: the highly novel, aria-like choral writing of 'Va pensiero' is violently countered by the energetic prophesy that follows, but the two halves of the scene are intimately linked by shared rhythmic and melodic motifs. Although, unusually for Verdi, *Nabucco* has no important tenor role, Nabucco and Zaccaria present magnificent opportunities for the baritone and bass, and Abigaille, though always problematic to cast, can prove effective for a forceful yet agile soprano. However, as has often been pointed out, the true protagonist of the opera is undoubtedly the chorus, which dominates several of the strongest scenes, and which enters with such stirring effect at climactic points in so many of the solo numbers.

I Lombardi alla prima crociata

('The Lombards on the First Crusade')

Dramma lirico in four acts set to a libretto by Temistocle Solera after Tommaso Grossi's poem *I Lombardi alla prima crociata*; first performed in Milan, Teatro alla Scala, on 11 February 1843. *I Lombardi* was revised in French in 1847, as *Jérusalem*.

The cast at the première included Giovanni Severi (Arvino), Prosper Dérivis (Pagano), Carlo Guasco (Oronte), and Erminia Frezzolini (Giselda).

Arvino } *sons of Folco, Lord of Rò*	tenor
Pagano }	bass
Viclinda, *Arvino's wife*	soprano
Giselda, *her daughter*	soprano
Pirro, *Arvino's squire*	bass
Prior of the City of Milan	tenor
Acciano, *tyrant of Antioch*	bass
Oronte, *his son*	tenor
Sofia, *Acciano's wife, a secret Christian convert*	soprano

Nuns, priors, populace, hired ruffians, armigers in Folco's palace, ambassadors from Persia, Media, Damascus and Chaldea, harem woman, knights and crusading soldiers, pilgrims, celestial virgins, Lombard women

Setting Milan, in and around Antioch, and near Jerusalem in 1096–97

As with Verdi's previous opera, *Nabucco*, there seems to be hardly any reliable information about the genesis of *I Lombardi*. No records exist of negotiations with La Scala, although popular rumour has it that, after the huge success of *Nabucco*, Bartolomeo Merelli (the impresario there) left to the composer's discretion the fee for his new opera, and that Verdi took advice on an appropriate sum from his future wife, Giuseppina Strepponi. Nor is there any surviving correspondence between Verdi and his librettist, Temistocle Solera. They were both in Milan during the period of composition (presumably the second half of 1842) and, if we are to trust Verdi's later recollections, the composer altered very little of Solera's initial draft. The opera was apparently frowned upon by the religious censors in Milan but eventually escaped with only a few unimportant changes. The first night was a wild public success. For a revival in Senigallia in July 1843, Verdi composed a new cabaletta in Act 2 for Antonio Poggi (as Oronte). His revised, French version of the opera was given as *Jérusalem* in Paris in 1847.

*   *   *

The prelude (the first Verdi wrote) is very short and follows the conventional strategy of attempting a kind of radical synopsis of the ensuing action.

ACT I 'THE VENDETTA' Scene i *The piazza of San Ambrogio, Milan* To a stage-band accompaniment, the opening chorus celebrates new friendship between the brothers Arvino and Pagano ('Oh nobile esempio!'); the two have been enemies ever since Pagano jealously attacked Arvino during the latter's wedding to Viclinda eighteen years ago. Pagano and Arvino appear with family and supporters to announce publicly their reconciliation. This leads to a concertato movement, 'T'assale un tremito! . . . padre che fia?', which is led off by Giselda, who anxiously asks why her father seems so ill at ease; as the ensemble develops, all the principals are musically differentiated. A prior of the city announces that Arvino will lead a group to the Crusades. All join in a bellicose chorus, 'All'empio che infrange', and process off to a robust march. An offstage chorus of nuns introduces Pagano, who, in the first movement of a double aria, 'Sciagurata! hai tu creduto', informs us that he can never forget Viclinda. A group of supporters enters, swearing to help him against Arvino, and he finishes the scene with a fierce cabaletta of revenge, 'O speranza di vendetta'.

Scene ii *A gallery in the Folco palace* Viclinda and Giselda are still uneasy. Arvino enters to inform Viclinda that his father, Folco, is in the adjoining room. Giselda offers a prayer for divine assistance, the subtly scored and harmonically bold Preghiera 'Salve Maria!'. As the women go off, Pagano and his henchman Pirro appear. Pagano enters Arvino's room, to emerge a little later, bloody dagger in hand, dragging Viclinda after him. But, as flames are seen through the windows, Arvino and his followers intercept the villain. The discovery that Pagano has killed his own father precipitates the central Andante mosso, 'Mostro d'averno orribile'. Arvino demands his brother's death while Giselda counsels mercy; Pagano tries unsuccessfully to kill himself, and all join in pronouncing his banishment in a final stretta, 'Va! sul capo ti grava'.

ACT 2 'THE MAN OF THE CAVE' Scene i *A room in Acciano's palace in Antioch* Months have passed; Viclinda has died and the Crusaders are at the gates of Antioch. Acciano and his supporters remain defiant in the chorus 'È dunque vero?'. The stage empties to leave Acciano's wife Sofia (who has converted to Christianity) and their son Oronte. Oronte has fallen in love with Giselda, who has been taken prisoner, and recalls her in an Andante ('La mia letizia infondere') remarkable for its motivic economy. At his mother's prompting, Oronte agrees to convert, celebrating his decision in the gentle, Donizettian cabaletta, 'Come poteva un angelo'.

Scene ii *The mouth of a cave on a mountain peak* A suitably sombre orchestral prelude introduces Pagano (now called 'The Hermit'), who emphasizes his newfound faith in the minor-major Romanza 'Ma quando un suon terribile'. Pirro enters and, failing to recognize his old accomplice, confesses his sins and seeks to atone by revealing Antioch's defences to the Crusaders. A distant stage-band march heralds the Crusaders, who appear with Arvino at their head. Arvino tells 'The Hermit' that Giselda has been captured, and Pagano swears to aid them in battle. The scene closes with a warlike chorus, 'Stolto Allhà!'.

Scene iii *Inside the harem at Antioch* A female chorus, complete with gestures towards 'eastern' local colour, introduces Giselda, who closes the act with a full-scale double aria billed as a 'Rondò Finale'. In the first movement, 'Se vano è il pregare', she prays to her dead mother. The middle section sees the stage suddenly filled with fleeing women and pursuing Crusaders. Sofia tells Giselda that Arvino has killed her husband and son, and in the closing cabaletta, 'No! . . . giusta causa non è d'Iddio', Giselda turns on her father for his ungodly violence.

ACT 3 'THE CONVERSION' Scene i *The valley of Jehoshaphat* A group of Crusaders and their followers cross the stage, singing the chorus,

'Gerusalem!', one of the simplest but most effective pieces in the opera. Giselda appears and is soon joined by Oronte, whom she had believed dead. The lovers' decision to run off together is played out in a traditional four-movement duet, notable for its second movement, 'Oh belle, a questa misera', in which the couple bid farewell to their homelands; and for an un-usually curtailed cabaletta, 'Ah, vieni, sol morte', punctuated by offstage cries from the Lombard soldiers.

Scene ii *Arvino's tent*   Arvino has discovered the disappearance of his daughter and calls down a curse on her. A group of Crusaders report that Pagano has been seen nearby and in a driving aria with chorus, 'Sì! del ciel che non punisce', Arvino vows to search Pagano out and kill him.

Scene iii *Inside a cave*   An elaborate orchestral prelude with solo violin, divided into three contrasting sections, begins the scene. Giselda helps Oronte, wounded by the Crusaders. Railing against God, she launches the first movement of an ensemble, 'Tu la madre mi togliesti'; but she is inter-rupted by Pagano (still 'The Hermit'), who brings holy water with which to bless the dying Oronte. The solo violin is still much in evidence (a sure sign that Oronte is destined for heaven) in the second lyrical movement, the Andantino 'Qual voluttà trascorrere'.

ACT 4 'THE HOLY SEPULCHRE' Scene i *A cave near Jerusalem*   A brief dialogue in the original printed libretto, not set to music, explains that Giselda has been brought back to her father by 'The Hermit', and that Arvino has forgiven his daughter. The scene then opens with Giselda, overtaken in sleep by a chorus of celestial spirits. A vision of Oronte ap-pears to sing the Andante 'In cielo benedetto', in which he tells his beloved that the Crusaders will find much-needed water at Siloim. When the vision vanishes, Giselda breaks into a brilliant cabaletta of joy, 'Non fu sogno!'— apparently one of the most popular numbers in the opera with contempo-rary audiences.

Scene ii *The Lombard camp near Rachel's tomb*   The Lombards, dying of thirst, conjure up visions of their distant homeland in the famous chorus 'O Signore, dal tetto natio', a number whose hymn-like slowness and pre-dominantly unison choral writing suggest that it was modelled on 'Va pen-siero' from *Nabucco*. Giselda announces that the Lombards can find water at Siloim, and they prepare for battle with the chorus 'Guerra! guerra!', first heard in Act 2 as 'Stolto Allhà!'.

Scene iii *Arvino's tent* 'The Hermit', gravely wounded, is supported by Giselda and Arvino; he reveals his true identity as Pagano and, on the point of death, leads off the final ensemble, 'Un breve istante'. The tent is thrown open to reveal Jerusalem, now in the hands of the Crusaders, and the opera ends with a grand choral hymn, 'Te lodiamo, gran Dio di vittoria'.

*   *   *

I Lombardi has often been compared to *Nabucco*, the immensely successful opera that preceded it in the Verdi canon. It is easy to see how such comparisons usually find the later opera less satisfactory. *I Lombardi* has a wider-ranging action than *Nabucco*, but Verdi, at this stage of his career, was less able or willing to depict various sharply contrasting locales, and many of the opera's choral sections (which traditionally carried the weight of such depictions) are somewhat routine. The great exception is the chorus 'O Signore, dal tetto natio', which rightly stands beside 'Va pensiero' as representative of Verdi's new voice in Italian opera. The opera's musical characterization is strangely uneven: the presence of two leading tenors seems to divide attention where it might usefully have been focussed; but the soprano, Giselda, stamps her personality on the drama at a very early stage, in particular with the original and colourful Preghiera 'Salve Maria!'.

Ernani

Dramma lirico in four acts set to a libretto by Francesco Maria Piave after Victor Hugo's play *Hernani*; first performed in Venice, Teatro La Fenice, on 9 March 1844.

The cast at the première included Carlo Guasco (Ernani), Antonio Superchi (Don Carlo), Antonio Selva (Silva), and Sophie Loewe (Elvira).

Ernani, *the bandit*	tenor
Don Carlo, *King of Spain*	baritone
Don Ruy Gomez de Silva, *a Spanish grandee*	bass
Elvira, *his niece and betrothed*	soprano
Giovanna, *her nurse*	soprano
Don Riccardo, *the King's equerry*	tenor
Jago, *Silva's equerry*	bass

Rebel mountaineers and bandits, knights and members of Silva's household, Elvira's maids-in-waiting, the King's knights, members of the *Lega*, Spanish and German nobles, Spanish and German ladies

Walk-on parts: Mountaineers and bandits, electors and nobles of the imperial court, pages of the imperial court, German soldiers, ladies, and male and female followers

Setting The Pyrenees, at Aix-la-Chapelle and at Saragossa, in 1519

Verdi's fifth opera was commissioned by the Teatro La Fenice, Venice, and was the first he wrote for a theatre other than La Scala. The Venetian authorities, impressed by the recent reception of *Nabucco* at La Fenice and of *I Lombardi* at La Scala, allowed the young composer to negotiate a sizable fee, and to make various unusual conditions, notably that he would have the right to choose from that season's company the singers for his new opera. A contract was signed in June 1843, and various subjects and librettists were mulled over; Verdi made it clear that he intended to break with the format of his previous two Milanese successes. A subject attributed to Sir Walter Scott and called *Cromvello* (or, sometimes, *Allan Cameron*) was initially decided upon, the librettist to be an unknown poet called Francesco Maria Piave; but Verdi became enthusiastic about Victor Hugo's *Hernani* and, in spite of worries that its political subject matter would create difficulties with the censor, persuaded Piave to switch course.

During autumn 1843 the correspondence between Verdi, Piave, and the theatre management makes it clear that the composer took an unusually active interest in shaping his libretto and intervened on several important points, insisting for example that the role of Ernani be sung by a tenor (rather than by a contralto, as had originally been planned). At least in part, this new concern for the poetic text was necessitated by his working with Piave, who was inexperienced in theatrical matters and occasionally made what Verdi deemed errors in broad dramatic planning, as well as succumbing to prolixity. Last-minute alterations to the cast caused Verdi to make various late changes to his score, notably in adding a cantabile for Silva to the Act 1 finale. The première run of performances was an enormous success.

Ernani quickly became immensely popular, and was revived countless times during its early years. In general, Verdi was adamant that no changes should be made to the score; but he did allow at least one exception. At the request of Rossini, who was acting on behalf of the tenor Nicola Ivanoff, he supplied an aria with chorus for Ernani as an alternative ending to the Act 2 finale. The piece was first performed in Parma on 26 December 1844. Although there is no direct evidence, it is possible that Verdi also sanctioned the addition of a cabaletta for Silva in Act 1. This piece, originally written for the bass Ignazio Marini as part of an additional aria in *Oberto* (1841–42, Barcelona), was inserted by Marini into performances of *Ernani* at La Scala in the autumn of 1844.

*   *   *

The prelude economically sets forth musical ideas connected with the two main dramatic issues of the opera: first, intoned on solo trumpet and trombone, the theme associated with Ernani's fatal oath to Silva; and then a lyrical idea whose initial rising 6th might plausibly be thought to suggest the love between Ernani and Elvira in its purest state.

ACT I 'THE BANDIT' Scene i *The Pyrenees; Silva's castle is seen in the distance* A simple opening chorus ('Evviva! beviam!') sets the scene by introducing the boisterous, carefree world of 'mountaineers and bandits'. Their leader Ernani (in reality Don Giovanni of Aragon) has been proscribed by the king, his enemy. He enters to tell of his love for Elvira; all agree to help him steal her away from Don Ruy Gomez de Silva, her uncle, guardian, and now fiancé. Ernani's cavatina is in the conventional double-aria format, although the first movement, 'Come rugiada al cespite', shows an expansion of the usual lyrical periods as Ernani dwells on his hatred of Silva. The cabaletta, 'O tu, che l'alma adora', makes prominent use of syncopation to suggest Ernani's impatience for action.

Scene ii *Elvira's richly furnished apartments in Silva's castle* Elvira's cavatina, during which she meditates on her beloved Ernani, repeats the double-aria format of Ernani's, though the entire scene is more expansively developed musically. The Andantino, 'Ernani! . . . Ernani involami', has an expanded but still highly schematic form that was becoming common in Verdi's early works and, again characteristically, shows a rigorous control of the soprano's ornamental gestures. A Spanish-sounding middle section, during which Elvira's entourage compliments her on her forthcoming marriage to Silva, leads to the cabaletta, 'Tutto sprezzo che d'Ernani', in which the opening phrase's vocal and expressive range gives some indication of the new demands that Verdi was placing on his principal interpreters. Elvira and her women sweep out and the stage is taken by a disguised Don Carlo, King of Spain. Carlo, also in love with Elvira and outraged that he has been passed over, sends Giovanna, Elvira's nurse, to fetch his beloved. Elvira enters to express outrage at the king's audacity and they settle into one of Verdi's most successful vehicles, the so-called dissimilar duet between baritone and soprano. The first movement, as usual, is rapid-fire dialogue with continuity preserved by the orchestra. But this soon gives way to a second movement in which the characters' opposing positions are explored: Carlo leads off with a lyrical outpouring, 'Da quel dì che t'ho veduta'; Elvira counters in the parallel minor with spiky dotted rhythms. The third movement offers a thoroughly Romantic *coup de scène*: Carlo impatiently tries to drag Elvira away, she grabs his knife to defend her honour, and at the peak of the action Ernani himself appears through a secret door. There is a shocked *declamato* from Carlo before Elvira and Ernani launch into the furious stretta of the duet-turned-trio, one that is full (perhaps too full) of syncopations to emphasize the young lovers' defiant energy.

The extended cadences of the stretta are immediately followed by the appearance of Elvira's third suitor, the aged Silva, and the start of the first finale. Silva is of course dismayed at the scene that greets him and, after angrily summoning his followers, engages in a sorrowful, chromatically inflected Andante, 'Infelice! e tu credevi'. (This is sometimes followed by the cabaletta 'Infin che un brando vindice'.) But there are more surprises to come. Soon after Silva has finished, emissaries reveal the true identity of the king. The revelation precipitates the central slow movement of the finale, which begins in utter confusion but gradually finds lyrical voice, notably through the repetition and development of a small cadential motif. As the movement ends, Silva kneels to ask the king's forgiveness, which the latter grants, explaining that he is there to canvass support for the forthcoming election of an emperor. In an aside the king offers to help Ernani—wishing to exact revenge himself rather than leaving it to Silva—and, openly announcing that the bandit is under royal protection, orders him to leave. Ernani's angry aside, in which he threatens to follow Carlo and fight to the death, leads off the stretta of the finale, which begins in a hushed but pointed minor and progresses to the major mode with a simple but highly effective crescendo.

ACT 2 'THE GUEST' *A magnificent hall in Silva's castle* After a scene-setting chorus praising Silva and Elvira, there occurs the kind of complex articulated scene Verdi often favoured in the middle of an opera. The number is called 'Recitativo e Terzetto' but enfolds within its trio a prolonged duet. As the chorus disperses, Silva grants entry to a 'pilgrim' who has asked for shelter. Elvira appears and Silva introduces her as his future bride, at which point the 'pilgrim' throws off his disguise, reveals himself as Ernani, and offers his own head as a wedding present. The ensuing Andante, 'Oro, quant'oro ogn'avido'—Ernani angry at Elvira's apparent betrayal, Elvira miserable, Silva (who has not recognized Ernani) simply confused—is dominated by Ernani and makes dynamic use of triplet figures. Silva assures his 'guest' of protection and speeds off to arm his castle. As soon as the lovers are alone, Elvira assures Ernani that she meant to kill herself on the wedding night, and their reconciliation is sealed by a brief Andantino with prominent harp and woodwind. When Silva returns he is horrified to find them in each other's arms. He learns that Don Carlo is waiting for Ernani outside the castle with hostile intent; but he will not

give up the bandit, wishing for a more personal revenge. In an angry
stretta he ushers Ernani into a secret hiding place as the lovers voice their
despair.

Carlo's entry heralds a long passage of accompanied recitative. The
king asks Silva to reveal Ernani's whereabouts and, on being denied, disarms the old man and orders a search of the castle. During the search
Carlo sings 'Lo vedremo, o veglio audace', the first movement of what is
formally an 'aria', but in which Silva joins freely. The king's anger mani-
fests itself in a wide-ranging, highly declamatory line while Silva denies
him with obsessively restricted rhythms and pitches. The middle movement, though often lyrical, is packed with stage action: Carlo's followers
return, having found nothing in the castle; the king threatens Silva; Elvira
'enters precipitously' and begs for mercy; Carlo takes her hostage. The
closing cabaletta, 'Vieni meco, sol di rose', is a magnificent dramatic stroke:
after all the action and conflict, Verdi ends with a passage of pure baritone
lyricism, full of gentle ornaments as the king invites Elvira to join him. The
stage clears to leave Silva alone. He releases Ernani from hiding and immediately challenges him to a duel. Ernani refuses, and reveals that the
king himself is pursuing Elvira. As honour demands, Ernani's life is now
forfeit to Silva. In order to join forces with Silva in taking revenge on
Carlo, Ernani offers the old man a hunting horn and proposes a deadly
pact, suitably emphasized with solemn brass chords: whenever Silva wishes
Ernani to kill himself, he must simply sound the horn. The deal is struck;
Ernani joins Silva and his followers in an explosive Prestissimo, 'In ar-
cione, in arcion', to close the act.

ACT 3 'CLEMENCY' *Subterranean vaults confining the tomb of Charlemagne
at Aix-la-Chapelle* Dark instrumental colours suitable to the setting introduce the act. Carlo enters with Riccardo, his equerry. It is the day of the
election of the Holy Roman Emperor, and Carlo has heard that conspiracy
is afoot. He instructs Riccardo to fire three cannon shots if the election goes
in his favour. Left alone 'to converse with the dead', the king bitterly reviews his misspent youth and resolves to rise in stature if he is elected. The
aria that illustrates this important turning point in the drama, 'O de'
verd'anni miei', is notable for its extreme change in atmosphere halfway
through: from sombre musical recollections of the florid baritone persona
who has characterized the previous acts, to a newfound strength and broadness of expression at the words 'e vincitor de' secoli'. Carlo conceals himself in Charlemagne's tomb as the conspirators enter: the sombre orchestral
colours reassert themselves as the plotters exchange the password and draw

lots for the task of assassinating the king. Ernani wins and, with the triplet figures that have been sprinkled through the scene gradually gaining ascendancy in the orchestra, all join in a grand chorus, 'Si ridesti il Leon di Castiglia'. In rhythmic stamp, this piece bears a relationship to 'Va pensiero' (*Nabucco*) and 'O Signore, dal tetto natio' (*I Lombardi*), but here the rhythmic vitality, and consequent spur to action, is far more immediate. The three cannon shots sound, and Carlo emerges triumphantly from the tomb as the stage fills with his followers. In a magnificent finale, Carlo forgives the conspirators and even consents to the marriage of Ernani and Elvira; his closing peroration to Charlemagne, 'Oh sommo Carlo', eventually draws everyone into his musical orbit.

ACT 4 'THE MASK' *A terrace in the palace of Don Giovanni of Aragon [Ernani] in Saragossa* As is often the case with Verdi and his contemporaries, the final act is by far the shortest. A chorus and a group of dancers tell us that wedding preparations for Ernani and Elvira are under way. The two lovers emerge for a brief but intense affirmation of their happiness, but are cut short by the sound of a distant horn. Ernani attempts to hide the truth from Elvira by complaining of an old wound and sending her for help. Left alone, he momentarily convinces even himself that the horn was an illusion. But Silva appears to demand the life that is owed him. Elvira returns as Ernani takes the proffered dagger; and so begins the final trio, 'Ferma, crudel, estinguere', justly one of the most celebrated pieces in the work, notable above all for its profusion of melodic ideas. The close of the trio is followed immediately by Silva's reminder of the pact of honour. In spite of Elvira's protests, Ernani takes the dagger and stabs himself. The lovers have time only for a last, desperate affirmation before the hero dies, leaving his bride to faint away as the curtain falls.

*　　　*　　　*

As Verdi himself stated more than once, *Ernani* represents an important change of direction in his early career. His two earlier successes, *Nabucco* and *I Lombardi*, had both been written for La Scala, one of the largest stages in Italy and well suited to the grandiose choral effects of those works. For the more intimate atmosphere of La Fenice, he created an opera that instead concentrated on personal conflict, carefully controlling the complex sequence of actions necessary to bring characters into intense confrontation. This new format brought about a fresh consideration of the fixed forms of Italian opera, in particular an expansion and enrichment of the solo aria and the duet, together with a more flexible approach to the musical sequences that bind together lyrical pieces. Most important, though, was Verdi's gathering sense of a musical drama's larger rhetoric. In Act 3 he extended to an entire act the kinds of musical continuities previously encountered only at scene level. The action unfolds in a continuous musical arc, one given direction by the development of various musical devices, some rhythmic, some melodic, some timbral: from the dark instrumental colours that begin the act, to Carlo's great turning point in the aria 'O de' verd'anni miei', to the conspirators' chorus 'Si ridesti il Leon di Castiglia', to the magnificent finale in which Carlo forgives all. In this respect, the third act of *Ernani* sets an imposing standard, one that is rarely equalled until the operas of the early 1850s.

I due Foscari

('The Two Foscari')

Tragedia lirica in three acts by set to a libretto by Francesco Maria Piave after Byron's play *The Two Foscari*, first performed in Rome, Teatro Argentina, on 3 November 1844.

The cast at the première included Achille De Bassini (Francesco Foscari), Giacomo Roppa (Jacopo), and Marianna Barbieri-Nini (Lucrezia).

Francesco Foscari, *doge of Venice*	baritone
Jacopo Foscari, *his son*	tenor
Lucrezia Contarini, *Jacopo's wife*	soprano
Jacopo Loredano, *member of the Council of Ten*	bass
Barbarigo, *senator, member of the Giunta*	tenor
Pisana, *Lucrezia's friend and confidante*	soprano
Officer of the Council of Ten	tenor
Servant of the Doge	bass

Members of the Council of Ten and the Giunta, Lucrezia's maids, Venetian women, populace, and masked figures of both sexes

Walk-on parts: Il Messer Grande, Jacopo Foscari's two small children, naval commanders, prison guards, gondoliers, sailors, populace, masked figures, pages of the Doge

Setting Venice in 1457

Soon after the première of *Ernani* in Venice, Verdi agreed to write a new opera with Piave for the Teatro Argentina in Rome. The first choice was

Lorenzino de' Medici, but this proved unacceptable to the Roman censors, and a setting of Byron's *The Two Foscari* was agreed upon. It is clear from Verdi's early descriptions that he conceived the opera in the *Ernani* vein (relatively small-scale, concentrating on personal confrontations rather than grand scenic effects), although he did urge Piave to attempt something grandiose for the first-act finale. The correspondence between composer and librettist again reveals the extent to which Verdi intervened in the making of the libretto, a good deal of the large-scale structure of the opera being dictated by his increasingly exigent theatrical instincts. Verdi was also concerned with matters of ambience and showed himself anxious to introduce certain moments in which scenic effects could be exploited.

Composing *I due Foscari* occupied Verdi for about four months (a long time by the standards of most of its predecessors). Its first performance was not received with great enthusiasm, possibly because the expectations of the audience had been driven too high by Verdi's enormous and widespread success with *Ernani*. In 1846 Verdi supplied the famous tenor Mario with a replacement cabaletta for Jacopo in Act 1 (first performed at the Théâtre Italien, Paris).

*   *   *

The prelude depicts an atmosphere of stormy conflict before introducing two themes from the opera, the first a mournful clarinet melody to be associated with Jacopo, the second an ethereal flute and string passage from Lucrezia's cavatina.

ACT 1 Scene i *A hall in the Doges' Palace in venice*   The curtain rises as the Council of Ten and the Giunta are gathering. Their opening chorus ('Silenzio . . . Mistero') immediately casts over the opera a subdued yet menacing atmosphere, suggested musically by dark instrumental and vocal sonorities and by tortuous chromatic progressions. The prelude's clarinet melody is heard as Jacopo, the Doge's son, falsely accused of murder and likely to be exiled from Venice, appears from the prisons to await an audience with the Council. In a delicately scored arioso, he salutes his beloved Venice and begins the first section of a two-movement cavatina. The first movement, 'Dal più remoto esilio', evokes local colour in its 6/8 rhythm, prominent woodwind sonorities, and unusual chromatic excursions. The cabaletta, 'Odio solo, ed odio atroce', is routinely energetic, although it defies convention in allowing the tenor to linger over a high A as the orchestra undertakes a reprise of the main theme.

Scene ii *A hall in the Foscari Palace* Lucrezia, Jacopo's wife, enters to a rising string theme, associated with her at intervals through the opera. She is determined to confront the Doge in an attempt to save her husband, but first she offers a prayer, 'Tu al cui sguardo onnipossente'. This Preghiera exhibits a more highly ornamental vocal style than is usual in early Verdi, although the decoration is—typically for the composer—always contained with the fixed phrase lengths. The ensuing cabaletta, 'O patrizi, tremate l'Eterno', is novel in formal design, beginning with an arioso-like passage in the minor and dissolving into open-structured ornamental writing at the end.

Scene iii *A hall in the Doge's Palace* (as 1.i) The Council has concluded its meeting and, in part with a return to the music of the opening chorus, informs us that Jacopo's crime must be punished with exile.

Scene iv *The Doge's private rooms* The Doge's 'Scena e Romanza' opens with yet another theme that is to recur through the course of the opera, this time a richly harmonized melody for viola and divided cellos. The Romanza 'O vecchio cor, che batti', in which the Doge apostrophizes his son, is clearly a companion piece to Jacopo's earlier 'Dal più remoto esilio' (note, for example, the identical opening accompaniment figures), although the baritone father sings with far more direct emotional appeal than his tenor son. The finale of Act 1 is a lengthy scene between Lucrezia and the Doge, in which Jacopo's wife begs the Doge to show mercy. One of Verdi's finest early soprano-baritone duets, the number falls into the conventional four-movement pattern, but individual sections boast considerable inner contrast, responding closely to the differing emotional attitudes of the principals.

ACT 2 Scene i *The state prisons* A loosely structured chromatic prelude for solo viola and cello introduces Jacopo, alone in prison. He has a terrifying vision of Carmagnola, a past victim of Venetian law, and in the Romanza 'Non maledirmi, o prode' begs the vision for mercy. 'Non maledirmi' is conventional in its move from minor to major, but has an unusual return to the minor as the vision of Carmagnola reappears to haunt the prisoner and eventually render him unconscious. Lucrezia, accompanied by her rising string theme, enters and, after reviving Jacopo, announces his sentence of exile. There follows one of Verdi's very rare love duets, this one laid out in the usual multimovement form though without an opening 'action' sequence. The closing portions of the duet see an injection of local colour: gondoliers singing in praise of Venice interrupt husband and wife, giving them fresh hope for the future. The Doge, powerless to affect the decision of the Council, whose ruling he must put into effect, now enters to bid a sad farewell to his son. The first lyrical movement of the ensuing trio, 'Nel tuo paterno amplesso', makes much of the contrast in vocal personalities—declamatory tenor, sustained baritone, breathless, distraught soprano—while the final stretta (in which the principals are joined by a gloating Loredano) simplifies matters by uniting Jacopo and Lucrezia in syncopated unison.

Scene ii *The hall of the Council of Ten*   An opening chorus, again partly built on material from Act 1 scene i, explains that Jacopo's crimes are murder and treason against the state. The Doge appears, soon followed by his son, who continues to protest his innocence. The Doge will not listen, but all are dumbfounded by the sudden appearance of Lucrezia, who has brought her children with her in a final plea for mercy. The stage is set for the slow movement of the concertato finale, 'Queste innocenti lagrime', led off by Jacopo, who is seconded by Lucrezia. This grandiose movement develops momentum right up to the final peroration (the passage sometimes termed 'groundswell'), but its last cadence is interrupted: Jacopo returns to the minor mode and the intimate musical language of his opening phrases, and is in turn interrupted by a further tutti repetition of the 'groundswell' idea. The extreme juxtaposition creates sufficient dramatic charge to close the act without a traditional fast stretta.

ACT 3 Scene i *The old Piazzetta di San Marco*   Local colour in the form of an 'Introduzione e Barcarola' begins the act, with gondoliers offering a more developed reprise of the music that had earlier interrupted the Jacopo-Lucrezia duet. Jacopo is brought forth for the final parting. His 'All'infelice veglio' is Romanza-like in its progress from minor to major but is enriched by contributions from Lucrezia and, eventually, from the chorus, making the scene a fitting grand climax to the tenor's role.

Scene ii *The Doge's private rooms* (as in 1.iv)   First comes a scena for the Doge in which he is presented with a deathbed confession revealing that Jacopo is innocent. But the message is too late: Lucrezia rushes on to announce that Jacopo died suddenly on leaving Venice. Lucrezia's aria 'Più non vive!' is, as befits this late stage of the drama, highly condensed, and is perhaps best considered a kind of bipartite cabaletta, allowing (as did her first-act aria) more room than is usual in early Verdi for ornamental flourishes. As she

leaves, the Council of Ten appear, led by Loredano, asking the Doge to re-
linquish his power on account of his great age. He answers in an impassioned
aria, 'Questa dunque è l'iniqua mercede'. In many ways the most powerful
moment of the opera, this 'aria' is really a duet between the Doge and the
male chorus: he in declamatory triplets demanding the return of his son;
they in inflexible unison. The great bell of St Mark's sounds to mark the election of a new Doge—not Loredano, in spite of his ambitions—and, after
a final apostrophe to Jacopo, the Doge falls lifeless to the ground.

*   *   *

I due Foscari, as Verdi himself was later to admit, suffers somewhat from
being too gloomy in general tone, and this in spite of periodic evocations
of the Venetian lagoon. But the opera nevertheless offers some interesting
experiments. Perhaps most striking is the use of recurring themes to iden-
tify the principals. These proto-'Leitmotifs' are here perhaps applied too
rigidly, serving ultimately to impede any sense of development or progression in the characters; but the experiment itself is significant, suggesting
that Verdi was anxious to explore new means of musical and dramatic articulation. The increased importance of local colour is also notable in light
of Verdi's future development. Although in *I due Foscar* the sense of a precise ambience seems externally imposed on the score rather than emerging
from it, Verdi's awareness of the potential of this added dimension in musical drama was decisive; from this time onwards he would rarely employ
local colour in quite the mechanical way he had in his earliest operas.

Giovanna d'Arco

('Joan of Arc')

Dramma lirico in a prologue and three acts set to a libretto by Temistocle Solera in part after Friedrich von Schiller's play *Die Jungfrau von Orleans*; first performed in Milan, Teatro alla Scala, on 15 February 1845.

The cast at the première included Antonio Poggi (Carlo), Filippo Colini (Giacomo), and Erminia Frezzolini in the title role.

Carlo VII [Charles VII], *King of France*	tenor
Giacomo, *a shepherd in Dom-Rémy*	baritone
Giovanna [Joan of Arc], *his daughter*	soprano
Delil, *an officer of the king*	tenor
Talbot, *supreme commander of the English army*	bass

King's officers, villagers, people of Reims, French soldiers, English soldiers, blessed spirits, evil spirits, nobles of the realm, heralds, pages, young girls, marshals, deputies, knights and ladies, magistrates, halberdiers, guards of honour

Setting Dom-Rémy, Reims and near Rouen in 1429

There is virtually no evidence, but it seems that Verdi had arranged to write an opera for the 1844–45 Carnival season at La Scala as early as December 1843, and that soon afterwards he suggested to the impresario Bartolomeo Merelli that Temistocle Solera be engaged as the librettist. Solera was duly hired, wrote a text, and then—with typical exaggeration—made much of the fact that his libretto on the life of Joan of Arc was 'original', owing nothing either to Shakespeare or to Schiller. Verdi's correspondence makes no mention of any changes to the libretto, and we must assume that, as with Solera's *Nabucco* and *I Lombardi*, the composer was willing to set the text more or less as it stood. The score was written during the autumn and winter of 1844–45. Its first performance at La Scala (preceded by a revival of *I Lombardi*) was a great public success, but the standards of production were far below Verdi's expectations and caused a serious rift between him and Merelli. The result was that there would be no Verdi premières at La Scala for many years to come.

*   *   *

The overture is in three movements. The first is stormy and uncertain; the second is an Andante pastorale featuring solo flute, oboe, and clarinet (with more than shades of Rossini's *Guillaume Tell* overture); the last returns to the stormy minor but concludes in a triumphant and bellicose major.

PROLOGUE Scene i *A great hall in Dom-Rémy* The opening scene is a conventional two-movement cavatina for the tenor, though with unusually important choral interventions (Verdi and Solera no doubt wished to sustain their image with the Milanese after the choral successes of *Nabucco* and *I Lombardi*). Even before the tenor enters, the unison chorus laments the sad fate of France in 'Maledetti cui spinge rea voglia', and choral forces are again prominent in the soloist's lyrical movements, particularly in an unusually long *tempo di mezzo*. Carlo, after admitting defeat, narrates a dream ('Sotto una quercia'): as he was lying beneath an oak tree, the Madonna told him to place before her his helmet and sword. On hearing that such an oak exists nearby, he decides to visit it, though insisting that he can no longer be king.

Scene ii *A forest* Giacomo appears for a brief scena, voicing fears that his daughter Giovanna may be in league with the devil. He retires to be replaced by Giovanna. In a highly ornamented, Bellinian first movement ('Sempre all'alba ed alla sera'), she prays for weapons in the coming battle. As she falls asleep, a chorus of devils (jauntily recommending sins of the flesh) and of angels (promising her glory as the saviour of her country) jostle for her attention. She awakes to find Carlo before her and immediately declares herself ready for battle. They join in a lively, syncopated cabaletta, during which Giacomo sees them together and concludes that his daughter has in some way bewitched the king.

ACT I Scene i *A remote place scattered with rocks* The English soldiers have been routed and fear that supernatural forces are against them. Talbot tries unsuccessfully to allay their fears. Giacomo, still convinced that his daughter is in the grip of evil forces, announces that the woman inspiring the French army can be their prisoner that evening. In an Andante sostenuto, 'Franco son io', he tells them of his dishonour at the hands of Carlo; the ensuing cabaletta, 'So che per via di triboli', explores a father's tender feelings. The usual progression from lachrymose Andante to energetic cabaletta is thus reversed, which allows for a moderate-paced, unusually touching, Donizettian cabaletta, quite lacking in characteristic Verdian rhythmic drive.

Scene ii *A garden in the court of Reims*   Giovanna has fulfilled her mission but is unwilling to leave Carlo and the court: the demon voices still torment her. She sings of her simple forest home in 'O fatidica foresta', another delightful example of Verdian pastoral, before Carlo arrives to initiate an impressive four-movement duet-finale in which he and Giovanna admit their love for each other. Particularly notable is the slow movement ('T'arretri e palpiti!'), which includes a remarkable range of emotional attitudes as Giovanna struggles with her conflicting voices, and as Carlo swings between unease at her behaviour and attempts to calm her with expressions of love.

ACT 2 *A square in Reims*   A somewhat routine 'Grand triumphal march' introduces the victorious troops, prominent among whom are Carlo and Giovanna. Giacomo looks on, giving vent to his religious zeal in a minor-major Romanza, 'Speme al vecchio era una figlia', which never seems to find its true point of climax. Then comes the grand concertato finale of the opera, in which Giacomo denounces his daughter. The most interesting movement is the Andante, 'No! forme d'angelo': unaccompanied duet fragments from Carlo and Giacomo are juxtaposed with an extended cantabile for Giovanna; even in the cadential close Verdi finds room to sketch her fragile musical persona. The remainder of the number offers high drama as Giovanna refuses three times to deny Giacomo's accusations of sacrilege; she is turned on by the crowd in the stretta, 'Fuggi, o donna maledetta'.

ACT 3 *Inside a fort in the English camp*   Giovanna, imprisoned, looks on as the English and French do battle, noting with dismay that Carlo has been surrounded. Her ardent prayers alert Giacomo to his mistake in accusing her, and they join in a duet of reconciliation, the most impressive section of which is the slow movement, 'Amai, ma un solo istante', in which a moving succession of melodic ideas underpins the father's gradual acceptance of his daughter's purity. Giovanna is released by her father and rushes to aid the French: now it is Giacomo's turn to comment on the battle, which with his daughter's help swings decisively against the English. Carlo enters victorious, forgives Giacomo, but learns that Giovanna has been mortally wounded. In the Romanza 'Quale più fido amico', delicately scored for solo English horn and cello, he bemoans his loss. Giovanna is brought in to the strains of a funeral march; she has enough strength to salute her father and the king, and to look forward to a welcome in heaven. She leads off the final ensemble with an elaborately ornamented solo accompanied by obbligato cello, and then expires as a long-breathed theme for the onlookers carries all before it.

*   *   *

Giovanna d'Arco is unlikely ever to be a mainstream repertory work, but there is nevertheless much to admire. Although the opera was probably intended as a sequel to the grand choral tableau works Verdi and Solera had previously created together, in the end it is dominated by the role of Giovanna—Verdi probably encouraged in this change by the extraordinary skills of his leading soprano, Erminia Frezzolini. In spite of the warrior-maiden character she impersonated, Frezzolini was by no means the typical early Verdian soprano, and was entrusted with the kind of delicate ornamentation the young composer so rarely lingered over. The other principals are perhaps less successfully projected, but they are involved in powerfully original ensembles, numbers which again and again make clear that the young Verdi was constantly experimenting with the formal vehicles through which his drama was projected.

Alzira

Tragedia lirica in a prologue and two acts set to a libretto by Salvadore Cammarano after Voltaire's play *Alzire, ou Les Américains*; first performed in Naples, Teatro San Carlo, on 12 August 1845.

The cast at the première included Filippo Coletti (Gusmano), Gaetano Fraschini (Zamoro), and Eugenia Tadolini (Alzira).

Alvaro, *father of Gusmano, initially Governor of Peru*	bass
Gusmano, *Governor of Peru*	baritone
Ovando, *a Spanish Duke*	tenor
Zamoro, *leader of a Peruvian tribe*	tenor
Ataliba, *leader of a Peruvian tribe*	bass
Alzira, *Ataliba's daughter*	soprano
Zuma, *her maid*	mezzo-soprano
Otumbo, *an American warrior*	tenor

Spanish officers and soldiers, Americans of both sexes

Setting Lima and other regions of Peru, about the middle of the sixteenth century

There were two reasons why *Alzira*, Verdi's eighth opera, was something of a special event. It was the first he had written specially for the famous Teatro San Carlo in Naples, and so offered him the opportunity to confront a significant public and theatre with whom he had so far had little success. More than this, it presented a chance to collaborate with Salvadore

Cammarano, resident poet at the San Carlo, certainly the most famous librettist still working in Italy, and renowned for his string of successes in the previous decade with Gaetano Donizetti. Because of Cammarano's fame, Verdi seems to have taken little active part in the formation of the libretto (this in contrast to the works he prepared with his principal librettist of the period, Piave), being for the most part happy to accept the dictates of Cammarano's highly professional instincts. Work on *Alzira*, begun in the spring of 1845, was delayed not only by illness but by the fact that Verdi had to add an overture when the work proved too short for a full evening's entertainment. Despite an unusually strong première cast, the first performances were at best only a partial success. Subsequent revivals fared little better, and the opera soon disappeared from the repertory. It has occasionally been revived in modern times, but remains one of the composer's two or three least-performed operas.

*   *   *

The overture is in three movements. The first is an Andante mosso in which woodwind and percussion attempt to impose a generic local colour on the exotic ambience; the second juxtaposes warlike calls to arms with a lachrymose clarinet solo; the third is a marchlike Allegro brillante.

PROLOGUE 'THE PRISONER' *A vast open plain, irrigated by the Rima River* A bloodthirsty tribe of 'Americans' led by Otumbo drag on Alvaro in chains, tie him to a tree, and mock him with the driving 6/8 chorus 'Muoia, muoia coverto d'insulti'. They are about to dispatch him horribly when a boat is sighted carrying Zamoro, their leader whom they believed dead. Zamoro, strangely moved by the sight of Alvaro, orders him to be released and returned to his people. With Alvaro gone, Zamoro's unusually extended narrative slow movement, 'Un Inca . . . eccesso orribile!', tells the tribe of his brutal treatment at the hands of the wicked Spaniard Gusmano. The movement over, Zamoro hears that his beloved Alzira is imprisoned with her father in Lima. Zamoro swears to rescue them, and he joins his warriors in a bellicose cabaletta, 'Dio della guerra'.

ACT I 'A LIFE FOR A LIFE' Scene i *The main piazza of Lima* A choral movement, reinforced by the *banda*, introduces Alvaro, who announces that he is ceding power to his son Gusmano. The latter immediately declares a general peace with the Inca chief Ataliba, reminding him that Ataliba's daughter Alzira has been agreed to as Gusmano's reward. But in the Andante of his double aria, 'Eterna la memoria', Gusmano admits that

Alzira's feelings for her former lover remain too powerful for him to over-come. Ataliba urges Gusmano to be patient; but the new Governor can brook no delay and in the cabaletta 'Quanto un mortal può chiedere' declares that he must possess Alzira immediately.

Scene ii *Ataliba's apartments in the Governor's palace*   Tremolando strings introduce a sleeping Alzira, who awakes to utter Zamoro's name and tell her attendants of a strange dream. 'Da Gusman, su fragil barca' narrates how she dreamt of escaping from Gusmano in a boat, being caught in a storm and rescued by her beloved; the aria boldly follows the pattern of the tale rather than duplicating the form of a conventional Italian slow movement. Despite the warnings of her entourage, she proudly declares her love for Zamoro in the ornamental cabaletta 'Nell'astro che più fulgido'. Ataliba enters, dismisses Zuma and the chorus, and in simple recitative begs Alzira to marry Gusmano. She will have none of this, and asks instead for death. As Ataliba leaves, Zuma announces a 'member of the tribe', and Alzira is ecstatic to see none other than Zamoro. The first movement of their duet, 'Anima mia!', comprises a rapid exchange of loving words, held together in the traditional manner by a driving orchestral melody. With little else needing to be said, Cammarano and Verdi moved immediately to the cabaletta, 'Risorge ne' tuoi lumi'. The lovers are discovered by Gusmano, Ataliba, and a host of attendants. Gusmano orders Zamoro to instant execution and, in a fiery Allegro, Zamoro taunts Gusmano with cowardice. The stage is now set for an unusually grand concertato slow movement, 'Nella polve, genuflesso', one that begins with a freer dialogue structure than usual and, perhaps for this reason, builds to an uncommonly impressive final climax. The movement over, wild, exotic music is heard in the distance: a messenger reports that a hostile army is without, demanding the return of Zamoro. Gusmano decides to release him, thus offering a life for the life of his father; but in leading off the concluding stretta, 'Trema, trema . . . a ritorti fra l'armi', he warns Zamoro that they will meet again on the battlefield.

ACT 2 'THE REVENGE OF A SAVAGE'   Scene i *Inside the fortifications of Lima*   The Incas have again lost the battle; victorious Spanish soldiers indulge in a brindisi, 'Mesci, mesci', interrupted only briefly by the mournful sight of Zamoro and his followers trudging across the stage. Gusmano promises his soldiers rich spoils and loudly pronounces a death sentence on Zamoro. At this Alzira rushes on to beg for clemency, and Gusmano offers her a polite version of Count di Luna's bargain in *Il trovatore*: Zamoro's life for Alzira's hand in marriage. The impasse is explored in a slow movement, 'Il pianto . . . l'angoscia', Alzira's breathless sobs contrasting with Gusmano's smooth (perhaps too smooth) cantabile. Eventually she agrees, and the pact is sealed by a duet cabaletta, 'Colma di gioia ho l'anima'.

Scene ii *A dreary cave* A sombre orchestral introduction, appropriate to the desolate scene, introduces Otumbo, who tells his friends that he has secured the release of Zamoro by bribing his Spanish guards. Zamoro appears, and in 'Irne lungi ancor dovrei' declares himself desolate without his beloved Alzira. Otumbo makes matters worse by telling him that Alzira is about to marry Gusmano. Nothing can restrain Zamoro's fury, and in the cabaletta 'Non di codarde lagrime' he resolves to take stern revenge.

Scene iii *A great hall in the Governor's residence* A bridal chorus, 'Tergi del pianto America', looks forward to the peace that marriage will bring; Gusmano welcomes all to the ceremony. He is about to take Alzira's hand when Zamoro (disguised as a Spanish soldier) bursts on the scene, plunges a dagger into Gusmano's heart, and awaits bloody retribution. But Gusmano has a surprise in store: he has learnt from Alzira the joys of peace and mercy, and in a final aria accompanied by the chorus ('I numi tuoi') gives the two lovers his blessing. It is an impressive close, with the chorus gradually taking the lyrical thread as Gusmano loses strength and the mode shifts from minor to major.

* * *

In later life, Verdi pronounced *Alzira* 'proprio brutta' ('downright ugly'), and the opera is without doubt one of his least-often performed, even in today's revival-conscious atmosphere. Perhaps, as happened on other occasions, the esteem in which Verdi held his librettist was a disadvantage, inhibiting him from following freely his dramatic instincts. Whatever the case, the articulation of the opera swings wildly between extremely economic closed forms and a much freer, 'declamatory' style, often triggered by narrative. Even its moments of comparative failure are interesting, coming as they often do in numbers such as Alzira's Act 1 narration, in which the composer attempted something startlingly new in formal terms. Zamoro's Act 1 aria 'Un Inca . . . eccesso orribile!', is another case in point: it starts off conventionally, breaks into angry declamation, and then closes by switching wildly between this style and tender recollections of his beloved Alzira, never settling on the lyrical synthesis we expect of a closed form aria. In this and other moments, Verdi seemed intent above all on mirroring a psychological process, responding to each nuance of the words rather than developing a rounded musical statement; he was, in other words, experimenting with a type of 'realism' in which attention to the individual meanings of words and phrases would substitute for the catharsis of the well-turned tune. In that sense *Alzira* is an opera decisively ahead of its time.

Attila

Dramma lirico in a prologue and three acts set to a libretto by Temistocle Solera (with additional material by Francesco Maria Piave) after Zacharias Werner's play *Attila, König der Hunnen*; first performed in Venice, Teatro La Fenice, on 17 March 1846.

The cast at the première included Ignazio Marini (Attila), Natale Costantini (Ezio), Sophie Loewe (Odabella), and Carlo Guasco (Foresto).

Attila, *King of the Huns*	bass
Ezio, *a Roman general*	baritone
Odabella, *the Lord of Aquileia's daughter*	soprano
Foresto, *a knight of Aquileia*	tenor
Uldino, *a young Breton, Attila's slave*	tenor
Leone, *an old Roman*	bass

Leaders, kings and soldiers, Huns, Gepids, Ostrogoths, Heruls, Thuringians, Quadi, Druids, priestesses, men and women of Aquileia, Aquileian maidens in warlike dress, Roman officers and soldiers, Roman virgins and children, hermits, slaves

Setting Aquileia, the Adriatic lagoons and near Rome, in the middle of the fifth century

Verdi had read Werner's ultra-Romantic play as early as 1844, and initially discussed the subject with Piave. However, for his second opera at La Fenice (a highly suitable subject, dealing with the founding of the city of Venice) the composer eventually decided on Solera, the librettist with whom—at least until then—he seems to have preferred working. Solera set about preparing the text according to his usual format, with plenty of opportunity for those grand choral tableaux found in *Nabucco* and *I Lombardi*; but the progress of the opera was beset with difficulties. First Verdi fell seriously ill, and then Solera went off to live permanently in Madrid, leaving the last act as only a sketch and necessitating help from the ever-faithful Piave. Verdi instructed Piave to ignore Solera's plans for a large-scale choral finale and to concentrate on the individuals, a change of direction of which Solera strongly disapproved. The première was coolly received, but *Attila* went on to become one of Verdi's most popular operas of the 1850s. After that it lost ground although recent times have seen several important revivals. In 1846 Verdi twice rewrote the Romanza for Foresto in Act 3: the first time for Nicola Ivanoff, the second for Napoleone Moriani.

*   *   *

The prelude follows a pattern that later became common in Verdi's work: a restrained opening leads to a grand climax, then to the beginnings of melodic continuity that are quickly fragmented. It is the drama encapsulated.

PROLOGUE Scene i *The piazza of Aquileia*   'Huns, Heruls, and Ostrogoths' celebrate bloody victories and greet their leader Attila who, in an impressive recitative, bids them sing a victory hymn. A group of female warriors is brought on, and their leader Odabella proclaims the valour and patriotic zeal of Italian women. Odabella's two-movement aria is a forceful display of soprano power, its first movement, 'Allor che i forti corrono' showing an unusually extended form that allows Attila to interject admiring comments. Such is the force of this movement that the cabaletta, 'Da te questo', merely continues the musical tone, although with more elaborate ornamentation. Impressed by her bravery, Atilla gives her his sword. As Odabella leaves, the Roman general Ezio appears for a multimovement duet with Attila. In the slow movement, 'Tardo per gli anni, e tremulo', he offers Attila the entire Roman Empire if Italy can be left unmolested and in Ezio's hands ('Avrai tu l'universo, resti l'Italia a me': 'For you the world, leave Italy to me'—a phrase with some resonance in the political struggles to come in the 1850s). Attila angrily rejects the proposal, and the warriors end with a cabaletta of mutual defiance, 'Vanitosi! che abbietti e dormenti'.

Scene ii *The Rio-Alto in the Adriatic lagoon*   The scene opens with a sustained exploration of local colour (strongly suggesting that Verdi now had his eye on the fashions of the French stage). First comes a violent orchestral storm, then the gradual rising of dawn is portrayed with a passage of ever increasing orchestral colours and sounds. Foresto leads on a group of survivors from Attila's attack on Aquileia; the settlement that they build there will eventually become Venice. In an Andantino that again shows unusual formal extension, 'Ella in poter del barbaro', his thoughts turn to his beloved Odabella, captured by Attila. In the subsequent cabaletta, 'Cara patria, già madre', the soloist is joined by the chorus for a rousing conclusion to the scene.

ACT 1 Scene i *A wood near Attila's camp* A melancholy string solo introduces Odabella, who, refusing a chance to escape and playing on Attila's obvious attraction to her, has remained in his camp in order to find an opportunity to murder him. In a delicately scored Andantino, 'Oh! nel fuggente nuvolo', Odabella sees in the clouds the images of Foresto and her dead father. Foresto himself appears: he has seen her with Attila and accuses her of betrayal. Their duet takes on the usual multimovement pattern: Foresto's accusations remain through the minor-major slow movement, 'Sì, quello io son, ravvisami', but Odabella convinces him of her desire to kill Attila, and they lovingly join in a unison cabaletta, 'Oh t'innebria nell'amplesso'.

Scene ii *Attila's tent, later his camp* Attila tells his slave Uldino of a terrible dream in which an old man denied him access to Rome in the name of God ('Mentre gonfiarsi l'anima'). But he dismisses the vision with a warlike cabaletta, 'Oltre quel limite'. A vocal blast from Attila's followers is interrupted by a procession of women and children led by Leone, the old man of Attila's dream (he is Pope Leo I, suitably disguised at the behest of the Italian censors). His injunction precipitates the slow movement of the concertato finale, 'No! non è sogno', which is led off by a terrified Attila, whose stuttering declamation is answered by a passage of sustained lyricism from Foresto and Odabella. The concertato takes on such impressive proportions that Verdi saw fit to end the act there, without the traditional stretta.

ACT 2 Scene i *Ezio's camp* The scene is no more than a conventional double aria for Ezio. In the slow movement, 'Dagl'immortali vertici', he muses on Rome's fallen state. Foresto appears and suggests a plan to destroy Attila by surprising him at his camp. In the cabaletta, 'È gettata la mia sorte', Ezio eagerly looks forward to his moment of glory.

Scene ii *Attila's camp*   Yet another warlike chorus begins the scene. Attila greets Ezio, the Druids mutter darkly of fatal portents, the priestesses
dance and sing. A sudden gust of wind blows out all the candles, an event
that precipitates yet another concertato, 'Lo spirto de' monti', a complex
movement during which Foresto manages to tell Odabella that Attila's cup
is poisoned. The formal slow movement concluded, Attila raises the cup to
his lips, but is warned of the poison by Odabella (who wishes a more personal vengeance); Foresto admits to the crime, and Odabella claims the
right to punish him herself. Attila approves, announces that he will marry
Odabella the next day, and launches the concluding stretta, 'Oh miei prodi!
un solo giorno'; its dynamism and rhythmic bite prefigure similar moments in *Il trovatore*.

ACT 3   *A wood*   Foresto is awaiting news of Odabella's marriage to Attila, and in a minor-major Romanza, 'Che non avrebbe il misero', bemoans
her apparent treachery. Ezio arrives, urging Foresto to speedy battle. A
distant chorus heralds the wedding procession, but suddenly Odabella herself appears, unable to go through with the ceremony. Soon all is explained
between her and Foresto, and they join Ezio in a lyrical Adagio. Attila now
enters in search of his bride, and the stage is set for a Quartetto finale. In
the Allegro, 'Tu, rea donna', Attila accuses the three conspirators in turn,
and in turn they answer, each with a different melodic line. At the climax
of the number, offstage cries inform us that the attack has begun. Odabella
stabs Attila, embraces Foresto, and the curtain falls.

*   *   *

As many have pointed out, *Attila* started life as a further example of
Verdi's grandiose, 'oratorio' vein, but as the opera develops the focus
turns to individuals, so much so that the closing scenes have minimal
choral participation and risk seeming rather perfunctory. This may in part
be due to the fact that Solera, the great architect of Verdi's 'oratorio'
style, deserted the project before it was completed, and that Piave had to
finish the libretto; perhaps Solera's original plan for a grand choral finale
would have been more apt. But it may also reflect an attempt on Verdi's
part to reconcile his two 'styles'—find new ways of grafting a drama of
individuals (such as *Ernani* or *I due Foscari*) onto one that is essentially
public (such as *Nabucco* or *I Lombardi*). The uncertainty about the
opera's genre may perhaps explain why two of the principals, Ezio and
Foresto, are somewhat vague and undefined, never managing to emerge
from the surrounding tableaux. On the other hand, Odabella and Attila,

both of whom assume vocal prominence early in the opera, are more powerful dramatic presences. As with all of Verdi's early operas, there are impressive individual moments, particularly in those grand ensemble movements that constantly inspired the composer to redefine and hone his dramatic language.

Macbeth

Opera in four acts set to a libretto by Francesco Maria Piave (with additional material by Andrea Maffei) after William Shakespeare's play; first performed in Florence, Teatro della Pergola, on 14 March 1847. The revised version, with a libretto translated by Charles-Louis-Etienne Nuitter and Alexandre Beaumont, was first performed in Paris, Théâtre Lyrique, on 21 April 1865.

The cast at the 1847 première included Felice Varesi (Macbeth) and Marianna Barbieri-Nini (Lady Macbeth). For the 1865 revised version the cast included Jean Vital Ismael (Macbeth) and Inez Rey-Balla (Lady Macbeth).

Duncano [Duncan], *King of Scotland*		silent
Macbeth,	*Generals in Duncan's army*	baritone
Banco [Banquo],		bass
Lady Macbeth, *Macbeth's wife*		soprano
Lady-in-waiting to Lady Macbeth		mezzo-soprano
Macduff, *a Scottish nobleman, Lord of Fife*		tenor
Malcolm, *Duncan's son*		tenor
Fleanzio [Fleance], *Banquo's son*		silent
A Servant of Macbeth		bass
A Doctor		bass
A Murderer		bass
The Ghost of Banquo		silent
A Herald		bass

Witches, messengers of the king, Scottish nobles and exiles, murderers, English soldiers, bards, aerial spirits, apparitions

Setting Scotland and the Anglo-Scottish border

Verdi's contract of 1846 with the impresario Alessandro Lanari and the Teatro della Pergola in Florence stipulated no particular opera, and in the summer of that year various possibilities, including *I masnadieri* and *Macbeth*, came under consideration. The final decision, Verdi made clear, would depend on the singers available. *Macbeth* would have no tenor lead but needed a first-class baritone and soprano; *I masnadieri*, on the other hand, was dependent on a fine tenor. By late September the cast had been secured, notably with the engagement of Felice Varesi, one of the finest actor-baritones of the day; accordingly, the choice fell on *Macbeth*. By this time, Verdi had already drafted the broad dramatic lines of the opera and had written encouraging letters to his librettist, Piave, emphasizing that this, his first Shakespearean subject, was to be a special case: 'This tragedy is one of the greatest creations of man! If we can't do something great with it, let us at least try to do something out of the ordinary . . . I know the general character and the *tinte* as if the libretto were already finished'.

As the première drew near, Verdi again and again demonstrated his particular interest in the opera: by bullying Piave into producing exactly the text he required; by engaging his friend Andrea Maffei to retouch certain passages; by taking unusual time in making sure the production was well rehearsed and true to his intentions; and by endlessly coaching the leading singers—in particular Varesi and Marianna Barbieri-Nini—to ensure that their every nuance was as he wished. The première was a great success, and the opera soon began to be performed around Italy; Verdi often advised those responsible for revivals of the special attention that the opera needed.

In 1864 the French publisher and impresario Léon Escudier asked Verdi to add ballet music for a revival of the opera at the Théâtre Lyrique, Paris. The composer agreed but also announced that he wanted to make substantial changes to some numbers that were 'either weak or lacking in character'. As well as the additional ballet and major or minor retouchings to various numbers, this revision eventually included a new aria for Lady Macbeth in Act 2 ('La luce langue'); substantial alterations to Act 3, including a new duet for Macbeth and Lady Macbeth ('Ora di morte'); a new chorus at the beginning of Act 4 ('Patria oppressa'); and the replacement of Macbeth's death scene with a final 'Inno di vittoria'. The Paris première was largely unsuccessful. The reception puzzled Verdi, and although the original version of the opera continued to be performed for some time in Italy, it is clear that he wished the 'Paris' version to supersede it. In spite of a recent revival of interest in the 1847 version, and in spite of the fact that it is clearly more unified stylistically, the Paris *Macbeth* is the one generally heard today. In the discussion below, the most substantial revisions will be considered as they appear.

*   *   *

The prelude is made up of themes from the opera. First comes a unison woodwind theme from the witches' scene at the start of Act 3, then a passage from the apparition music in the same act. The second half is taken almost entirely from Lady Macbeth's Act 4 'sleepwalking' scene.

ACT I Scene i *A wood*   The witches' chorus that opens the act divides into two parts, the first ('Che faceste?') in the minor, the second ('Le sorelle vagabonde') in the parallel major. Both partake of the musical 'colour' associated throughout with the witches, among which are prominent woodwind sonorities (both dark and shrill), mercurial string figures, and a tendency for rhythmic displacement. Macbeth and Banquo enter and are hailed by the witches with their threefold prophecies (Macbeth shall be thane of Cawdor; he shall be king; Banquo's descendants shall be kings), darkly scored and with prominent tritones. A brisk military march then introduces messengers, who inform Macbeth of Cawdor's death and hence the fulfilment of part of the prophecy. As Verdi admitted to his principal baritone, Varesi, this sequence would traditionally have called for a double aria for Macbeth, but instead the composer supplied a one-movement duettino for Macbeth and Banquo, 'Due vaticini', full of broken lines and suppressed exclamations as the two men examine their consciences. The witches' closing stretta, 'S'allontanarono', is far more conventional, though it does find room for yet more 'characteristic' colour.

Scene ii *A room in Macbeth's castle*   Lady Macbeth's cavatina generates great dramatic power from a conventional outward form. After a stormy orchestral introduction, she enters to read a letter from her husband describing the events we have just witnessed. The first movement of her double aria, 'Vieni! t'affretta!', bids Macbeth hurry home so that she can instil in him her bloody thoughts; it is remarkable for its avoidance of formal repetition and for its adventurous harmonic excursions. A messenger announces that Macbeth and Duncan are expected that night, and Lady Macbeth exults in the cabaletta 'Or tutti sorgete', whose moments of agility are woven into the restricted formal structure. The cabaletta over, Macbeth appears and in a brief recitative Lady Macbeth unfolds her plans for Duncan. The couple are interrupted by the arrival of the king himself, whose parade around the stage is accompanied by a 'rustic' march from the stage-band. The 'Gran Scena e Duetto' that follows begins with Macbeth's extended arioso 'Mi si affaccia un pugnal?!', during which he sees a vision of a dagger and steels himself to murder Duncan. The passage is rich in musical invention, as sliding chromatic figures jostle with distorted 'religious' harmonies and fugitive reminiscences of the witches' music; it will set the tone for the great recitatives of Verdi's later career. Macbeth enters the king's room, and Lady Macbeth appears, soon to be rejoined by her husband. Macbeth's motif at 'Tutto è finito!' ('All is finished!') furnishes the accompaniment material for the first movement of a four-movement duet, the Allegro 'Fatal mia donna! un murmure'. This movement involves a rapid exchange between the characters, with musical continuity mostly supplied by the orchestra. As Macbeth describes the inner voice that has denied him sleep, a second, more lyrical movement, 'Allor questa voce', begins: the singers again have dissimilar musical material, although they eventually come together for an extended passage 'a 2'. A short transitional movement, 'Il pugnal là riportate', sees Lady Macbeth return the dagger to the king's room and emerge with blood on her hands that she has smeared on his sleeping servants. The duet closes with a short cabaletta, 'Vieni altrove! ogni sospetto', which in the 1847 version quickly turns to the major mode but which in 1865 Verdi revised to keep subdued and in the minor throughout. The first-act finale begins with the arrival of Macduff and Banquo, the latter singing a solemn apostrophe to the night. Macduff discovers the murder of Duncan and calls everyone on stage announce the dreadful news. This launches the Adagio concertato, 'Schiudi, inferno': an outburst of group anguish, a quiet unaccompanied passage in which all pray for God's guidance, and a final soaring melody in which divine vengeance is called down on those who are guilty. Following the pattern of the preceding duet, the final stretta is extremely short, functioning more as a coda than as a movement in its own right.

ACT 2 Scene i *A room in the castle*   An orchestral reprise of part of the Act 1 Macbeth-Lady Macbeth duet leads to a recitative between the couple. Malcolm has fled and is suspected of Duncan's murder, but Macbeth, obsessed by the witches' prophesy that Banquo's sons will be kings, decides that more blood must flow. In the 1847 version, Lady Macbeth closes the scene with the cabaletta 'Trionfai! securi alfine', a conventional two-verse movement in the manner of Elvira in *Ernani*. In 1865 Verdi replaced this with 'La luce langue', a multisectional aria whose chromaticism is consistently that of his later style.

Scene ii *A park*   The quiet, staccato chorus of murderers, 'Sparve il sol', in Verdi's traditional manner for depicting sinister groups, leads to a Romanza for Banquo, in the coda of which the assassins strike him down but cannot prevent his son Fleance from escaping.

Scene iii *A magnificent hall*   Festive music underpins the assembling of noble guests, after which Macbeth summons his wife to sing a brindisi. She obliges with 'Si colmi il calice', and (as will happen in Act i of *La traviata*) is answered by the unison chorus. The closing strains of the song echo in the orchestra as Macbeth learns from an assassin of Banquo's death and Fleance's escape. The festive music resumes, but Macbeth has a horrible vision of Banquo at the banquet table (this and the second hallucination were revised and chromatically intensified in the 1865 version). Lady Macbeth calms him and repeats her brindisi, but the vision returns. The king's terror precipitates the concertato finale, 'Sangue a me', which is led off and dominated by Macbeth, though with frequent interjections from his wife. There is no formal stretta, the act ending with the general sense of stunned surprise intact.

ACT 3 *A dark cavern*   After a stormy orchestral introduction, the witches' chorus, 'Tre volte miagola', brings back the opening idea of the prelude as the first of a series of increasingly lively, rhythmically bumpy 6/8 melodies, ones clearly intended to depict the 'bizarre' element of the supernatural. The ballet that follows, written for the 1865 Paris version, is broadly in three movements. In the first, various supernatural beings dance around the cauldron to an Allegro vivacissimo. Hecate is called forth and, in an Andante second movement full of the rich chromaticism of Verdi's later style, mimes that Macbeth will come to ask of his destiny and should be answered (Verdi insisted that this section be mimed rather than danced). The final movement is a sinister waltz, the spirits dancing even more wildly around the cauldron.

The Apparition Scene, substantially revised in the 1865 version to intensify its harmonic and orchestral effect, has little sustained melodic writing and consists of brief but telling musical episodes. The first introduces the three apparitions, who make their predictions of Macbeth's fate: the armed head is that of Macbeth himself, the bloody child represents

Macduff 'from his mother's womb ripp'd', the crowned child holding a bough is Malcolm with the trees of Birnam Wood. Then, to Macbeth's arioso 'Fuggi, regal fantasima', come the eight kings, the last of whom is in the form of Banquo and precipitates Macbeth's 'Oh! mio terror! dell'ultimo', at the end of which he faints. A gentle chorus and dance of the aerial spirits, 'Ondine e silfidi', precedes the finale, which was completely rewritten for 1865. In the 1847 version the act finished with a cabaletta for Macbeth, 'Vada in fiamme', very much in the early Verdi style though with an unusual minor-major key scheme. In 1865 Verdi replaced this with a duettino for Macbeth and Lady Macbeth, 'Ora di morte e di vendetta': the added subtlety of articulation perhaps results in a loss of sheer rhythmic energy.

ACT 4 Scene i *A deserted place on the border of England and Scotland* The 1847 version of the opening, 'Patria oppressa', not least in its lamenting of the 'lost' homeland, is reminiscent of the 'patriotic' choruses that became so famous in Verdi's early operas, although the minor mode gives it a different colour. The 1865 replacement is one of the composer's greatest choral movements, with subtle details of harmony and rhythm in almost every bar. Macduff's 'Ah, la paterna mano', which follows, is a conventional minor-major Romanza. The scene is rounded off by a cabaletta-like chorus, 'La patria tradita', as Malcolm's troops prepare to attack Macbeth.

Scene ii *A room in Macbeth's castle* (as 1.ii)   Lady Macbeth enters, sleepwalking. Her famous aria, 'Una macchia', is justly regarded as one of the young Verdi's greatest creations. Preceded by an atmospheric instrumental depiction of Lady Macbeth's guilty wandering, the aria itself is distinguished by its expanded formal and harmonic structure and—most important—by a marvellously inventive orchestral contribution.

Scene iii *Another room in the castle*   A noisy orchestral introduction leads to Macbeth's confessional Andante sostenuto 'Pietà, rispetto, amore', a slow aria with some surprising internal modulations. Soldiers rush on to announce the seeming approach of Birnam Wood; a pseudo-fugal orchestral battle ensues during which Malcolm overcomes Macbeth in single combat. In 1847 the opera ended with a short, melodramatic scene for Macbeth, 'Mal per me', full of declamatory gestures that recall motivic threads from earlier in the drama. For the 1865 version Verdi replaced this with a Victory Hymn, 'Macbeth, Macbeth ov'è?', a number in his most modern

style, with more than a hint of Offenbach in its dotted rhythms, and perhaps even a gesture to the *Marseillaise* in its final bars.

*   *   *

There is no doubt that Verdi's frequently voiced perception of the 1847
Macbeth as an especially important work, ennobled by its Shakespearean
theme, was one that he successfully converted into dramatic substance.
Much of the opera displays an attention to detail and sureness of effect
unprecedented in earlier works. This holds true as much for the 'conventional' numbers, such as Lady Macbeth's opening aria or the subsequent
duet with Macbeth, as for formal experiments like the Macbeth-Banquo
duettino in Act 1. *Macbeth* is, for this reason, often considered a watershed
in Verdi's early career. But what also singles the opera out is an element
that recent commentators have found troublesome: its exploitation in the
witches' music of the 'genere fantastico' (the fantastic or supernatural
genre). There are early attempts in this vein in *Giovanna d'Arco*, but in
Macbeth this alternative 'colour' is vividly explored and placed in juxtaposition to the dark, personal world of Macbeth and his wife, thus expanding
the range of the opera by centring it around a violent conflict between two
musically distinct worlds. (Incidentally, this experiment might also be
linked to Verdian interest—never very strong—in the trappings of Romanticism, which tended to be more a style than a full-fledged movement
in Italy, in spite of periodic importations from France and elsewhere.)

The 1865 revisions undoubtedly enrich the score, supplying several of
its most effective pieces, notably 'La luce langue' and the opening chorus
of Act 4. Clearly the sense of stylistic disparity the revisions create did not
concern Verdi; indeed, for the most part he made little attempt to match the
replacement numbers with the main body of the score, instead producing
pieces that are among the most harmonically advanced of his later career.
Nor should such disparity unduly concern us: we may well overestimate
the importance of stylistic consistency in opera, and the 1865 revision will
surely continue to be the most commonly performed version of this magnificent work.

I masnadieri

('*The Bandits*')

Melodramma in four acts set to a libretto by Andrea Maffei after Friedrich von Schiller's play *Die Räuber*; first performed in London, Her Majesty's Theatre, on 22 July 1847.

The cast at the première included Jenny Lind (Amelia), Italo Gardoni (Carlo), Filippo Coletti (Francesco), and Luigi Lablache (Massimiliano).

Massimiliano, Count Moor	bass
Carlo, *his son*	tenor
Francesco, *brother to Carlo*	baritone
Amalia, *orphan, the Count's niece*	soprano
Arminio, *the Count's treasurer*	tenor
Moser, *a pastor*	bass
Rolla, *a companion of Carlo Moor*	tenor

Wayward youths (who become bandits), women, children, servants

Setting Bohemia, at the beginning of the eighteenth century

The lucrative contract to compose an opera for Her Majesty's Theatre in London was an important sign of Verdi's burgeoning international reputation and allowed him to write for some of the most famous singers of the age. More than that, the librettist was his friend Andrea Maffei, a distinguished man of letters with a reputation far above that of Piave or Solera, who had between them supplied most of Verdi's earlier librettos. All this notwithstanding, *I masnadieri* had a troublesome birth: Maffei's lack of experience in theatrical matters was a considerable trial; Verdi quarrelled with the publisher of the opera, Francesco Lucca (with whom he never had the generally cordial relations he enjoyed with his usual publisher, Ricordi); and when he arrived in London to supervise the production, he seems to have been oppressed beyond all reason by the detested English weather. The première was a magnificent gala occasion—Queen Victoria headed the guests of honour—and a triumphant success, aided by the fame of the singers, especially Lind and Lablache, the latter one of the great names of the previous generation of Italian singers. But the enthusiastic reception was short-lived, and the opera fared rather badly in Italy. Modern revivals are not uncommon but they remain special occasions: it seems unlikely that the work will find a permanent place in the international repertory.

*　　　*　　　*

A lachrymose cello solo, written expressly for Alfredo Piatti, the principal cellist at Her Majesty's Theatre, forms a brief but effective prelude.

ACT I Scene i *A tavern on the frontier of Saxony* In a formally conventional but carefully crafted double aria with chorus, Carlo muses on his distant homeland and his beloved Amalia (the Andantino 'O mio castel paterno') before learning, through a letter from his brother, that he is forbidden to return home. He and his friends decide to become bandits and swear an oath of blood brotherhood (the cabaletta 'Nell'argilla maledetta').

Scene ii *Franconia: a room in Massimiliano's castle* A rapid change of locale is effected for a second two-movement aria, this time for Carlo's wicked brother Francesco. In the angular Andante sostenuto, 'La sua lampada vitale', Francesco threatens to hasten the end of his father's life. He then orders that Massimiliano be told of Carlo's death in battle, hoping that shock and grief will finish the old man off. In a forceful cabaletta, 'Tremate, o miseri!', he eagerly looks forward to assuming power.

Scene iii *A bedroom in the castle* After a prelude in which solo woodwinds are prominent, Amalia looks at the sleeping Massimiliano and thinks back over past joys in 'Lo sguardo avea degli angeli'. The aria was clearly written with Jenny Lind in mind: it is far more highly ornamented than the usual Verdian model and, to accommodate the free flow of decoration, formally far more discursive. Massimiliano awakes and, in a short duet movement with Amalia, 'Carlo! io muoio', laments that he will die without seeing his favourite son. Arminio and Francesco enter to deliver the false news of Carlo's death, saying that Carlo's last words accused his father and instructed Amalia to marry Francesco. This revelation precipitates the quartet 'Sul capo mio colpevole': Massimiliano is both repentant and furious with Francesco; Amalia (joined by a reformed Arminio) offers religious consolation; Francesco eagerly looks forward to his triumph. It is a powerfully effective clash of emotions and ends as Massimiliano, seemingly lifeless, falls to the ground.

ACT 2 Scene i *An enclosure adjoining the castle chapel*   Time has passed; Francesco is lord of the castle. Amalia visits Massimiliano's grave and in a simple Adagio, 'Tu del mio Carlo in seno', imagines him and Carlo together in heaven. Arminio rushes in to reveal that Carlo and Massimiliano are both alive. Amalia rejoices in a jubilant, distinctly old-fashioned cabaletta, 'Carlo vive?', which again gave ample opportunity for Jenny Lind to demonstrate her famed agility. Francesco enters to declare his love for Amalia. they launch into a four-movement soprano-baritone confrontation duet, a type of dramatic situation at which Verdi almost always succeeded. But for once the format proves disappointing: the Andantino 'Io t'amo, Amalia' dissolves too quickly into rhythmic unison at the 3rd or 6th, and the cabaletta, 'Ti scosta, o malnato', in which Amalia defies Francesco's attempts to take her by force, deals somewhat unimaginatively with the clash of tessituras that many of Verdi's best examples exploit so powerfully.

Scene ii *The Bohemian forest near Prague*   The 'Finale Secondo' begins with a typical slice of bandit life, though the choral writing is more complex than Verdi usually ventured. Rolla, condemned to be hanged, is rescued by Carlo and his followers, who rejoice in their carefree life. They leave Carlo alone to lament his outcast state in a minor-major Romanza, 'Di ladroni attorniato'. His companions return to report that they are under attack; all join in a warlike chorus.

ACT 3 Scene i *A deserted place adjacent to the forest near Massimiliano's castle*   Amalia has escaped from Francesco but is now alone and terrified to hear the sound of bandits nearby. She begs for mercy from the first man she sees: miraculously, this turns out to be Carlo; the lovers are blissfully united in a duet. The slow movement, 'Qual mare, qual terra', is perhaps a trifle dull, although colouristic vocal effects make up for a lack of the usual confrontational tension. Amalia tells Carlo of his father's death and of Francesco's attempts on her virtue. They end the scene in a cabaletta,

'Lassù risplendere', in which Amalia has yet more opportunity to display her trills and agility.

Scene ii *Inside the forest*   A further bandits' chorus precedes the 'Finale Terzo'. Carlo wrestles with his Byronic soul and even contemplates suicide, but is interrupted by Arminio, whom he sees delivering food to someone imprisoned in a deserted tower. Carlo intervenes, bringing forth from the tower an emaciated old man who reveals himself as Massimiliano. In an impressive minor-major narrative, 'Un ignoto, tre lune or saranno', Massimiliano (who has not recognized his son) tells how Francesco had confined him there after he recovered from his collapse. Carlo is outraged, and calls on his fellow bandits to join him in swearing a solemn oath of vengeance against Francesco.

ACT 4 Scene i *A suite of rooms in Massimiliano's castle*   Francesco's 'Pareami che sorto da lauto convito' describes a frightening vision of divine retribution; it is a movement that prefigures the great soliloquies of Verdi's middle-period operas. He summons Moser and asks forgiveness for his sins: only God can grant forgiveness, the pastor answers. Prompted by signs that the castle is under attack, Francesco rushes off to meet his fate.

Scene ii *The forest* (as 3.ii)   Carlo will not reveal his identity to Massimiliano but nevertheless asks 'a father's blessing'. In a gentle duet 'Come il bacio d'un padre amoroso', father and son are vocally united. The robbers appear, having captured Amalia; Carlo's identity is revealed. In a final trio 'Caduto è il reprobo!', reminiscent of the parallel number in Act 4 of *Ernani*, Carlo rails against his commitment to a life of crime while Amalia offers to stay with him no matter what. But Carlo's robber companions are near at hand, impossible to ignore: in a final declamatory outburst, he stabs Amalia and rushes off to the gallows that await him.

*   *   *

I masnadieri is one of the most intriguing of Verdi's early works. It should have been a great success: a foreign commission of great prestige, a high Romantic foundation in Schiller (one of the composer's favourite sources), a distinguished man of letters as the librettist, a cast of international standing. What is more, Verdi and his librettist consciously tried to break with certain long-standing traditions in order to make their creation more romantically intense: no other early opera dispenses with an opening chorus, for example, or with a concertato finale. But all these ingredients proved problematic. Verdi felt out of touch and out of sympathy with the English environment and may have been unsure of the audience's taste and requirements; the drama proved somewhat unwieldy, particularly in its lack of opportunities for character confrontation; Maffei, in spite of his poetic skills and willingness to experiment, was unsure in dramatic pacing; and the cast, Jenny Lind in particular, inspired music that, though distinguished enough on its own, proved difficult to subsume under an overall dramatic colour, the achievement of which was so crucial to Verdian success.

Jérusalem

('Jerusalem')

Opéra in four acts set to a libretto by Alphonse Royer and Gustave Vaëz after Temistocle Solera's and Verdi's earlier opera *I Lombardi alla prima crociata*; first performed in Paris, Opéra, on 26 November 1847.

The cast at the première included Gilbert Louis Duprez (Gaston), Charles Portheaut (the Count), Adolphe Alizard (Roger), and Esther Julian van Gelder (Hélène).

Gaston, *Viscount of Béarn*	tenor
The Count of Toulouse	baritone
Roger, *the Count's brother*	bass
Hélène, *the Count's daughter*	soprano
Isaure, *her companion*	soprano
Adhemar de Monteil, *the papal legate*	bass
Raymond, *Gaston's squire*	tenor
A Soldier	bass
A Herald	bass
The Emir of Ramla	bass
An Officer of the Emir	tenor

Knights, ladies, pages, soldiers, pilgrims, penitents, an executioner, Arab sheiks, women of the harem, people of Ramla

Setting Toulouse and Palestine, in 1095 and 1099

The great Paris opera house, the Académie Royale de Musique (often simply called the Opéra), had been making overtures to Verdi for some two years when, in the summer of 1847, he signed a contract to supply the theatre with a 'new' work by November of that year. As had Rossini and Donizetti, Verdi offered for his début at the Opéra a revision of one of his earlier Italian operas; with the help of Royer and Vaëz, both of whom had considerable experience in such matters, he fashioned a French version from *I Lombardi alla prima crociata*, first performed in 1843 and not previously seen in Paris. The librettists retained little of the original plot apart from its basis in a crusade: in vocal terms, the lovers Giselda and Oronte become Hélène and Gaston, the warring brothers Arvino and Pagano become the Count of Toulouse—now a baritone rather than tenor—and Roger. As well as adding the obligatory ballet, Verdi decided on some wide-ranging structural changes, adding much new music, cutting what he considered weak or inappropriate, and leaving only a few of the original numbers in their former positions. *Jérusalem* was well received in Paris. However, and in spite of being in many ways superior to *I Lombardi*, the opera failed to establish itself in either the French repertory or (retranslated as *Gerusalemme*) on Italian stages. It is today only occasionally revived. The following summary will mention musical detail only in passages new to the revised opera.

*   *   *

The prelude is new; in contrast to the juxtaposition of disparate musical elements in *I Lombardi*, it sets out to develop in a systematic manner aspects of its opening theme.

ACT 1 *A gallery connecting the Count of Toulouse's palace and his chapel*
As the curtain rises, Hélène and Gaston bid each other farewell, Gaston assuring his beloved that he will be reconciled to the Count (who killed his father) if permission is granted for their marriage. Their brief duet, 'Adieu, mon bien-aimé', is unaccompanied except for solo horn. As Gaston leaves, Isaure appears and the two ladies kneel in prayer, Hélène offering a French version of 'Salve Maria' from *I Lombardi*, now called 'Vierge Marie'. Hélène and Isaure depart and, as the orchestra depicts a sunrise, the stage fills with lords and ladies who join in a chorus celebrating the end of civil war, 'Enfin voici le jour propice'. The Count and all other principals appear. They are about to go on a Crusade, and the Count offers peace to Gaston and his family, sealing the pact with his daughter's hand. All rejoice except Roger, who incestuously desires Hélène for himself. The principals explore their individual feelings in the quintet 'Je tremble encor, j'y crois à peine', a number that required some vocal redistribution from its

model in *I Lombardi*. In a newly composed linking passage, Gaston swears allegiance to the Count, who is pronounced leader of the crusading army. The scene closes with a grand chorus, 'Cité du Seigneur!'.

An organ sounds from inside the chapel; Roger appears and, in the slow movement 'Oh! dans l'ombre, dans le mystère', muses on his incestuous love. The aria over, Roger instructs a soldier to seek out two knights in golden armour and to murder the one not wearing a white cloak. After a warlike chorus looking forward to the Crusade, he anticipates the murder of Gaston in a cabaletta new for the French version, 'Ah! viens! démon! esprit du mal!'. The action scene that follows is also new. Cries of 'Murder!' in the chapel precede the appearance of Gaston: it is the Count who has been attacked. Roger's hired assassin accuses Gaston of instigating the violence and all join in an accusatory concertato, 'Monstre, parjure, homicide!'. The papal legate sentences Gaston to exile and in a final stretta, 'Sur ton front est lancé l'anathème', all pronounce a solemn curse on him.

ACT 2 Scene i *The mountains of Ramla in Palestine*   Four years have passed. At the opening, corresponding with Act 2 scene ii of *I Lombardi*, the disguised Roger is outside his cave, singing the Adagio 'O jour fatal! ô crime!'. Raymond enters, dying of thirst. At the news that others are in a similar plight, Roger hurries to the rescue. Hélène now appears, recognizes Raymond as Gaston's squire and learns that her beloved is alive and imprisoned in Ramla. She breaks into a joyous cabaletta, originally in Act 4 of *I Lombardi* and here retitled 'Quelle ivresse! bonheur suprême!', and leaves to seek out Gaston. A band of pilgrims, weak from lack of water, struggle on to deliver 'O mon Dieu! Ta parole est donc vaine!' (the French version of 'O Signore, dal tetto natio'). As in *I Lombardi*, a lively march introduces the Count (marvellously recovered, he tells us, from the assassination attempt), who asks the hermit's blessing. Instead, though, Roger (still unrecognized) elects to accompany them into battle. All depart after a lively final chorus, 'Le Seigneur nous promet la victoire', new for the French version.

Scene ii *A room in the Emir's palace at Ramla*   Gaston, a prisoner, muses on Hélène in a revised version of his Act 2 Andante from *I Lombardi*, now called 'Je veux encor entendre'. The Emir appears, quickly followed by Hélène, who has been captured nearby. The Act 3 lovers' duet from *I Lombardi* then ensues; Hélène and Gaston are about to escape to join the Crusaders but are at the last moment surrounded by guards.

ACT 3 Scene i *The gardens of the harem at Ramla*   This scene corresponds to Act 2 scene iii of *I Lombardi*, except that the opening chorus is followed by a full-length ballet. By the time the dancing is over, Crusaders are at the gates. Hélène prays for deliverance, Gaston appears at her side. The Crusaders rush in, and the Count denounces Hélène for consorting with Gaston, the presumed assassin. Hélène, like her Italian counterpart, responds with a cabaletta, 'Non . . . votre rage', at the close of which the Count drags her away.

Scene ii *The public square at Ramla*   In an impressive ensemble scene, new for the French version, Gaston is led on to the strains of a funeral dirge. The Legate informs the crowd that he is to be dishonoured and executed; Gaston pleads for mercy in the Andante mosso, 'O mes amis, mes frères d'armes'. But the accusers are unmoved: he will be executed the following day. In a closing stretta, 'Frapper bourreaux!', Gaston asks for immediate death, proud before God of his innocence.

ACT 4 Scene i *On the edge of the Crusaders' camp in the valley of Jehoshaphat*   The scene is based on the 'Coro della Processione' that opens Act 3 of *I Lombardi*, although the chorus is preceded by a recitative from Roger, who gazes over the valley at Jerusalem. As the procession moves away, Roger and Hélène remain to offer Gaston a final blessing. The tenor appears, and so the new plot links to the famous trio that ends Act 3 of *I Lombardi*: it is now called 'Dieu nous sépare, Hélène!', is shorn of its violin solo and boasts an exciting coda in which offstage sounds of battle cause Gaston and Roger to rush off to the fray.

Scene ii *The Count's tent*   The Count, accompanied by an unknown knight who has distinguished himself in battle, announces victory. The knight reveals himself as Gaston. Roger is now brought on, mortally wounded. The music links into the final scene of *I Lombardi*, with Roger's revelation of his true identity, and his pleas that mercy be shown to Gaston, answered by the closing Hymne Général, 'A toi gloire ô Dieu de victoire'.

*   *   *

Although *Jérusalem* was soon converted into the Italian *Gerusalemme*, and published in Italy, Verdi's revision failed to oust *I Lombardi* from the Italian stage and gradually disappeared from the repertory. This is in some ways regrettable, as the French opera simplifies the complex action of its

Italian original, adds convincing new music (in particular the crowd scene of Act 3 scene ii), cuts some of the weaker portions and, by converting Arvino from a tenor to a baritone, solves one of the problems of vocal distribution that always plagues *I Lombardi*. Whatever its ultimate merits, *Jérusalem* serves as a fascinating first document in charting Verdi's relationship with the French stage, a relationship that was to become increasingly important during the next decade.

Il corsaro

('The Corsair')

Opera in three acts set to a libretto by Francesco Maria Piave after Byron's poem *The Corsair*; first performed in Trieste, Teatro Grande, on 25 October 1848.

The cast at the première included Gaetano Fraschini (Corrado), Achille De Bassini (Seid), Carolina Rapazzini (Medora), and Marianna Barbieri-Nini (Gulnara).

Corrado, *Captain of the corsairs*	tenor
Giovanni, *a corsair*	bass
Medora, *Corrado's young beloved*	soprano
Seid, *Pasha of Coron*	baritone
Gulnara, *Seid's favourite slave*	soprano
Selimo, *an Aga*	tenor
A Black Eunuch	tenor
A Slave	tenor

Corsairs, guards, Turks, slaves, odalisques, Medora's maids, Anselmo (a corsair)

Setting An island in the Aegean and the city of Coron, at the beginning of the nineteenth century

Verdi had toyed with setting Byron's poem as early as 1844 and kept the subject in mind during the years immediately following. In 1845 he considered using it to fulfil a commission from Her Majesty's Theatre in London: Piave wrote the libretto, but the London trip was postponed. A year later

Verdi showed his continuing enthusiasm for the topic by asking Piave not to give the libretto to any other composer. Eventually, he wrote the opera to honour the final part of a long-standing contract with Giovanni Ricordi's rival publisher Francesco Lucca, a man with whom Verdi had had unfortunate dealings ever since Lucca and Ricordi had come to legal blows over the rights to *Nabucco* in 1842. Anxious above all to be rid of his obligation, Verdi set Piave's libretto in the winter of 1847–48, giving the opera to Lucca without any idea of where or when it would first be performed. For a composer who in all previous operas had taken an enormous, often fanatical interest in the details of his creations' first staging, such indifference is suspicious: many have seen it as an indication that Verdi had little faith in his new creation. Lucca eventually placed the opera at the Teatro Grande in Trieste, but Verdi did not even trouble to attend the first performances. The première was poorly received and managed only a few revivals before it disappeared from the repertory. The opera has rarely been revived in modern times.

*   *   *

The prelude, based on material from the opera, is one of extreme contrasts, with the opening orchestral storm music followed by a lyrical subject of great simplicity.

ACT I Scene i *The corsairs' island in the Aegean* A boisterous offstage chorus of corsairs introduces Corrado, who bemoans his life of exile and crime in 'Tutto parea sorridere', an aria that delicately hovers between the Italian norm and the French two-verse variety. A letter containing military intelligence is presented to Corrado, who resolves to set sail, rallying his troops with the cabaletta 'Sì: de' Corsari il fulmine'; in the manner of Verdi's earliest successes, the chorus joins the soloist for the final lines.

Scene ii *Medora's apartments in the old tower* Medora, awaiting Corrado's arrival, takes up her harp and sings a two-verse Romanza, 'Non so le tetre immagini', full of vague forebodings but not without elaborate vocal ornament. Corrado enters and a conventionally structured duet finale closes the act. The first lyrical movement, 'No, tu non sai', a dissimilar type in which Medora's disturbed chromatic line is settled by Corrado's reassuring melodic stability, is unusual in its progressive deceleration of tempo; the cabaletta, 'Tornerai, ma forse spenta', which sees Corrado about to depart yet again, is more traditionally paced, with a faster final section in which the lovers sing an extended passage in 3rds and 6ths.

ACT 2 Scene i *Luxurious apartments in Seid's harem*   A chorus of odalisques, graced with high woodwind local colour, introduces Gulnara, who hates Seid and seeks to escape from the harem. Her Andantino, 'Vola talor dal carcere', is conventionally scored but has much of that harmonic and orchestral density we expect from post-*Macbeth* Verdi. She agrees to attend a banquet of Seid's and in the cabaletta 'Ah conforto è sol la speme' prays that Heaven will take pity on her.

Scene ii   *A magnificent pavilion on the shores of the harbour of Coron*   After a brief chorus, Seid salutes his followers and joins them in a solemn hymn, 'Salve, Allah!', a number whose rhythmic cut is more than a little reminiscent of the famous choruses in *I Lombardi* and *Ernani*. A dervish appears, asking for protection from the corsairs. He and Seid have time for the brief first movement of a duet, 'Dì: que' ribaldi tremano', before flames and offstage cries signal an attack. The dervish throws off his disguise to reveal himself as Corrado, who calls for his followers. In an extended battle sequence, Corrado and his troops attempt to save the women of the harem, a delay that causes him to be wounded and the attack to fail. In the ensuing Andante of the concertato finale, 'Audace cotanto mostrati pur sai?', Seid derides the fallen hero, Corrado is defiant, and Gulnara and the odalisques find their amorous feelings aroused by these handsome would-be saviours. More prisoners are brought on, but Seid is above all happy to have Corrado in his power. He leads off the stretta 'Sì, morrai di morte atroce', promising his prisoner an agonizing death.

ACT 3 Scene i *Seid's apartments*   The baritone has so far had little of the vocal limelight; room is now made for a full-scale double aria. In the Andantino, 'Cento leggiadre vergini', Seid regrets that of all the women available to him, the one whom he loves has spurned him. As in Corrado's Act 1 aria, though even more economically, the aria is notable for its orchestral reprise of the main melody. In the cabaletta 'S'avvicina il tuo momento', a movement more reminiscent of *Oberto* than of the post-*Macbeth* style, Seid looks forward to Corrado's grisly death.

Gulnara enters to plead for Corrado's life. The first movement of the ensuing duet, 'Vieni, Gulnara!', is a free dialogue over a complex orchestral melody, a type later to be made famous in the Rigoletto-Sparafucile duet. But Seid will not be persuaded and eventually concludes that Gulnara must love Corrado. His anger bursts forth in the duet cabaletta, 'Sia l'istante maledetto'.

Scene ii   *Inside a prison tower*   A sombre prelude featuring solo cello and viola introduces Corrado, alone and in chains. Before falling asleep, he laments his fate in a spare but expressive recitative. Gulnara steals in and awakens him. In the long and unusually free first movement of their duet, 'Seid la vuole', Gulnara offers Corrado a means of escape, saying that she herself will kill Seid. Corrado's personal honour obliges him to refuse her help, and he further distresses her by admitting his love for Medora. Gulnara departs, and the orchestra sounds a reprise of the stormy music first heard in the prelude to Act 1. As the storm subsides, Gulnara returns to announce that Seid is dead. Corrado now assures her of his protection and in the cabaletta 'La terra, il ciel m'abbomino' they prepare to escape together.

Scene iii *The corsairs' island* (as 1.i)   An orchestral prelude featuring fragments of Medora's Act 1 Romanza introduces Corrado's beloved, near death and without hope of seeing him again. But suddenly a ship is sighted, Corrado and Gulnara arrive, and the lovers fall into each other's arms. Corrado and Gulnara narrate something of their adventures before Medora leads off the concertato, 'O mio Corrado, appressati', whose opening melody had appeared in the prelude to the opera. Corrado and Gulnara raise the emotional temperature by protesting at fate, but Medora's strength fails. In an agony of despair, Corrado flings himself from the cliffs.

*   *   *

It is important to recall that the libretto of *Il corsaro* (and therefore its essential dramatic structure) was fixed as early as 1846, some time before Verdi worked on *Macbeth:* small wonder, then, that much of the opera seems rather old-fashioned in relation to the works that surround it. It is also—perhaps for this reason, perhaps (as mentioned earlier) because of Verdi's feud with the publisher Lucca—an uneven work, with an element of the routine in certain passages. On the other hand, there are many moments, particularly in the final act, that stand comparison with the best operas of this period, and some formal experiments—strange and elliptical as they may be in their dramatic context—that will bear much fruit in the years to come.

La battaglia di Legnano

('The Battle of Legnano')

Tragedia lirica in four acts set to a libretto by Salvadore Cammarano after Joseph Méry's play *La Bataille de Toulouse*; first performed in Rome, Teatro Argentina, 27 January 1849.

The cast at the première included Filippo Colini (Rolando), Teresa De Giuli Borsi (Lida), and Gaetano Fraschini (Arrigo).

Federico Barbarossa	bass
First Consul of Milan	bass
Second Consul of Milan	bass
Mayor of Como	bass
Rolando, *a Milanese leader*	baritone
Lida, *his wife*	soprano
Arrigo, *a soldier from Verona*	tenor
Marcovaldo, *a German prisoner*	baritone
Imelda, *Lida's maid*	mezzo-soprano
Arrigo's Squire	tenor
A Herald	tenor

Knights of Death, magistrates and leaders of Como, Lida's maids, Milanese people, Milanese senators, soldiers from Verona, Novara, Piacenza, and Milan, German army

Setting Milan and Como in 1176

The revolutions that swept through Italy and much of the rest of Europe in 1848—and in particular Milan's 'cinque giornate', when in five days of tough street fighting the Milanese forced the Austrians temporarily from their city—inspired Verdi to attempt an opera in which the theme of patriotism would be overt. Together with his librettist Cammarano, he decided to compose an opera set in twelfth-century Italy, the epoch of the Lombard league, adapting for the purpose a recent French drama. Work on *La battaglia di Legnano* took up most of 1848, and by the time it was finished Milan and many other cities were long back in Austrian hands. But Rome was still a beleaguered republic, and the première of the opera took place there in what must have been highly charged circumstances. It was a clamorous success, with the entire final act encored. Understandably, though, the opera was extremely difficult to get past the censors in the repressive, counterrevolutionary atmosphere of the 1850s; and it is in this context hardly surprising that *La battaglia* failed to make its way in the 1850s. Even before the first performance, Verdi's publisher Ricordi had approached Cammarano about a 'sanitized' version (that is, with a setting removed from Italy), and although *L'assedio di Arlem* (set in the Flemish-Spanish wars) had a few outings, it never established itself. In the mid-1850s Verdi voiced an intention of rehabilitating *La battaglia* by subjecting it to a thorough revision; but his ideas came to nothing, and the work virtually disappeared from the theatre until its occasional modern revival.

*   *   *

The overture has the usual three-part structure, with the middle section slower and (in the manner of the *Guillaume Tell* overture) dominated by solo woodwind. But its inner workings and its sheer scale far outstrip any of Verdi's previous efforts; the piece deserves revival in today's concert halls.

ACT I 'HE LIVES!' Scene i *A part of rebuilt Milan, near the city walls* Soldiers from various parts of northern Italy congregate and sing an unaccompanied patriotic hymn, 'Viva Italia! Sacro un patto' (already heard as the opening subject of the overture). Arrigo emerges from the troops to greet his beloved Milan in 'La pia materna mano', an aria whose subtlety of orchestral detail and distant modulations immediately alert us to the developments taking place in Verdi's musical language. After a brief reprise of the hymn, Rolando joyously greets Arrigo, having thought him killed in battle. His Romanza, 'Ah! m'abbraccia d'esultanza', functions dramaturgically as a cabaletta but is actually a French-influenced ternary form. The scene is rounded off by a solemn 'giuramento' in which all swear to defend Milan to the last drop of blood.

Scene ii *A shady place*   A female chorus celebrating the arrival of the soldiers introduces Lida, who explains in an Andante, 'Quante volte come un
dono', that she cannot be happy now that her father and brothers have
been slain in battle. Again, unusually detailed orchestration and harmonic
excursions underline a new manner in Verdi's style. Marcovaldo pays un-
welcome court to Lida, but is interrupted by Imelda, who announces that
Rolando has returned, bringing with him Arrigo. Lida's attempts to restrain her joy at the news that Arrigo is alive coalesce into her cabaletta
'A frenarti, o cor nel petto'.

Rolando ushers in Arrigo, saying that his friend must remain in the
house as a guest. Left alone, Arrigo and Lida engage in a long, single-
movement duet finale, 'È ver? . . . Sei d'altri?', a piece quite unlike the
usual multi-movement sequence and gaining its cohesion more from juxtapositions of key than from contrasting formal units.

ACT 2 'BARBAROSSA!' *A magnificent room in the town hall of Como*   In
the chorus 'Sì, tardi ed invano' the people of Como, ancient enemies of the
Milanese, rejoice to hear of their rivals' difficulties with Barbarossa. Arrigo
and Rolando enter to request military assistance, urging their cause with a
passionate duet, 'Ben vi scorgo'. Hardly has the duet finished than Barbarossa
himself appears, his impressive entrance immediately precipitating the concertato finale. The Adagio, 'A che smarriti e pallidi', is made up of patterned
exchanges between Barbarossa and the two Milanese warriors, first in a hesi-
tant minor, then in a more lyrically extended major, with the chorus firmly on
Barbarossa's side. Barbarossa then has the windows thrown open to display
the mass of German troops; but Arrigo trusts the power of the people. In the
stretta, 'Il destino d'Italia son io!', the musical opposition between the two
sides continues, Verdi lavishing much orchestral and harmonic detail on a
part of the finale that had traditionally been of the most straightforward.

ACT 3 'DISGRACE!' Scene i *A subterranean vault in the basilica of San
Ambrogio, Milan*   In a sombre opening chorus, 'Fra queste dense tene-
bre', the Knights of Death celebrate a pact to avenge the deaths of their
forefathers. Arrigo is admitted to their ranks before all join in the solemn
oath of allegiance, 'Giuriam d'Italia por fine ai danni'. The scene is reminiscent of *Ernani* Act 3, though regularly punctuated with French-
influenced atmospheric effects.

Scene ii *Apartments in Rolando's castle*   Lida has heard of Arrigo's enlist-
ment with the Knights of Death and has written him a letter which she

now gives to Imelda. Her scene has no formal aria but is full of those lyrical outpourings that will become one of Verdi's greatest strengths in the years to come. Rolando enters to bid farewell to his wife and child, and joins Lida in the tender duet 'Digli ch'è sangue italico'. As Lida and the child leave, Arrigo appears and Rolando confesses his fears for the coming battle. In the gentle, Bellinian Andante, 'Se al nuovo dì pugnando', he entrusts his family to the care of Arrigo should he die in battle. The friends embrace; Arrigo leaves. Marcovaldo now enters: he has intercepted Lida's letter, and shows it to Rolando. In a furious cabaletta, 'Ahi scellerate alme d'inferno', Rolando swears vengeance on his wife and friend.

Scene iii *A room high in the tower*   Arrigo, alone on the balcony as the curtain rises, decides to write a letter of farewell to his mother. Lida enters and the couple confess their love in a simple recitative. They are interrupted by Rolando's offstage voice, which causes Lida to hide on the balcony. Rolando appears and immediately discovers Lida, thus precipitating the Terzetto finale. The first movement, 'Ah! d'un consorte, o perfidi', is all flux and change; in the central Andante, 'Vendetta d'un momento', the two lovers desperately call for death. But Rolando has other plans. Once the set piece has finished, Arrigo hears trumpets calling him to the Knights of Death and prepares to leave; but Rolando has decided that his punishment will be 'disgrace' and rushes out, locking the door behind him. Arrigo cannot stand the shame that will result if he fails to join the Knights, and with a final cry of 'Viva Italia!' throws himself from the balcony into the moat below.

ACT 4 'TO DIE FOR THE HOMELAND!' *The vestibule of a church, giving on to a piazza in Milan*   As a choir is heard singing inside the church, Imelda tells Lida how Arrigo survived his fall and reached the Knights of Death. They join the chorus in a prayer. Distant sounds of rejoicing announce victory over the German army. All unite in a celebratory hymn, but at its close a funeral march is heard in the distance. Arrigo is brought in, mortally wounded. He again protests Lida's innocence and begins the final trio of reconciliation, 'Per la salvata Italia'. The last, soaring phrase, sung by Arrigo, Lida and then by the entire company, sums up the opera's message: 'Chi muore per la patria alma sì rea non ha!' ('He who dies for the homeland cannot have an evil soul!').

*   *   *

La battaglia di Legnano was from the start dogged by the special circumstances of its creation: in the early years by problems with the censor, and later perhaps by its too intense association with a particular historical period. But Verdi's plans to revise the work in the 1850s are surely significant, suggesting that he thought the opera comparable to *Macbeth, Stiffelio,* and *Luisa Miller. La battaglia* is impressive above all in its inner workings, which show a concern for orchestral and harmonic detail that never left Verdi after his decisive encounter with French operatic style. But it also experiments on the larger, structural level. The first scene is a good case in point: it is set out in a kind of arch-form, with brief arias for two of the principals embedded in a symmetrical sequence of choral and orchestral numbers: orchestral marches begin and end the scene, these are flanked by a pair of choruses, inside of which are the two solos. And then, at the centre of the arch comes yet another chorus. Such an organization is very different from a typical Italian opening scene (such as those that start *Nabucco* or *Ernani,* for example), in which the central event will be a two-movement aria for a single character, around which are arranged choral interventions. What the layout powerfully resembles, however, are the operas that were then much on Verdi's mind and to which he was listening nightly in Paris: the works of Auber, Meyerbeer, and their lesser contemporaries. His new, 'Italian' style was, in other words, borrowed directly from the French.

The musical atmosphere established in this first scene, what Verdi would later call the 'colorito' of his score, is rarely abandoned, and this whether in the 'public' sections of the work (mostly added by Verdi and his librettist), or during the 'domestic' sections (surviving from Méry's original play). True, the Act 3 choral 'Giuramento' partially returns to the manner of Verdi's earlier choruses, and the principals indulge in two rather traditional cabalettas (for the soprano Lida in the second scene of Act 1, and for the baritone in Act 3). But most of the other set pieces tend towards a far looser, less predictable organization. A magnificent example is the duet between Arrigo and Lida that closes Act 1, in which there is hardly a hint of the classic four-movement structure, the musical tension between the characters thus being preserved until almost the final bars. In today's climate, in which almost all Verdi's early operas are occasionally revived, *La battaglia* stands as one of Verdi's most unjustly neglected works.

Luisa Miller

Melodramma tragico in three acts set to a libretto by Salvadore Cammarano after Friedrich von Schiller's play *Kabale und Liebe;* first performed in Naples, Teatro San Carlo, on 8 December 1849.

The cast at the première included Marietta Gazzaniga (Luisa), Achille De Bassini (Miller), Antonio Selva (Walter), and Settimio Malvezzi (Rodolfo).

Count Walter	bass
Rodolfo, *his son*	tenor
Federica, *Duchess of Ostheim, Walter's niece*	contralto
Wurm, *Walter's steward*	bass
Miller, *a retired old soldier*	baritone
Luisa, *his daughter*	soprano
Laura, *a peasant girl*	mezzo-soprano
A Peasant	tenor

Federica's ladies-in-waiting, pages, retainers, archers, villagers

Setting The Tyrol, in the first half of the seventeenth century

Verdi's relationship with Naples, never entirely happy, continued inauspiciously during the late 1840s: in 1848, despite his efforts to withdraw, the Neapolitan authorities held him to a long-standing contract for a new opera at the San Carlo. The librettist was to be Salvadore Cammarano, resident poet at the theatre and a man of vast experience in both the practical and the artistic side of operatic production. Verdi's first idea was for a setting of Francesco Guerrazzi's recent historical novel, *L'assedio di Firenze*, a large-scale subject designed to suit the dimensions of the San Carlo and, one imagines, intended to follow the line of Verdi's current preoccupation, *La battaglia di Legnano*. However, by April 1849 this idea—hardly surprisingly given the counterrevolutionary political climate—had been rejected by the Neapolitan censors. Cammarano then suggested using Schiller's *Kabale und Liebe*, a play the composer himself had earlier considered. Verdi accepted, although not without asking for a considerable number of structural alterations to the synopsis Cammarano sent him (not all of which the poet, who was no Piave in matters of acquiescence, agreed to).

Negotiations had thus far been undertaken with Verdi in Paris, where he had set up house with Giuseppina Strepponi while supervising the première of *Jérusalem*. In the late summer of 1849 he returned to Italy to work on *Luisa Miller* (as Schiller's play had been retitled); he arrived in Naples in late October to supervise the staging of the opera, first performed some five weeks later. The première was, it seems, greeted with some skepticism (though there are few press reports to go on), and even though the opera received a respectable number of revivals, it never attained the popularity of *Nabucco* or *Ernani* and faded from the repertory later in the century. *Luisa Miller* was 'rediscovered' in the 1920s as part of the German Verdi renaissance and has subsequently become—with *Nabucco*, *Ernani*, and *Macbeth*—one of the few Verdi operas written before 1850 to enjoy a firm place in the international repertory.

*   *   *

The overture, in C minor, is unlike any other Verdi wrote in that it is monothematic and built primarily around a process of modulation rather than on a succession of contrasting melodies. The composer's clear intention was to emulate a Germanic, 'symphonic' movement rather than the usual, Italian potpourri overture. Moments such as the feint towards G minor in the exposition, or the unusual modulations of the retransition, show that Verdi was perfectly able to understand and reproduce such symphonic devices when the mood took him.

ACT I 'LOVE' Scene i *A pleasant village* A pastoral atmosphere is immediately created by the orchestra's 6/8 movement and prominent woodwind writing, and is confirmed by the chorus's simple, rocking melody 'Ti desta o Luisa', which bids Luisa awake on a beautiful April dawn. Miller and Luisa enter, Miller casting doubts on his daughter's relationship with

'Carlo', an unknown young man who has arrived with the new Count. Luisa expresses her naïve love in the cavatina 'Lo vidi, e il primo palpito', which is simple and cabaletta-like, continuing elaborate woodwind effects in the accompaniment. Villagers present Luisa with flowers and 'Carlo' (Rodolfo in disguise) emerges from the crowd. The lovers join Miller in a closing Terzetto, 'T'amo d'amor ch'esprimere', Miller avoiding the main melody to mutter his suspicions and discontent in a staccato countertheme. As the stage clears, Miller is detained by Wurm, who angrily demands Luisa's hand in marriage. In the spacious, conventionally organized Andante maestoso, 'Sacra la scelta è d'un consorte', Miller insists that his daughter will make her own choice of husband. But Wurm reveals the true identity of 'Carlo' and Miller bursts into a cabaletta of rage and grief, 'Ah! fu giusto il mio sospetto!'.

Scene ii *A room in Walter's castle*   Walter and Wurm are in mid-conversation, Wurm having told the Count of Rodolfo's involvement with Luisa. When Wurm leaves, Walter releases his confused paternal feelings in the minor-major Romanza 'Il mio sangue, la vita darei', another expanded form in which the major section takes an unexpected plunge back into minor-mode reflections. Rodolfo appears and his father orders him to marry the recently widowed Duchess Federica. Before Rodolfo can explain his predicament Federica herself appears, heralded by a delicate chorus, 'Quale un sorriso d'amica sorte'. Federica and Rodolfo are left alone, and the Duchess admits her love in the first movement of a two-movement duet (the Andantino 'Dall'aule raggianti'), which begins lyrically but diverts into fragmentary dialogue as Rodolfo admits he loves another. The cabaletta, 'Deh! la parola amara', confirms their divided position.

Scene iii *A room in Miller's house*   An offstage chorus tells of a hunt in progress. Luisa is anxiously awaiting 'Carlo' but is instead confronted by her father, who reveals her lover's true identity and his forthcoming marriage. Rodolfo intervenes to swear his continuing love, telling Miller he knows a terrible secret that will protect them from the Count's wrath. Walter himself arrives to precipitate the first movement of the concertato finale, an Allegro dominated by a driving violin melody reminiscent of the overture theme. Walter summons soldiers and orders the arrest of Miller and his daughter, ignoring both the protests of Miller and Rodolfo and the entreaties of Luisa. The ensuing Andantino, the central lyrical movement 'Fra mortali ancora oppressa', allows the principals to present their differing reactions with unusual definition. The act then quickly comes to a close: in an arioso of gathering intensity Rodolfo pleads with his father and, at the climax, threatens to reveal the dreadful secret. Walter immediately frees Luisa, the chorus thanks heaven, and the curtain falls with no concluding stretta.

ACT 2 'THE INTRIGUE' Scene i *A room in Miller's house* (as 1.iii)   Villagers rush on and in a formal narrative tell Luisa that her father has been taken to prison. As they disperse, Wurm enters and tells Luisa that, to save her father, she must write a letter at Wurm's dictation, saying that she never loved Rodolfo and now wishes to elope with Wurm. Before signing the letter, Luisa offers a prayer, the famous 'Tu puniscimi, o Signore', an Andante agitato remarkable for its lack of formal repetition. Wurm continues his demands: that she will swear the letter is her own and that she loves Wurm. She closes the scene with a cabaletta, 'A brani, a brani, o perfido', that swings from minor to major as she moves from anticipation of death to thoughts that her father will be on hand to minister to her final moments.

Scene ii *Walter's room in the castle*   Walter, brooding, is joined by Wurm, who tells him about the progress of their plot against Luisa. They join in a narrative duet, 'L'alto retaggio non ho bramato', recalling their murder of the old Count and Rodolfo's discovery of the secret. The duet begins with a formality typical of operatic narrative but becomes increasingly fragmented as the description of events unfolds; it culminates in the cabaletta-like 'O meco incolume', in which Walter vows to protect Wurm or accompany him to the gallows. Federica appears and Wurm is dismissed. Walter tells her that Rodolfo is now ready to marry, and produces Luisa, who in a dialogue movement controlled by orchestral melody rejects Rodolfo and declares her love for Wurm. This last statement precipitates the Andante 'Come celar le smanie', a quartet unusual for its complete lack of orchestral accompaniment.

Scene iii *The castle gardens*   Rodolfo now has Luisa's infamous letter, and sorrowfully reminisces in the famous Andante 'Quando le sere, al placido', an early example of Verdi's use of the French *couplet* form. Wurm appears and Rodolfo challenges him to a duel, which Wurm evades by firing his pistol into the air and rushing off. Walter appears with some followers and, after Rodolfo has told him of Luisa's 'betrayal', Walter persuades his son to marry Federica as revenge. Rodolfo, in a confusion of distress, closes the act with the cabaletta 'L'ara, o l'avello apprestami'.

ACT 3 'THE POISON' *A room in Miller's house* (as 1.iii)   An orchestral reminiscence of past themes introduces the chorus 'Come in un giorno solo', in which the villagers lament Luisa's sorrowful countenance. Luisa, who exchanges words with the chorus while writing a letter, is joined by Miller, who has learnt from Wurm the true nature of her sacrifice. Their ensuing duet is in the usual four movements, during the first of which Miller discovers that Luisa's letter proposes a suicide pact with Rodolfo. In the second movement, 'La tomba è un letto', Luisa returns to her naïve, first-act musical style as she looks forward to an innocent grave; Miller counters with an impassioned plea in the parallel minor. The movement ends with Luisa tearing up the letter; there is a heartfelt reconciliation, and father and daughter join in a cabaletta, 'Andrem, raminghi e poveri', in which they look forward to leaving the village to live a simple, wandering existence.

As Miller departs, Luisa hears an organ from a nearby church; she kneels in prayer. Rodolfo enters and in a long, passionate recitative full of violent orchestral interjections forces her to admit to writing the letter; then he shares with her a drink that he has surreptitiously poisoned. The duet moves into regular musical periods at the Andante, 'Piangi, piangi . . . il tuo dolore', whose lyricism seems all the more intense for having so long been denied. Rodolfo admits that he has poisoned them both; Luisa at last feels free to confess her deception, and they join in the stretta, 'Maledetto il dì che nacqui', Rodolfo cursing the day he was born, Luisa trying to comfort him. The arrival of Miller, who quickly discovers all, leads to a Terzetto finale, 'Padre! ricevi l'estremo . . . addio', at the close of which Rodolfo, seeing Luisa fall dead, kills Wurm before himself collapsing by the side of his beloved.

$$*\qquad*\qquad*$$

Many modern commentators have seen in *Luisa Miller* a radical break, marking a new type of Verdian opera, albeit one he was to deploy only sparingly in the years to come. In one sense this is hard to sustain: it is difficult to see in the formal aspect of *Luisa* a stylistic turning point, particularly when compared with *Macbeth,* which had appeared two years earlier. However, for that perceptive early critic of Verdi, Abramo Basevi, *Luisa Miller* marked the beginning of Verdi's 'second manner', one in which he drew more deeply on Donizetti's example and less on Rossini's, and in which his musical dramaturgy took on a more subtle and varied form. Certainly the relationship to Donizetti's *Linda di Chamounix* (1842) is evident in many places; but ultimately the debt is less to a specific composer or work than to a genre, that of *opera semiseria*—a 'mixed' genre that partook both of comic and serious elements. Again this called for stylistic expansion, a broader musical canvas on which to play out the drama, one enriched by extensive attention to depiction of the Alpine setting so typical of *semiserie*.

Few would, then, argue about the opera's important position among pre-*Rigoletto* operas. And we should also recall that its control of conventional musical forms, especially the grand duet, is exemplary; in this respect, the middle-period work *Luisa* most resembles is not *Rigoletto* but *Il trovatore*, whose driving energy within conventional contexts is apparent in many scenes, perhaps particularly in the final act. Ultimately, though, *Luisa Miller*'s *semiseria* genre suggests for it more profound links to a different, less grandiose Verdian line: to the delicate, urban world of *La traviata*, and (particularly) to *Un ballo in maschera*, in which the play of genres will be at its most poignant and intense.

Stiffelio

Opera in three acts set to a libretto by Francesco Maria Piave after Emile Souvestre's and Eugène Bourgeois' play *Le Pasteur, ou L'Évangile et le foyer;* first performed in Trieste, Teatro Grande, on 16 November 1850.

The cast at the première included Gaetano Fraschini (Stiffelio), Marietta Gazzaniga (Lina), and Filippo Colini (Stankar).

Stiffelio, *an Ahasuerian preacher*	tenor
Lina, *his wife*	soprano
Stankar, *an old colonel, count of the Empire*	
and Lina's father	baritone
Raffaele von Leuthold, *a nobleman*	tenor
Jorg, *an old preacher*	bass
Federico di Frengel, *Lina's cousin*	tenor
Dorotea, *Lina's cousin*	mezzo-soprano

The Count's friends, Stiffelio's disciples, Ahasuerians, Fritz (a servant)

Setting Austria, in and around Stankar's castle by the river Salzbach, at the beginning of the nineteenth century

As was becoming the pattern, Verdi's April 1850 contract for the work that became *Stiffelio* was signed not with a theatre but with a publisher, in this as in most other cases Ricordi. The librettist was again to be Piave, who himself suggested an adaptation of *Le Pasteur,* a French play that had received its première only the previous year but was already available in Italian translation. It was a bold choice, a far cry from the melodramatic plots of Byron (*Il corsaro, I due Foscari*) and Hugo (*Ernani*): modern, 'realistic' subjects were unusual in Italian opera, and the religious subject matter seemed bound to cause problems with the censor. Giovanni Ricordi decided to have the première staged at Trieste—the theatre that had recently given such a lukewarm reception to *Il corsaro*—and, true to expectation, the local censors insisted on a number of important changes, in particular muting the action of the final scene so as (in the composer's view) to make it ridiculous. The work's reception was better than that accorded *Il corsaro*, although there were reservations about the opera's novel shape and subject matter. *Stiffelio* had occasional revivals in subsequent years, but it was continually dogged by censorship difficulties; in the mid-1850s Verdi decided to 'rescue' his music by revising it to fit a different, less sensitive plot: *Aroldo*.

The original *Stiffelio* disappeared from the repertory and won its first modern revival only in the 1960s. Since then it has received a fair number of performances, and is ranked by many as Verdi's most unjustly neglected opera.

*   *   *

The overture is of the potpourri type: a sequence of contrasting melodies, some of which return in the subsequent action. Its predominantly martial atmosphere (even the main cantabile melody is scored for solo trumpet) seems, curiously, better suited to *Aroldo* than to the original subject.

ACT I Scene i *A hall on the ground floor of Stankar's castle* The opera immediately pronounces its unusual formal exterior by beginning without the customary introductory chorus. Instead, Jorg offers up an intense, chromatic prayer on behalf of Stiffelio, who has just returned from a mission. Stiffelio appears, surrounded by his family and friends, and in the ensuing narration, 'Di qua varcando sul primo albore', relates that a boatman reported to him how at first light he saw a young man and woman at an upstairs window of the castle, clearly up to no good, and how the man threw himself from the window into the river, dropping some papers as he did so. Stifled outbursts from Lina and Raffaele suggest their guilty consciences, but Stiffelio puts their fears to rest by magnanimously casting the documents into the fire. All join in a septet, 'Colla cenere disperso', after which Stiffelio's friends sing a welcoming chorus, 'A te, Stiffelio, un canto', based on a theme heard in the overture.

The crowd disperses, leaving Stiffelio alone with his wife. The first part of his double aria shifts rapidly from mood to mood, responding as it does to Lina's reactions. First comes 'Vidi dovunque gemere', in which he describes the moral collapse he has seen everywhere on his journey; then he has a reassuring word for his wife in 'Ah no, il perdono è facile'; and finally come the loving words of 'Allor dunque sorridimi' as he takes her hand and asks for a smile such as she gave him on their wedding day. But his melody suddenly breaks off as he sees that her ring is missing. She can give no answer to his inquiries about it, and his suspicions burst out in the cabaletta 'Ah v'appare in fronte scritto'. The final bars are interrupted by Stankar, who asks Stiffelio to join his friends; with a reminder that he will soon return, the pastor hurries away.

Lina offers a prayer, 'A te ascenda, oh Dio clemente', delicately scored and with those elaborate cadential harmonies so characteristic of the later Verdi. She decides to write her husband a letter of confession but is interrupted by Stankar, who reads the first line and is confirmed in his suspicions of her infidelity. Their ensuing duet follows the conventional four-movement pattern. The first movement is dominated by an accusing Stankar, while the second, the Andante 'Ed io pure in faccia agl'uomini', is of the 'dissimilar' type, Lina answering his impassioned declamation with obsessively repeated 'sobbing' figures. Stankar, fearful of family dishonour, forbids Lina to reveal the truth; she reluctantly agrees, and they seal the bargain with the cabaletta 'Or meco venite', sung *sotto voce* almost throughout. In a brief *scena*, Raffaele conceals a letter to Lina inside a book, Klopstock's *Messias*. Federico enters to take the book away and, observed by Jorg, he and Raffaele depart.

Scene ii *A reception hall in the castle*   The jubilant opening chorus, 'Plaudiam! di Stiffelio s'allegri', fashioned on a waltz-time variant of one of the overture's main themes, is interspersed with fragments of conversation as Jorg tells Stiffelio of the hidden letter and his (mistaken) suspicions about Federico. Stiffelio is called upon to describe his forthcoming sermon, and with bitter declamation says it will concern the evils of betrayal. As if to illustrate his point, he asks Federico for the *Messias*. But the book is locked, and Stiffelio's demand for Lina's key leads to the Adagio of the concertato finale, 'Oh qual m'invade ed agita', a magnificently imposing movement that builds to a climax of rare power. Stiffelio forces the lock; the letter falls out, but Stankar seizes it and, in spite of the preacher's protests, tears it up. Stiffelio's anger bursts out in the stretta 'Chi ti salva, sciagurato', Lina pleading for her father's protection while Stankar challenges Raffaele to a duel.

ACT 2 *An ancient graveyard*   The sombre orchestral prelude is one of Verdi's most evocative to date. Lina, drawn by an 'unknown force', finds the tomb of her mother and in the Largo 'Ah! dagli scanni eterei'—whose luminous scoring makes a striking contrast to the prelude—begs for divine support. Raffaele appears, refusing to renounce his love for Lina even when she directs at him the imploring cabaletta 'Perder dunque voi volete'. But they are interrupted by Stankar, who provokes Raffaele to a duel. They defy each other and clash swords as Stiffelio appears, calling on them to stop in the name of God. The intervention is too much for Stankar, who blurts out that Raffaele is Lina's seducer. This precipitates a magnificent concertato movement, the quartet 'Ah no . . . è impossibile!', one that prefigures the famous quartet in *Rigoletto* in its melding of strongly contrasting musical material. It is dominated by Stiffelio, who develops an imposing musical presence through his powerful declamatory style. Stiffelio continues to control the next movement, in which he takes upon himself Stankar's challenge to Raffaele. At the height of the action, a chorus within the church is heard singing of divine forgiveness. In spite of the others' pleading, Stiffelio cannot renounce his thirst for vengeance; eventually he falls down in a faint at the sight of a nearby cross.

ACT 3 Scene i *An antechamber with doors leading to various rooms*   First comes a two-movement aria for Stankar in which his sense of dishonour leads him to thoughts of suicide. After an unusually complex recitative, the Andante 'Lina, pensai che un angelo' shows Verdi already along the road to the baritone cantabile movements of his later works, while the cabaletta 'Oh gioia inesprimibile', performed almost entirely *sotto voce*, approaches the level of suppressed energy so pervasive in *Il trovatore*. As Stankar leaves, Stiffelio appears with Jorg, whom he immediately sends off to warn the congregation of his arrival. He meets Raffaele and, questioning him about Lina's future, leads him to a side room where, Stiffelio says, he will 'hear all'. Lina herself now appears before Stiffelio. This is the key confrontation in the opera: a duet difficult to understand in terms of the standard four-movement pattern, so closely are its various stages fashioned around the rapidly changing reactions of the main characters. First comes Stiffelio's 'Opposto è il calle', in which, to a deceptively simple melody charged with harmonic tension, he demands divorce. Lina's violent response is countered by a yet more restricted period from Stiffelio, but then Lina takes over and in 'Non allo sposo volgomi' begs him to listen as a priest if not as a husband. Her final plea, 'Egli un patto proponea', accompanied by solo English horn, is the most touching of all: she declares that her love for Stiffelio has never wavered. Stiffelio, understanding that Raffaele is to blame, goes to the side room to confront him. But Stankar appears, bloody sword in hand, to announce that honour is now satisfied. The closing cabaletta, 'Ah sì, voliamo al tempio', is (as befits the moment) of the 'dissimilar' type, and concludes as Stiffelio is dragged by Jorg towards the church.

Scene ii   *The interior of a Gothic church*   This very brief final scene is remarkable in being based almost entirely on stage effect: there are hardly any sustained melodies, merely declamation and atmospheric choral interpolations. The congregation, Lina included, is at prayer as Stiffelio and Jorg appear. Stiffelio opens the Bible, determined to take inspiration from whatever passage he finds. He reads the episode of the woman taken in adultery and, when he utters the phrase 'and she rose up, forgiven', the congregation repeats his words in a stirring choral close.

*   *   *

Much has been made of *Stiffelio* in recent times, some commentators even claiming that it deserves an equal place beside the operas it immediately precedes, *Rigoletto*, *Il trovatore*, and *La traviata*. Its 'modern' plot and subject matter are certainly in tune with contemporary sensibilities, and the tendency of its most powerful moments to avoid or radically manipulate the traditional forms has been much praised. There are, though, a few drawbacks, not least that the progress of the action is occasionally unclear and that the reason for Lina's adultery is never established. What is more, even the 'forward-looking' dramaturgical structures seem at times to lack necessary durational weight, almost as though the composer were working out new modes of formal balance as he progressed. It is, for instance, significant that many of the alterations made for *Aroldo* are not governed by the new plot but are inserted because Verdi felt he could improve on *Stiffelio*'s dramatic articulation.

   However, we should not overemphasise these problematic issues. The opera has many powerful aspects, in particular those that collect around the protagonist, one of Verdi's most challenging tenor roles. Stiffelio is a character who feels profoundly at odds with the world in which he must act, but who cannot express himself in isolation. He sings primarily in ensembles, every one of which he leads off and then dominates with his vocal presence; he is, then, in constant and painful proximity to his fellows, and it is small surprise that these ensembles are commonly agreed to be the high points of the opera. In this and many other senses, *Stiffelio* is best seen as an important document in a larger development that Verdi was undergoing. Especially after his extended stay in cosmopolitan Paris during 1847–49, Verdi could never again take Italian romantic *melodramma* entirely on its own terms; he was constantly seeking to enlarge and enrich the genre from within, and also to challenge its basic dramatic conventions (the lyric tenor, the villainous baritone). As modern revivals allow us to know *Stiffelio* better, perhaps even to establish it in 'the repertory', our understanding of—and respect for—Verdi as a musical dramatist cannot fail to increase.

Rigoletto

Melodramma in three acts set to a libretto by Francesco Maria Piave after Victor Hugo's play *Le Roi s'amuse;* first performed in Venice, Teatro La Fenice, on 11 March 1851.

The cast at the première included Raffaele Mirate (Duke), Felice Varesi (Rigoletto), and Teresa Brambilla (Gilda).

The Duke of Mantua	tenor
Rigoletto, *his court jester*	baritone
Gilda, *Rigoletto's daughter*	soprano
Sparafucile, *a hired assassin*	bass
Maddalena, *his sister*	contralto
Giovanna, *Gilda's duenna*	soprano
Count Monterone	bass
Marullo, *a nobleman*	baritone
Borsa, *a courtier*	tenor
Count Ceprano	bass
Countess Ceprano	mezzo-soprano
Court Usher	bass
Page	mezzo-soprano
Noblemen	

Walk-on parts: Ladies, pages, halberdiers

Setting In and around Mantua during the sixteenth century

Verdi first mentioned the idea of setting a version of Victor Hugo's drama (with Salvadore Cammarano as the librettist) as early as September 1849, shortly after he had returned to Italy from Paris; but it was a contract with the Teatro La Fenice, Venice, signed in April 1850, that eventually brought the opera into being. Perhaps encouraged by the presence in Venice of the accomplished baritone Felice Varesi (who had created the title role of *Macbeth* in 1847), Verdi suggested to Piave, the resident poet at La Fenice, that they adapt Hugo's *Le Roi s'amuse*, 'one of the greatest creations of the modern theatre'. He had fears that there might be problems with the censor, but Piave—after seeking advice in Venice—managed to reassure him and the plan went ahead under the working title of *La maledizione*. By summer 1850, however, signs from Venice over the suitability of the subject were not encouraging. Verdi insisted on continuing, saying that he had now found the musical colour of the subject and so could not turn back.

By early October 1850 the cast for the première had been fixed, and Piave had submitted a draft libretto. Verdi, still involved with *Stiffelio* at Trieste, had little time to begin composition in earnest and probably did not start drafting the score until late November. Soon after that, however, the Venetian censors intervened: calling attention to the 'disgusting immorality and obscene triviality' of the libretto, they imposed an absolute ban on its performance in Venice. Verdi was enraged, blamed Piave, and, refusing to consider writing a fresh opera, offered La Fenice *Stiffelio* instead. Piave, whose doglike devotion to the composer never wavered, hastened to make an acceptable adaptation; called *Il duca di Vendome*, this accommodated the censor's objections and was officially approved on 9 December. But Verdi remained steadfast. In a long letter of 14 December he went into great detail about the dramatic essentials of the subject, insisting (among many aspects that *Il duca di Vendome* had obscured or excised) that the principal tenor retain absolute power over his subjects, and that Triboletto (as the protagonist was then called) remain a hunchback. By the end of the month, a compromise had been reached with the authorities at La Fenice—one which in effect allowed Verdi to retain what he considered dramatically essential—and, soon after, the opera acquired a new title, *Rigoletto*.

Verdi spent the first six weeks of 1851 busy with his score; he arrived in Venice in mid-February to begin piano rehearsals with the principals and complete the orchestration. The première was an enormous success, and the opera, in spite of continuing problems with local censors, almost immediately became part of the core operatic repertory, being revived more than 250 times in its first ten years.

*   *   *

The prelude, as was to become common in mature Verdi, is a kind of synopsis of the opera's dramatic essentials. The brass, led by solo trumpet and trombone, intone a restrained motif later to be associated with the curse placed on Rigoletto; this builds in intensity and eventually explodes into a passionate sobbing figure for full orchestra; the figure peters out, the brass motif returns, and simple cadences effect a solemn close.

ACT I Scene i *A magnificent hall in the ducal palace*   The opening scene begins with a lengthy sequence of dance tunes played by an offstage band, over which the Duke and his courtiers converse casually. The Duke has seen a mysterious young woman in church and is determined to pursue her. To drive home his libertine character, he sings a lively, two-verse ballad in praise of women, 'Questa o quella'. The Duke then turns his attention to Countess Ceprano, courting her to the accompaniment of a graceful minuet, before Rigoletto enters to mock her unfortunate husband, Count Ceprano. To a reprise of the opening dance sequence, two conversations take place: Marullo tells the courtiers that Rigoletto has been seen with a mistress, and Rigoletto advises the Duke to banish or even execute Ceprano. The ensuing ensemble (Ceprano and others muttering vengeance against Rigoletto, whose mockery they have often endured) is interrupted by Monterone, come to upbraid the Duke for dishonouring his daughter. Rigoletto's sarcastic reply brings down on him Monterone's terrifying anathema; the scene ends in a further ensemble, with Rigoletto visibly shaken by the old man's curse. This opening sequence is clearly based on the traditional *introduzione* format, but with the difference that it boasts an unprecedented level of musical variety: from the brash dances of the stage-band, to the Duke's light, comic-opera ballad, to the elegant minuet, to Rigoletto's grotesque musical parodies, to Monterone's high drama and the stunned reaction it provokes. But there are also connecting devices (for example the descending melodic motif that opens the dance sequence) and a superb sense of dramatic economy; these serve to bind the episode together, making it one of the richest and most complex opening scenes hitherto attempted in nineteenth-century Italian opera.

Scene ii *The most deserted corner of a blind alley*   Rigoletto, returning home, meets the hired assassin Sparafucile, who offers his services. Rigoletto questions him but eventually sends him away. This brief duet, which is preceded by Rigoletto's intoned reminiscence of Monterone's curse, 'Quel vecchio maledivami!!', bears little relation to the formal norms of Italian opera. It is in a single movement, and the primary continuity is supplied by an orchestral melody played on solo cello and bass. Over this, the voices converse with the greatest naturalness, indeed with a restraint that belies the violence of the subject matter. The effect is calm, sinister, and seductive: a necessary pause after the preceding hectic activity, but one that adds an important new colour to the dramatic ambience.

Rigoletto reaches his house and offers the first of his long, freely structured soliloquies, 'Pari siamo!', in which the contrasting aspects of his personality are tellingly explored: the flexibility of utterance is that of recitative, but the emotional charge is that of an aria. The ensuing duet with Gilda returns us to the formal world of early-nineteenth-century opera, with a conventional four-movement sequence. An opening movement, dominated by a syncopated violin melody, gives way to 'Deh non parlare al misero', in which Rigoletto's increasingly agonized reminiscences of Gilda's mother are answered by his daughter's broken sixteenth notes and sobbing appoggiaturas. The *tempo di mezzo* transition section, as will happen increasingly in later Verdi, also develops lyrical ideas, notably 'Culto, famiglia, patria', in which Rigoletto tells Gilda that she is everything to him. But Gilda wishes for freedom to leave the house. Rigoletto, horrified, calls Giovanna and, in the cabaletta 'Ah! veglia, o donna', enjoins her to watch carefully over her charge. This final movement has none of the driving energy of the typical early Verdian cabaletta, being far more reminiscent of the relaxed, Donizettian type. But there is room for a remarkable intrusion of stage action: having reached the reprise of the main melody, Rigoletto breaks off, hearing a noise outside; as he goes to investigate, the Duke slips in unnoticed. The cabaletta then continues, but with a hidden presence that will lead the action forward.

Left alone with Giovanna, Gilda muses on the young man she has seen at church, hoping that he is poor and of common blood. The Duke emerges from his hiding place to declare his love and so initiate a further four-movement duet, albeit one much reduced in scope and duration in comparison with the preceding number. After a hectic dialogue movement in which Gilda begs him to leave, the Duke declares his love in a simple 3/8 Andantino, 'È il sol dell'anima', at the end of which he is joined by Gilda in an elaborate cadenza 'a 2'. In a brief connecting movement he declares himself to be 'Gualtier Maldè', a poor student; Ceprano and Borsa appear in the street outside, and Giovanna, who has not taken her employer's injunction very seriously, warns the lovers to part. The cabaletta of farewell, 'Addio, addio . . . speranza ed anima', is extremely condensed, the principals sharing the exposition of melodic material.

Gilda, again left alone, muses on her lover's name in the famous aria 'Caro nome'. The opening melodic phrases, as befits the character, are of extreme simplicity, but the aria develops in a highly unusual manner, as a contrasting series of tightly controlled ornamental variants, quite unlike the 'open'-structured ornamental arias of the previous generation. The aria is further held together by its delicately distinctive orchestration, in which solo woodwinds play an important part. As the opening melody returns in a coda-like ending, Marullo, Ceprano, Borsa, and other courtiers again appear outside and can be heard preparing Gilda's abduction.

Rigoletto returns to the scene, and briefly recalls Monterone's curse before Marullo tells him that they are planning to abduct Countess Ceprano, who lives nearby. While fitting Rigoletto with a mask, Marullo succeeds in blindfolding him. The courtiers sing a conspiratorial chorus, 'Zitti, zitti', mostly *pianissimo* but full of explosive accents. Rigoletto holds a ladder as the courtiers emerge with Gilda, her mouth stopped by a handkerchief. He does not hear her cries for help, but soon tires of holding the ladder and takes off the mask to find his house open and Gilda's scarf lying in the street. To an inexorable orchestral crescendo he drags Giovanna from the house but is unable to speak except once more to recall Monterone's curse, 'Ah! ah! ah! . . . la maledizione!'.

ACT 2 *A hall in the Duke's Palace* First comes a Scena ed Aria for the Duke: a necessary close focus on a character who will see no more of the action during Act 2. 'Ella mi fu rapita!' ('She was stolen from me!'), he cries, and in a lyrical Adagio pours out his feelings at the presumed loss of Gilda. 'Parmi veder le lagrime' is formally structured along familiar lines but is intricately worked, proving not for the first or the last time that formal conventionality in no sense blunted Verdi's musical or dramatic powers of invention. The courtiers enter to announce in a jaunty narrative that they have duped Rigoletto and have his 'mistress' (actually of course Gilda) nearby; this change of perspective immediately allows the Duke, who is aware of her identity, to launch into a cabaletta of joy and expectation, 'Possente amor mi chiama'. This movement's rather backward-looking melodic and orchestral brashness causes it often to be cut in performance, although doing so unbalances both the scene and the characterization of the Duke, who needs its somewhat vulgar catharsis to be fully convincing in his Act 3 persona.

The Duke exits in search of Gilda, and Rigoletto enters for a very different kind of Scena ed Aria. Affecting indifference before the courtiers, he mixes a nonchalant, public 'La ra, la ra'—though one in which the 'sobbing' accents are all too apparent—with stifled asides as he searches for his daughter. The innocent questions of a page eventually reveal to him that

Gilda is with the Duke; against the background of a string figure of gathering intensity he reveals that Gilda is his daughter and demands access to her. The courtiers block his way, and in frustration he hurls at them a remarkable outburst. 'Cortigiani, vil razza dannata', unclassifiable in conventional formal terms, is in three distinct parts, each marking a stage in Rigoletto's psychological progress. First, against an obsessively repeated string figure, he rails against the courtiers with fierce declamatory force. Then comes fragmentation, a breaking of the accompaniment rhythm, and of the voice: a frightening disintegration. And finally, the third stage, Rigoletto gains a new dignity and continuity: accompanied by a solo cello and English horn he asks pity for a father's sorrow.

Gilda enters, throws herself into her father's arms, and so begins yet another four-movement duet. Rigoletto solemnly dismisses the courtiers and bids her tell her story. 'Tutte le feste al tempio', unlike the parallel duet movements of Act 1, is begun by Gilda: it is she who now achieves a new status from the circumstances that have befallen her. And as with Rigoletto's previous monologue, the duet progresses through strongly contrasting sections: from her opening narration, a kind of duet with solo oboe; to Rigoletto's obsessively fixed response; and finally to a clarifying third stage, in which Rigoletto bids his daughter weep and in which she joins him with a completely new kind of vocal ornamentation, only superficially resembling that found in Act 1. Monterone passes by on his way to prison; this time Rigoletto assures him that vengeance will be had. Staring at a portrait of the Duke, the jester joins with his daughter in a cabaletta, 'Sì, vendetta, tremenda vendetta'.

ACT 3 *A deserted bank of the River Mincio* An orchestral prelude, in Verdi's most severe, 'academic' vein, leads to a brief exchange between Rigoletto and Gilda. Time has passed, but Gilda still loves the Duke (in the play, she has become the Duke's mistress; but this is passed over in the opera). Rigoletto, promising to show her the true man, has her gaze into Sparafucile's house through a chink in the wall. The Duke appears, asks loudly for wine and the woman of the house (Maddalena), and breaks into a song in praise of women's fickleness. 'La donna è mobile' is certainly the best-known piece in the score, perhaps unfortunately, as its brashness and simplicity make their full effect only in the surrounding gloomy context. The Duke's song dies away, to be followed by the famous quartet, 'Un dì, se ben rammentomi'. The first half of this remarkable set piece is dominated by a violin melody that carries reminiscences of earlier material (in particular Gilda's 'Caro nome'), over which the Duke and Maddalena converse lightheartedly. Then comes the main lyrical portion, 'Bella figlia del-l'amore', led off by the Duke's amorous approaches to Maddelana, but soon joined by her and by Rigoletto and Gilda, all of them in contrasting emotional states. The dramatic aptness of this section is made especially powerful by the manner in which the three principals involved all offer a kind of digest of their vocal characters elsewhere in the opera: the Duke (who carries the main melodic thread) ardent and lyrical, Gilda overcome with appoggiatura 'sobbing', Rigoletto declamatory and unmoving.

A storm is gathering as Sparafucile emerges. Over fragmentary bursts of orchestral colour he and Rigoletto agree on a price for the murder of the Duke: Rigoletto will return at midnight to take delivery of the body. The hunchback retires, and the Duke is conducted to a room, there dreamily re-calling 'La donna è mobile' before falling asleep. As the storm gathers force, Maddalena, attracted to the Duke, tries to persuade Sparafucile to spare him. Professional honour forbids that he kill Rigoletto instead, but he agrees that, if another person should come along before the time allot-ted, a substitution can be made. Gilda overhears this and, in a trio charac-terized by its relentless rhythmic drive ('Se pria ch'abbia il mezzo'), decides to sacrifice herself. She enters the house; a terrifying orchestral storm depicts the gruesome events that occur within.

The final scene shows great economy of means. The storm subsides as Rigoletto reappears to claim the body, which has been placed in a sack for easy disposal. He is about to dispatch it into the river when he hears the voice of the Duke, again singing 'La donna è mobile'. Horrified, he opens the sack to find Gilda, on the point of death. Their final duet, 'V'ho ingan-nato!', is necessarily brief, leaving time only for Gilda to anticipate her ar-rival in heaven—with obligatory flute arpeggios—and for Rigoletto to declaim in ever more broken lines. He recalls the curse one last time before the curtain falls.

*   *   *

Commonplace though it may be to say so, *Rigoletto* breaks decisive new ground in Verdi's career. This special placing is often seen as exemplified in the striking formal freedom of various scenes. But to concentrate overmuch on formal matters risks a certain distortion: most of the opera's formal inno-vations have been prefigured in earlier works, and many of its most powerful moments exist unambiguously and comfortably within the formal conven-tions of the time. In addition, there are further levels on which *Rigoletto* is exceptional: in its new 'expansion' of genre, with comic opera elements (notably that of French *opéra comique*) constantly intruding on the tragic atmosphere; and in its daring appropriation of Hugolian character types, with the outwardly disfigured baritone father claiming more sympathy than the romantic tenor lead.

Even more important is that, for the first time, the differences between *Rigoletto*'s main characters are articulated through the very nature of their musical discourse. It is significant that Rigoletto, the emotional centre of the drama, has no formal arias but instead typically sings in the declamatory style that Verdi had experimented with in *Alzira*. The Duke, on the other hand, perpetually inhabits highly conventional formal numbers, both his charm and superficiality being projected through this relative predictability. Caught between these two styles, forever responding to one and then the other, is Gilda, whose discourse moves from the most simple and naïve to the most fragmentary and anguished as she grows, painfully, through the drama. This new level of dramatic articulation was as much a technical as an emotional conquest: it entailed not only a mature acceptance of conventional discourse but also an acutely developed perspective on precisely when the traditional forms could be ignored, when exploited.

Il trovatore

('The Troubadour')

Dramma in four acts set to a libretto by Salvadore Cammarano (with additions by Leone Emanuele Bardare) after Antonio García Gutiérrez's play *El trovador*; first performed at Rome, Teatro Apollo, on 19 January 1853. The revised version, *Le Trouvère*, was first performed at the Paris Opéra on 12 January 1857.

The cast at the première included Giovanni Guicciardi (Count), Rosina Penco (Leonora), Emilia Goggi (Azucena), and Carlo Baucardé (Manrico).

Count di Luna, *a young nobleman of Aragon*	baritone
Leonora, *a lady-in-waiting to the Princess of Aragon*	soprano
Azucena, *a gypsy*	mezzo-soprano
Manrico, *an officer in the army of Prince Urgel, and the supposed son of Azucena*	tenor
Ferrando, *a captain in the Count's army*	bass
Ines, *Leonora's confidante*	soprano
Ruiz, *a soldier in Manrico's service*	tenor
An Old Gypsy	bass
A Messenger	tenor

Leonora's female attendants, nuns, servants and armed retainers of the count, gypsies, followers of Manrico, etc.

Setting Biscay and Aragon, in 1409

Verdi was still in Venice enjoying the success of *Rigoletto* (in March 1851) when he wrote to Cammarano suggesting García Gutiérrez's play (first performed in 1836) as a subject for his next opera. It is clear from his early letters that he saw the drama as a sequel to *Rigoletto*, this time with an unconventional female character, the gypsy Azucena, at the centre of the action. Azucena, like Rigoletto, was to be fired by two opposing passions: filial love and a desire for vengeance. More than this, it is clear that Verdi wished to develop further the experiments, formal and otherwise, he had tried out in parts of *Rigoletto*. In an early letter to Cammarano he urged: 'As for the distribution of the pieces, let me tell you that when I'm presented with poetry to be set to music, any form, any distribution is good, and I'm all the happier if they are new and bizarre. If in operas there were no more cavatinas, duets, trios, choruses, finales, etc., etc., and if the entire opera were, let's say, a single piece, I would find it more reasonable and just.' But, as so often with Verdi, these revolutionary sentiments in his writings were considerably toned down when it came to practical matters. Cammarano's draft libretto turned out to be fashioned along conventional lines, and Verdi made little objection.

In part owing to personal difficulties, work on the new opera moved along rather slowly. Verdi, who had become the most famous and frequently performed Italian composer in Europe, and who could by now write for more or less whichever theatre he chose in Italy, considered a number of places for the première, being particularly concerned with the availability of a first-rate Azucena. Eventually, in the middle of 1852, the Teatro Apollo in Rome was decided upon. But then, in July 1852, Cammarano died, leaving a draft of *Il trovatore* with many details in need of attention. Leone Emanuele Bardare was brought in, and was particularly involved in the expansion of Leonora's role, which Verdi had originally wished to minimize but now fashioned as a dramatic equal to Azucena, thus forming a symmetry with the pair of opposed male roles, Manrico and the Count.

The opera's première was a huge success, and *Il trovatore* very soon became the most popular of Verdi's works, both in Italy and around the world. In the mid-1850s Verdi created a revised version for performances at the Paris Opéra, in part to ensure his French rights to the score. *Le Trouvère*, in a translation by Emilien Pacini, included a ballet (placed after the opening chorus of Act 3), omitted Leonora's Act 4 cabaletta, 'Tu vedrai che amore in terra', and involved a substantial rewriting of the end of the opera (in which the 'Miserere' music returned in a lengthy coda).

*   *   *

ACT I 'THE DUEL' Scene i *A hall in the Aliaferia palace*   There is no overture or formal prelude, merely a series of martial arpeggios and horn-calls to set the scene. Ferrando bids the sentries and servants keep alert: the count fears that the troubadour who has been seen in the garden is his rival in love. At the chorus's bidding, Ferrando narrates the story of Garzia, the Count's brother. One day, when still a baby, Garzia was found with an old witch at his cradle. She was driven off, but the boy sickened and was thought to have been given the evil eye. The witch was sought out and burnt at the stake, but her daughter exacted a terrible revenge: on the day of the execution young Garzia disappeared, and the charred remains of a baby were found in the embers of the witch's funeral pyre. All this is told in a two-stanza narrative, each stanza divided into a relatively free introductory passage ('Di due figli'), and then a more formal 'aria' ('Abbietta zingara') in which violins double the voice in octaves (a typical trait of 'gypsy' style). The chorus rounds off each stanza with horrified comments. In freer recitative, with a good deal of winding chromaticism, Ferrando continues his narration. The old count fell into a decline and died; nothing more was heard of the gypsy's daughter, though the old witch herself is said still to roam the skies at night. The chorus joins Ferrando in 'Sull'orlo dei tetti', a rapid stretta that conjures up the ghostly forces around them. At the climax, the chiming of the midnight bell causes universal panic; all hurriedly disperse.

Scene ii *The palace gardens*   Leonora, restlessly wandering, tells her maid Ines how she fell in love with a mysterious knight at a tournament and how he vanished when civil war broke out between the house of Aragon and Prince Urgel of Biscay's supporters. This is for the most part delivered in the spare, functional recitative typical of the opera, a style that makes the moments of arioso all the more effective. Leonora continues her story in the formal mould of a two-stanza Andantino, 'Tacea la notte placida', a piece that moves from minor to major, flowering into an angular rising line as she describes how her lover has now returned as a troubadour to serenade her with melancholy songs. Ines suggests that Leonora should forget her lover, but in a highly ornamental cabaletta, 'Di tale amor', Leonora swears that she will die rather than lose him.

As the women depart, the Count enters to declare his consuming passion for Leonora. He is about to climb up to her apartment when he hears a distant serenade: Manrico's 'Deserto sulla terra', a simple two-stanza Canzone. Leonora hurries down to greet the troubadour; in the darkness she mistakenly addresses the Count and is then accused of treachery by Manrico. The three principals finish the act with a two-movement trio, first an Allegro agitato ('Qual voce!') dominated by a breathless, disjointed figure from the violins, and then—ignoring the usual lyrical slow movement—straight to a furious stretta ('Di geloso amor sprezzato'). The final curtain sees the Count and Manrico striding off to fight a duel as Leonora falls senseless to the ground.

ACT 2 'THE GYPSY' Scene i *A ruined hovel on the lower slopes of a mountain in Biscay* The tonality, rhythms, and melodic gestures of the orchestral introduction bring us back to the musical world of Act 1 scene i as the gypsies celebrate their return to work with the famous 'anvil' chorus, 'Vedi, le fosche notturne'. This is immediately juxtaposed with Azucena's Canzone, 'Stride la vampa!', an invocation of fire and destruction that hovers obsessively around the note B'. The gypsies retire (to a muted reprise of their chorus); Azucena tells Manrico of her mother's death at the stake, and of how she planned to take revenge by casting the old count's son onto the embers of the fire. Her narrative, 'Condotta ell'era in ceppi', starts out in regular periods; but as the tale unfolds the music breaks out of its tonal and rhythmic confines, coming to an intense declamatory climax as Azucena admits that she mistakenly threw her own baby onto the fire.

Manrico asks whether he is, then, Azucena's son, but the gypsy diverts him with assurances of love and encourages him, in turn, to tell a story. Manrico's 'Mal reggendo all'aspro assalto' recounts his duel with the Count and how a strange voice commanded him not to strike the fatal blow; but with Azucena's answer this piece turns into the first lyrical movement of a 'dissimilar' duet (in which each singer has individual musical material). They are interrupted by Ruiz, who bears a letter telling Manrico that Leonora, thinking him dead, is about to enter a convent. Manrico resolves to go to her immediately, and so begins the duet cabaletta, 'Perigliarti ancor languente', in which Azucena begs him not to court danger yet again.

Scene ii *The cloister of a convent near Castellor* The Count is resolved to steal Leonora away from the steps of the convent and apostrophizes her in 'Il balen del suo sorriso', an 'aristocratically' graced Largo that exposes the baritone's full expressive range. A bell from the convent urges action, and the Count and his followers disperse to hide, the male chorus's 'Ardir, andiam' serving as a frame for the Count's vigorous cabaletta of expectation, 'Per me ora fatale'. A chorale-like chant from offstage nuns mingles with a restrained reprise of the chorus's 'Ardir, andiam' to introduce Leonora. Her affecting arioso is cut short by the Count and then, to general amazement, by Manrico, whose sudden appearance precipitates the slow movement of the concertato finale, 'E deggio e posso crederlo?'. Led off by a breathless, sobbing Leonora, continued by the patterned opposition of the two male principals, the movement comes to a magnificent climax with Leonora's rising line, 'Sei tu dal ciel disceso, o in ciel son io con te?'. Action once more boils up as Manrico's followers surround the Count's men. With a final reprise of 'Sei tu dal ciel' (whose lyrical power functions in place of the usual stretta movement), Leonora rushes off with Manrico.

ACT 3 'THE GYPSY'S SON' Scene i *A military encampment*   The Count's men are eager to mount an attack on Castellor; when Ferrando tells them they will move at dawn the next day, they celebrate with the famous chorus 'Squilli, echeggi la tromba guerriera'. The Count, still in agony over his loss of Leonora, is interrupted by Ferrando, who brings news that Azucena has been captured nearby. She is led on and, to divert attention under interrogation, she lapses into her 'gypsy' mode, singing 'Giorni poveri vivea', a simple minor-mode song that unexpectedly flowers into the major as she mentions the love she has for her son. But Ferrando guesses her true identity and in a concluding stretta, 'Deh! rallentate, o barbari', she begs for mercy, the Count exults, and Ferrando and the chorus look forward to her death at the stake.

Scene ii *A room adjoining the chapel at Castellor, with a balcony at the back*   We move to the rival camp, where Leonora and Manrico are about to be married. Manrico calms his bride's fear with the Adagio 'Ah! sì, ben mio, coll'essere', in which the tenor approaches most closely the 'aristocratic' musical world of Leonora and the Count. The lovers indulge in a brief duet but are interrupted by Ruiz, who tells Manrico of Azucena's capture. Manrico immediately summons his followers and prepares to mount a rescue operation, pausing only to sing the cabaletta 'Di quella pira'. This movement, which rudely casts Manrico back into the more direct musical world of the gypsies, and is probably best known for its (inauthentic) high Cs, hides within its blunt exterior a good number of those subtle harmonic and orchestral gestures that Verdi seemed so effortlessly to integrate into even his most energetic music.

ACT 4 'THE EXECUTION' Scene i *A wing of the Aliaferia palace*   It is now too late in the drama for even brief narratives; we must grasp by deduction that Manrico's attack failed and that he is now a prisoner of the

Count. Leonora arrives to try to save him, and from outside the prison sings of her love in the Adagio 'D'amor sull'ali rosee', which retains her 'aristocratic' ornamental style, but now colours it with dark instrumental sonorities and a predominantly falling line. The ensuing *tempo di mezzo*, perhaps the most famous in Italian opera, combines three contrasting musical ideas: a solemn 'Miserere' sounding from within the palace; Leonora's fragmented response, underpinned by a quiet yet insistent 'death' rhythm from the full orchestra; and Manrico's farewell to his beloved, 'Ah! che la morte ognora', a simple melody that recalls his Act 1 serenade. The number concludes with Leonora's reiteration of her love in the cabaletta 'Tu vedrai che amore in terra' (sometimes omitted in performance for fear of overtaxing the soprano).

The Count appears, determined to execute both Manrico and Azucena. The arrival of Leonora initiates a conventionally structured though powerfully condensed four-movement duet. The first movement involves rapid dialogue over an orchestral melody; then the opponents move to a formally fixed statement of their opposing positions (the Andante mosso 'Mira, di acerbe lagrime'), Leonora begging for the life of Manrico, the Count obstinate in his desire for revenge. But then, in the third movement, Leonora strikes a Tosca-like bargain: she offers herself in exchange for her lover's life. The Count jubilantly agrees, failing to see that Leonora has secretly taken poison. They join in the celebratory cabaletta 'Vivrà! . . . Contende il giubilo'.

Scene ii *A grim prison*   The Finale Ultimo finds Manrico and Azucena languishing in prison. Azucena has a frightening vision of the death that awaits her, the orchestra recalling her 'Stride la vampa' of Act 2. With reassurance from Manrico, sleep gradually overtakes her. They join in the narcotic duet 'Sì . . . la stanchezza m'opprime', which begins in the minor but moves to the parallel major for Manrico's 'Riposa o madre' and Azucena's picture of the simple gypsy life, 'Ai nostri monti'. Leonora appears, telling Manrico that he is free to go; but he quickly guesses the nature of her bargain with the Count. In the concertato 'Parlar non vuoi?' he accuses her; Leonora frantically attempts to defend herself and, in the later part, we hear Azucena's somnolent reprise of 'Ai nostri monti'. Leonora collapses at Manrico's feet as the ensemble finishes; the poison begins to take effect, and soon the truth is out. In a second ensemble, 'Prima . . . che d'altri . . . vivere', Manrico and Leonora bid a tender farewell, the Count entering to add his comments in the later stages. As Leonora dies, the Count assumes control: Manrico is led off to the scaffold, and Azucena is forced to watch his execution. As the fatal blow falls, she tells the Count that he has just killed his own brother, and brings down the curtain with a final, exultant cry: her mother has been avenged.

*   *   *

Il trovatore, although it has remained one of the two or three most popular Verdi operas, has until recently fared rather badly with critics and commentators, mostly because of its unabashed formal conservatism in comparison with the works on either side of it, *Rigoletto* and *La traviata*. As we saw earlier, the opera clearly started life as a sequel to *Rigoletto*, this time with an outcast female protagonist (the gypsy Azucena) claiming centre stage. But the drama's eventual operatic manifestation proved very different. There is none of that mixing of genres found in *Rigoletto*, nor many examples of the earlier opera's taste for formal experiment: all the main characters express themselves in the stock forms of serious Italian opera of the previous generation; the symmetries of the overall organization (four acts, each divided into two) are precisely echoed in their patterned confrontations.

More recently, however, the achievement of the opera has been seen to lie precisely in this conservatism of formal discourse, the emotional energy of the drama being constantly channelled through tightly controlled, predictable units. Indeed, many of the most important stages in the critical rehabilitation of *Il trovatore* have concentrated attention on just those aspects that were earlier castigated. The libretto, for example, with its immovable character types and 'unrealistic' stage action, has been seen as one of the work's great strengths, its economy of dramatic means and immediacy of language forming a perfect base on which to build Verdian musical drama. Similarly, the extreme formalism of the musical language has been seen as concentrating and sharply defining the various stages of the drama, above all channelling them into those key confrontations that mark its inexorable progress.

If one musical feature can be singled out that best accounts for *Il trovatore*'s success, it is probably sheer musical energy. Time and again we find a relentless rhythmic propulsion in the accompaniments, and a tendency for melodic lines to be forced into a restrictive rhythmic compass, freeing themselves rarely but with consequent explosive power. This internal energy often runs through entire numbers, engendering a sense of progress across the various formal stages—from arioso to slow movement to cabaletta— that is just as convincing as the more radical, 'external' experiments with form encountered in the surrounding operas. The success of *Il trovatore* should, in other words, remind us that it is dangerous to see Verdian development in too simple a line, still less to tie it unthinkingly to a gradual 'emancipation' from formal restrictions: in spite of its celebration of traditional forms, *Il trovatore* is anything but a throwback to earlier achievements.

La traviata

('The Fallen Woman')

Melodramma in three acts set to a libretto by Francesco Maria Piave after Alexandre Dumas *fils'* play *La Dame aux camélias*; first performed in Venice, Teatro La Fenice, on 6 March 1853.

The cast at the première included Fanny Salvini Donatelli (Violetta), Ludovico Graziani (Alfredo), and Felice Varesi (Giorgio Germont).

Violetta Valéry, *a courtesan*	soprano
Flora Bervoix, *her friend*	mezzo-soprano
Annina, *Violetta's maid*	soprano
Alfredo Germont	tenor
Giorgio Germont, *his father*	baritone
Gastone, Vicomte de Letorières, *friend of Alfredo*	tenor
Baron Douphol, *Violetta's protector*	baritone
Marchese D'Obigny, *friend of Flora*	bass
Doctor Grenvil	bass
Giuseppe, *Violetta's servant*	tenor
Flora's Servant	bass
Commissioner	bass

Ladies and gentlemen, friends of Violetta and Flora, matadors, picadors, gypsies, servants of Violetta and Flora, masks, etc.

Setting In and around Paris, about 1700

By April 1852 Verdi had agreed to write a new opera for the Carnival 1853 season at the Teatro La Fenice in Venice, with Francesco Maria Piave as librettist. But even as late as October no subject had been decided upon: the unusually tight schedule was due in part to Verdi's continuing work on *Il trovatore*, the première of which in Rome eventually took place less than two months before that of *La traviata*. By the beginning of November, however, Verdi and Piave had elected to base their opera on Dumas *fils'* play, which had first been performed in Paris earlier that year. The working title of the opera, later changed at the insistence of the Venetian censors, was *Amore e morte* ('Love and Death'). As Verdi wrote to his friend Cesare De Sanctis on 1 January 1853, it was 'a subject of the times. Others would not have done it because of the conventions, the epoch and for a thousand other stupid scruples'. The composer even proposed that, contrary to custom, the opera should be performed in modern costume; but again the Venetian authorities would not agree, and the period was put back to the beginning of the eighteenth century.

La traviata, it seems, was written in something like record time. Even though the above-quoted letter to De Sanctis dates from just over two months before the première, it is primarily concerned with compositional problems surrounding the still unfinished *Il trovatore*; it is clear that *La traviata* was largely unwritten at the time. Its première, while not the outright fiasco that Verdi declared it to be, had a mixed reception, probably caused more by the singers than by the music: Salvini Donatelli was physically unsuited to the role of Violetta but generally applauded; Varesi was past his prime and found the part unsympathetic; Graziani was in bad health. Verdi was reluctant to allow further performances until he could find a more suitable cast, but he eventually allowed a second staging (on 6 May 1854) at the Teatro San Benedetto, Venice, making various alterations to the score, the most important of which were to the central Act 2 duet between Violetta and Germont. This time success was unequivocal, and the opera soon became one of the composer's most popular works. It has retained this position into modern times, in spite of the fact that the heroine's role is one of the most feared in the soprano repertory.

*   *   *

The prelude to *La traviata* is a curious narrative experiment: it paints a three-stage portrait of the heroine, but in reverse chronological order. First comes a musical rendering of her final decline in Act 3, with high, chromatic strings dissolving into 'sobbing' appoggiaturas; then a direct statement of love, the melody that will in Act 2 become 'Amami, Alfredo'; and finally this same melody repeated on the lower strings, surrounded by the delicate ornamentation associated with Violetta in Act 1.

ACT 1 *A salon in Violetta's house* It is August. In a festive atmosphere, the action underpinned by a sequence of lively orchestral dances, Violetta and friends greet their guests, among whom is Alfredo Germont, a young man who for some time has loved Violetta from afar. Eventually all sit down to supper and Violetta calls for a toast. Alfredo takes up the cup to sing the famous brindisi 'Libiamo ne' lieti calici', a simple, bouncing melody repeated by Violetta and finally (with judicious transposition) by the entire chorus. A band in an adjoining room now starts up a succession of waltzes and the guests prepare to dance; but Violetta feels unsteady (the symptoms suggest she is consumptive) and begs the others to go on without her. Alfredo remains behind and, with the dance music still sounding, warns Violetta that her way of life will kill her if she persists. He offers to protect her and admits his love in the first movement of their duet. 'Un dì felice eterea' begins hesitantly but builds to the passionate outpouring of 'Di quell'amor ch'è palpito', a melody that will reappear later as a kind of emblem of Alfredo's devoted love. Violetta answers with an attempt to defuse the situation, telling him he will soon forget her, and surrounding his passionately insistent melody with showers of vocal ornamentation. The dance music (which disappeared during the duet) now returns as Violetta playfully gives Alfredo a flower, telling him to return when it has faded. To round off the scene the returning guests, seeing dawn approaching, prepare to leave in the stretta, 'Si ridesta in ciel l'aurora'.

Left alone, Violetta closes the act with a two-movement aria. She muses fondly of her new conquest in the Andantino 'Ah fors'è lui', which—like Alfredo's declaration—begins hesitantly but then flowers into 'Di quell'amor'. This sequence is then literally repeated (in the style, that is, of a French *couplets* rather than an Italian cantabile) before Violetta violently shrugs off her sentimental thoughts and resolves that a life of pleasure is her only choice. She closes the act with the cabaletta 'Sempre libera degg'io', full of daring, almost desperate coloratura effects. But in the closing moments her melody is mixed with 'Di quell'amor', sung by Alfredo from beneath the balcony.

ACT 2 Scene i *A country house near Paris* It is the following January; three months have passed since Violetta and Alfredo set up house together in the country. Alfredo sings of his youthful ardour in 'Dei miei bollenti spiriti', an unusually condensed Andante with no repetition of the initial melodic phrase. Annina then hurries in to inform Alfredo that Violetta has been selling her belongings to finance their country life together. Alfredo immediately decides to raise money himself and rushes off to Paris after expressing his despair in the cabaletta 'Oh mio rimorso!' (often cut in modern performances).

Violetta appears and is soon joined by a visitor who announced himself as Giorgio Germont. Their ensuing duet is unusually long; typically for Verdi, the formal expansion is concentrated on the opening movement of the conventional four-movement sequence. After an initial passage of recitative, this first movement involves three main subsections: a kind of lyrical dialogue between the principals. First comes an Allegro moderato ('Pura siccome un angelo') in which Germont describes the plight of his daughter, whose forthcoming marriage is threatened by Alfredo's scandalous relationship with Violetta. After a brief transition, Violetta reveals the seriousness of her illness and protests that Alfredo is all she has in the world (the breathless 'Non sapete quale affetto'). But Germont is adamant and in 'Bella voi siete e giovine' assures Violetta that she will find others to love. Eventually Violetta capitulates: the second movement of the duet, 'Dite alla giovine', begins with her heartbroken agreement to leave Alfredo and gives ample opportunity for the voices to interweave. The final two movements are relatively brief and conventional: Violetta agrees to break the news to Alfredo in her own way, begging Germont to remain to comfort his son; and then, in the cabaletta 'Morrò . . . la mia memoria', she asks Germont to tell Alfredo the truth after her death.

As Germont retires, Violetta begins to write a letter to Alfredo but has not finished by the time her lover reappears. He is disturbed by her agitation, but she answers his questions with a simple, passionate declaration of love, 'Amami, Alfredo' (the melody that served as the basis for the opera's prelude) before rushing out. The remainder of the scene might well, of course, focus on Alfredo, but operatic convention requires a two-movement aria for the baritone (who has no other opportunity in the opera for an extended solo); Alfredo's reactions are thus sandwiched into the transition passages. Soon after Violetta has left, a servant brings Alfredo her letter saying that she must leave him forever; his anguished response is immediately countered by Germont's lyrical Andante mosso, 'Di Provenza il mar, il suol', which conjures up a nostalgic picture of their family home. But Alfredo will not be consoled and at the end of Germont's cabaletta, 'No, non udrai rimproveri', his anger boils over: knowing that she has received an invitation to a party in Paris, he assumes that Violetta has deserted him to return to her old friends.

Scene ii *A salon in Flora's town house* A boisterous orchestral opening, over which Flora and her new lover discuss the separation of Violetta and

Alfredo, is followed by a two-part *divertissement*: a chorus of gypsies (with more than an echo of the musical world of *Il trovatore*) and then of matadors, dance and sing. Alfredo enters and, to an obsessively repeated motif which begins low in the strings and clarinets, begins recklessly betting on cards, apparently uncaring when Violetta appears on the arm of Baron Douphol. As Alfredo and the Baron bet against each other with barely concealed hostility, Violetta repeatedly laments her position in an anguished melody that cuts across the repeated motif. Supper is served, and Violetta manages a private meeting with Alfredo. In answer to his accusations she desperately claims that she now loves the Baron, at which Alfredo calls the guests together and, in a declamatory passage of rising fury, denounces Violetta and throws his winnings in her face as 'payment' for their time together. This precipitates a rapid passage of choral outrage before Germont, who has just arrived, leads off the Largo concertato ('Di sprezzo degno'). This large-scale movement depicts the contrasting moods of the main characters: Germont reproachful and lyrically contained; Alfredo distressed and remorseful with a fragmentary line; and Violetta, privately begging Alfredo to understand her distress with a line that eventually dominates through its simplicity and emotive power. Such is the charge of the movement that the act can end there, without the conventional concluding stretta.

ACT 3 *Violetta's bedroom*   It is February. The orchestral prelude opens with the idea that began the entire opera, and then develops into an intense solo for the first violins, full of 'sobbing' appoggiaturas. In the spare recitative that follows we learn from a doctor that Violetta is near death. To a restrained orchestral reprise of 'Di quell'amor', Violetta reads a letter from Germont, telling her that Alfredo (who fled abroad after fighting a duel with the Baron) now knows the truth about her sacrifice and is hurrying back to her side. But she knows that time is short, and in the aria 'Addio, del passato' bids farewell to the past and to life, the oboe solo adding poignancy to her painfully restricted vocal line. A chorus of revellers is heard outside, underlining the gloom of Violetta's isolation; but then, to a sustained orchestral crescendo, Alfredo is announced and throws himself into Violetta's arms. After the initial greeting Alfredo leads off the Andante mosso movement of their duet, 'Parigi, o cara': a simple waltz-time melody reminiscent of Act 1, in which the lovers look forward to a life together away from Paris. It is significant, though, that Violetta's attempts at Act 1-style ornamentation are now severely restricted in range.

Violetta decides that she and Alfredo should go to church to celebrate his return, but the strain even of getting to her feet is too much and she repeatedly falls back. This painful realization of her weakness precipitates the cabaletta 'Gran Dio! . . . morir sì giovine', in which Violetta gives way to a despair that Alfredo can do little to assuage. Germont appears, and a brief but passionate exchange between him and Violetta leads to the final concertato, 'Prendi, quest'è l'immagine', in which Violetta gives Alfredo a locket with her portrait, telling him that, should he marry, he can give it to his bride. The movement begins with an insistent, full-orchestra rhythmic figure, similar to that used in the Act 4 'Miserere' scene of *Il trovatore* and clearly associated with Violetta's imminent death; later, Violetta develops the simple, intense vocal style that has characterized her in this act. A last orchestral reprise of 'Di quell'amor' sounds as the final blow approaches. Violetta feels a sudden rush of life, sings a last 'Oh gioia!', but then collapses dead onto a sofa.

*   *   *

As we have seen, *La traviata* was written in great haste, its genesis thoroughly entangled with the creation of Verdi's previous opera, *Il trovatore*. Perhaps not surprisingly, there are some startling musical resemblances between the two works. But these similarities are on what one might call the musical surface; in dramatic structure and general atmosphere they are remarkably different, in some senses even antithetical. *La traviata* is above all a chamber opera: in spite of the 'public' scenes of the first and second acts, it typically acts out in an intimate setting, where there can be maximum concentration on those key moments in which the heroine's attitude to her surroundings are forced to change. Perhaps for this reason, the cabalettas, those 'public' moments that are so inevitable and essential to the mood of *Il trovatore*, tend to sit uneasily; we remember *La traviata* above all for its moments of lyrical introspection.

The opera is in many other ways a new adventure. It gestures towards a level of 'realism' very rare in earlier works (*Stiffelio* is its nearest cousin in this respect): the contemporary world of waltzes pervades the score, and the heroine's death from disease is graphically depicted in the music—from the first bars of the prelude to the gasping fragmentation of her last aria, 'Addio, del passato'. Within this radically new atmosphere there are, though, many surprising continuities: a reliance on conventional formal models, for example, even when—as in the case of Germont's two-movement aria in Act 2—their presence seems to interrupt the focus of the drama. But such harking back should not surprise us. One of Verdi's greatest strengths was his ability to balance formal and other continuities—his conservatism of attitude—against his desire always to try new dramatic solutions.

From all this, it is easy to see why *La traviata* is among the best loved of Verdi's operas, perhaps even *the* best loved. Cultural ambience and musical expression are very closely related: no suspension of disbelief is required to feel how the waltz tunes that saturate the score are naturally born out of the Parisian setting. And, perhaps most important, this sense of 'authenticity' extends to the heroine, a character whose psychological progress through the opera is mirrored by her changing vocal character: from the exuberant ornamentation of Act 1, to the passionate declamation of Act 2, to the final, well-nigh ethereal qualities she shows in Act 3. Violetta— Rigoletto and Gilda notwithstanding—is Verdi's most complete musical personality to date.

Les Vêpres siciliennes

('The Sicilian Vespers') [I vespri siciliani]

Opéra in five acts set to a libretto by Eugène Scribe and Charles Duveyrier after their libretto *Le Duc d'Albe*; first performed in Paris, Opéra, on 13 June 1855.

The cast at the première included Marc Bonnehée (Montfort), Louis Guéymard (Henri), Louis-Henri Obin (Jean Procida), and Sophie Cruvelli (Hélène).

Guy de Montfort (Monforte), *Governor of Sicily* *under Charles d'Anjou, King of Naples*	baritone
Le Sire de Béthune, *French officer*	bass
Comte de Vaudemont, *French officer*	bass
Henri (Arrigo), *a young Sicilian*	tenor
Jean Procida, *a Sicilian doctor*	bass
Duchess Hélène (Elena), *sister of Duke* *Frédéric of Austria*	soprano
Ninetta, *her maid*	contralto
Daniéli, *a Sicilian*	tenor
Thibault (Tebaldo), *French soldier*	tenor
Robert (Roberto), *French soldier*	baritone
Mainfroid (Manfredo), *a Sicilian*	tenor

Sicilian men and women, French soldiers, monks, *corps de ballet*

Setting In and around Palermo, 1282

After the performances of *Jérusalem* at the Opéra in 1847 Verdi had intended to produce an entirely new opera for Paris's leading theatre, but the revolutions of 1848 caused the plan to be shelved. He renewed negotiations with the Opéra, however, in 1852, and a contract was drawn up for a full-scale French grand opera in five acts, with a libretto by Eugène Scribe, the acknowledged poetic master of the genre. After various subjects had been proposed, poet and composer eventually agreed to use a revised version of an existing libretto, *Le Duc d'Albe*, written by Scribe and Charles Duveyrier for Halévy (who did not use it) and partly set to music by Donizetti in 1839.

Verdi spent most of 1854 working at the score, making a reluctant Scribe undertake some important revisions and complaining about the sheer length demanded by audiences at the Opéra. The première was well received, even by such severe critics as Berlioz, but the work failed to enter the standard repertory of the Opéra. What is more, its revolutionary subject caused difficulties with the Italian censors, and it was first performed in Italian at Parma in a bowdlerized version translated by Eugenio Caimi and called *Giovanna de Guzman*. Later performances as *I vespri siciliani* retained most aspects of Caimi's translation and, at least until recently, it was almost invariably in this Italian version that the opera was encountered. For a revival at the Opéra in 1863, Verdi replaced 'O jour de peine' with the tenor Romance 'O toi que j'ai chéri'.

*   *   *

The overture, the longest Verdi wrote and still sometimes revived in the concert hall, follows convention in being made up of themes drawn from the opera. It falls into two movements: a Largo, full of rhythmic 'death' figures, even in its more lyrical, major-mode section; and an Allegro agitato, whose main theme is taken from the Henri-Montfort duet in Act 3 and is repeated twice before a noisy Prestissimo brings the piece to a close.

ACT 1 *The main piazza in Palermo* The opening chorus, 'Beau pays de France!' ('Al cielo natio'), musically juxtaposes the victorious French soldiers with the resentful Sicilian people; it includes a brief episode in which a drunken soldier, Robert, looks forward to claiming his share of the vanquished Sicilian women. Hélène enters dressed in mourning; Béthune explains to Vaudemont that she is a hostage of Montfort and has come to pray for her brother Duke Frédéric, executed by Montfort a year ago. Robert staggers up, asking her for a song; she complies with a freely structured aria made up of three brief episodes and a closing cabaletta, 'Courage! . . . du courage!' ('Coraggio, su, coraggio'), in which she rallies the Sicilians around her. As the cabaletta draws to a close, the Sicilians advance on the

French; but they are interrupted by the appearance of Montfort, who precipitates a largely unaccompanied quartet 'Quelle horreur m'environne!' ('D'ira fremo all'aspetto'), in which Hélène and Montfort explore their conflicting positions. Henri now arrives and, unaware of Montfort's presence, explains to Hélène that he has inexplicably been released from prison by the Governor of Sicily but would dearly love to meet the tyrant face to face. At this Montfort reveals his identity and dismisses the women, thus preparing the ground for the closing duet finale. Like Hélène's aria, the duet passes through a number of short contrasting sections (as Montfort learns of Henri's history, offers him a commission in the French army and advises him to avoid Hélène) before closing with a cabaletta, 'Téméraire! téméraire!' ('Temerario! qual ardire!'), in which the characters' mutual defiance is reflected in a clash of strongly contrasting individual themes.

ACT 2 *A delightful valley near Palermo*   An orchestral introduction suggesting the movement of a boat accompanies the disembarkment of Procida. He greets his homeland in a brief recitative before beginning the famous Largo, 'Et toi, Palerme' ('O tu, Palermo'), fashioned in ternary form with a striking level of orchestral detail in the middle section. Procida's followers appear and together they sing the cabaletta 'Dans l'ombre et le silence' ('Nell'ombra e nel silenzio'), in which a stealthy, staccato choral passage precedes the main solo melody. Henri and Hélène arrive and are told by Procida that Spanish forces have agreed to aid the Sicilian cause, but that the Spaniards will not act unless there is a local uprising. Procida departs, leaving Henri and Hélène to embark on a two-movement duet—the first half of the traditional four-movement Italian model. In the first movement, the Allegro 'Comment, dans ma reconnaissance' ('Quale, o prode'), rapid dialogue precedes Henri's declaration of love; in 'Prés du tombeau peut-être' ('Presso alla tomba'), the couple sing together (though with differentiated lines), Hélène agreeing to accept Henri if he will avenge her brother's death.

Béthune appears, summoning Henri to a ball at Montfort's house that evening; when Henri refuses he is surrounded and dragged away. Hélène explains to Procida what has happened, but he is determined to continue his plan of attack. To the strains of a festive tarantella, the stage fills with young Sicilian men and women, among them twelve brides and their prospective husbands. Some French soldiers arrive and Procida encourages them to take advantage of the local women—to such good effect that at the end of the dance the soldiers abduct the young brides at sword point.

The chorus of outrage that follows, 'Interdits, accablés' ('Il rossor mi coprì!'), again obsessively repeating rhythmic 'death' figures, is interrupted by offstage voices singing a barcarolle: a boat is seen in the distance carrying French officers and Sicilian women. In a brief interlude, Procida decides that Montfort will be assassinated that very night; the two very different choruses then join in cleverly worked counterpoint to bring the act to a close.

ACT 3 Scene i *A study in Montfort's palace*   A brief orchestral prelude introduces Montfort, alone and brooding on his past: the woman he abducted many years ago has died, but she brought up their son Henri (who does not know his father's identity) to hate Montfort. The governor summons Henri to his presence before singing the famous 'Au sein de la puissance' ('In braccio alle dovizie'), a freely structured aria full of surprising harmonic excursions, in which he muses on his outward power and inward emptiness. Henri, entering, begins a lengthy duet, 'Quand ma bonté toujours nouvelle' ('Quando al mio sen'), which departs notably from standard Italian formal practice. There is a rapid alternation of tempos and moods in which Montfort presents Henri with proof of their relationship and, to a statement of the main theme of the overture (a melody that also dominates the final section of the duet), rejoices in his revelation. Henri is shocked, fears he must now lose Hélène and, in spite of Montfort's continued pleading, rejects the embrace of his father.

Scene ii *A magnificent hall laid out for a grand ball*   The long ballet that begins this scene is called 'Les Quatre Saisons' ('Le quattro stagioni') and, at least at the first production, entailed an elaborate mixture of mime and dance, with gods, zephyrs, naiads, fauns, and a final dance to Bacchus. Verdi's succession of brief contrasting movements shows the requisite instrumental invention and rhythmic vitality, though the ballet is perhaps too one-dimensional to be of much interest outside its immediate context.

The Act 3 finale is a large choral tableau, typical of French grand opera in its setting of private emotions within a public frame. The festive opening chorus, 'O fête brillante' ('O splendide feste!'), is interrupted by various dance tunes as Procida and Hélène approach Henri to tell him of the plot to murder Montfort. Henri warns Montfort of the danger but still refuses to side with his father. However, when Hélène tries to stab Montfort, Henri defends him and the conspirators are immediately arrested. The ensuing Adagio concertato, 'Coup terrible' ('Colpo orrendo'), which closes the act, is made up of two contrasting musical segments: first, a section of stunned surprise in which a tiny rhythmic motif is isolated and repeated; and then, its antithesis, a long lyrical melody in which all participants join to effect a stirring close.

ACT 4 *The courtyard of a fortress* A robust orchestral introduction presents Henri, who has a pass allowing him to visit the prisoners. He laments his position in 'O jour de peine' ('Giorno di pianto'), a strophic aria the angular melodic arch and harmonic underpinning of which are quite unlike the Verdian norm and which ends with a fast coda. Hélène then arrives to precipitate the first movement of their duet, 'De courroux et d'effroi' ('O sdegni miei'), in which fragmentary responses coalesce into a patterned melody as Henri begs for understanding, the melody momentarily breaking into recitative when he admits the identity of his father. The second movement, 'Ami! . . . le coeur d'Hélène' ('Arrigo! ah parli a un core'), is a miniature minor-major Romanza for Hélène, in which she reconciles herself to Henri, though with no hope of their union; the duet closes with a curtailed cabaletta, 'Pour moi rayonne' ('È dolce raggio').

Procida enters; he has been informed that Spanish forces are ready to aid the revolutionaries. He is quickly followed by Montfort, who orders the prisoners' immediate execution. Procida then leads off the quartet, 'Adieu, mon pays' ('Addio, mia patria'), in which the principals explore their differing emotions. Montfort offers clemency if only Henri will call him 'father'. A *De profundis* is heard offstage, the place of execution is revealed and eventually, to a slow, high violin melody, Henri submits. The prisoners are released and all join in a final stretta.

ACT 5 *Luxurious gardens in Montfort's palace in Palermo* The final act begins with three 'atmospheric' numbers in which the plot is barely advanced but local colour is richly explored. First comes the chorus 'Célébrons ensemble' ('Si celebri alfine'), quickly followed by Hélène's *sicilienne*, 'Merci, jeunes amies' ('Mercè, dilette amiche'), a *couplet* form entailing considerable virtuosity. Finally, there is Henri's lightly scored *mélodie* 'La brise souffle au loin' ('La brezza aleggia'), a song in praise of the evening breezes. Procida, his fanatical hatred undimmed, enters to announce the imminent uprising, which will begin at the sound of the wedding bells. He upbraids Hélène when he sees her love for Henri; she is horrified at the coming massacre. Henri leads off the first movement of the final trio, 'Sort fatal!' ('Sorte fatal!'). Hélène tries to stop the progress of events by refusing to go through with the wedding, but in spite of her pleading Henri will not leave the scene. In the closing stretta of the trio,

'Trahison! imposture!' ('M'ingannasti, o traditrice'), the principals' conflicting positions are again explored. Montfort enters and signals for the wedding bells to sound. The Sicilians rush in with daggers drawn and fall on Montfort and the French.

*   *   *

Les Vêpres siciliennes, in common with almost all French grand operas, has fallen from the repertory, its sheer length and the complexity of its vocal and scenic demands placing severe pressure on modern opera-house economics. There may also be purely musical reasons for the opera's comparative neglect: with a very few exceptions, its main lyrical numbers lack the melodic immediacy of the trio of Italian operas *(Rigoletto, Il trovatore* and *La traviata)* that immediately preceded it. However, for those wishing to understand Verdi's musical development during the 1850s, *Les Vêpres siciliennes* is enormously important, constituting as it does Verdi's most radical break with the tradition of Italian opera that had sustained his works thus far. Some aspects of the score suggest almost a pastiche experiment on Verdi's part: a conscious attempt to write a different kind of opera, one that would compete in the Parisian arena. This entailed aspects as large as the sprawling five-act structure typical of the genre, with a corresponding weakening of concentration on individuals; but it also engaged stylistic traits as basic as adaptation to French prose rhythms—not only in recitative but in lyric forms, where the relative weakness of French accentuation encouraged Meyerbeerian diffuseness and a slackening of the characteristic rhythmic incisiveness of Verdi's early manner. There were, of course, continuities, moments in which that early manner is recalled: not least in passages of individual contemplation such as Montfort's 'Au sein de la puissance', in which Verdi's experiments with the French manner are powerfully wedded to the arioso style of his most famous baritone protagonists.

Simon Boccanegra

Opera in a prologue and three acts set to a libretto by Francesco Maria Piave (with additions by Giuseppe Montanelli) after Antonio García Gutiérrez's play *Simón Bocanegra*; first performed in Venice, Teatro La Fenice, on 12 March 1857. The revised version, with additions and alterations by Arrigo Boito, was first performed in Milan, Teatro alla Scala, on 24 March 1881.

The cast at the 1857 première included Leone Giraldoni (Boccanegra), Giuseppe Echeverria (Fiesco), Luigia Bendazzi (Amelia) and Carlo Negrini (Gabriele). For the 1881 revised version the cast included Victor Maurel (Boccanegra), Edouard de Reszke (Fiesco), Anna D'Angeri (Amelia), and Francesco Tamagno (Gabriele).

PROLOGUE

Simon Boccanegra, *a corsair in the service of the Genoese Republic*	baritone
Jacopo Fiesco, *a Genoese nobleman*	bass
Paolo Albiani, *a Genoese goldsmith*	bass
Pietro, *a Genoese popular leader*	baritone

Sailors, populace, Fiesco's servants, etc.

DRAMMA

Simon Boccanegra, *the first Doge of Genoa*	baritone
Maria Boccanegra, *his daughter, under the name Amelia Grimaldi*	soprano

Jacopo Fiesco, *under the name Andrea*	bass
Gabriele Adorno, *a Genoese gentleman*	tenor
Paolo Albiani, *the Doge's favourite courtier*	bass
Pietro, *another courtier*	baritone
A Captain of the Crossbowmen	tenor
Amelia's Maidservant	mezzo-soprano

Soldiers, sailors, populace, senators, the Doge's court, African prisoners of both sexes

Setting In and around Genoa, about the middle of the fourteenth century; between the Prologue and Act 1, twenty-five years pass

Verdi was approached to write a new opera for the Teatro La Fenice in Venice, in the spring of 1856, at the instigation of the librettist Francesco Maria Piave. (His last première there had been another Piave opera, *La traviata* in 1853.) By May of that year a contract had been agreed with the theatre, the subject to be Gutiérrez's play *Simón Bocanegra;* Piave set to work according to precise instructions from the composer. In fact, Verdi himself supplied a complete prose sketch of the action, one so detailed that he insisted that his sketch rather than a draft of the libretto be submitted to the censors for approval. From August 1856 Verdi was in Paris, and in part because communication was difficult with Italy-based Piave, he took on a local collaborator, the exiled revolutionary Giuseppe Montanelli, who drafted several scenes. Verdi began composing in the autumn of 1856; as the date of the première approached, he showed his usual close concern with the staging and choice of performers. The première was only a moderate success; the libretto in particular received some harsh criticism. Subsequent revivals in the late 1850s were occasionally successful, although the 1859 La Scala première was a complete fiasco.

Doubtless in reaction to this lack of public acclaim, Verdi considered revising the score during the 1860s; but it was not until 1879 that he finally decided to make substantial alterations, in part to test the possibility of working with Arrigo Boito as librettist on the larger project of *Otello*. Looking over the 1857 score, Verdi pronounced it 'too sad' and decided that, although the prologue and final two acts could remain more or less unchanged, the first act needed a thorough overhaul, in particular by the injection of contrast and variety. This idea eventually gave rise to the famous Council Chamber scene; but in the end Verdi (somewhat reluctantly) found it necessary to make large adjustments to several other portions of the score (details are given below). The revised version had a resoundingly successful première at La Scala, directed by Franco Faccio.

*   *   *

PROLOGUE *A square in Genoa*   The 1857 version begins with a prelude in which various themes from the opera are briefly juxtaposed; the opening scene is the barest of declamatory recitatives. In 1881 Verdi underpinned the conversation between Paolo and Pietro with an undulating string theme, rich in harmonic inflections and clearly meant to introduce the maritime flavour of the score. The two men discuss who is to be the next Doge, Pietro persuading Paolo to support the corsair Boccanegra. As Pietro departs to rally the plebeian vote, Boccanegra himself appears. He is at first indifferent to the assumption of high office, but is persuaded to seek it by Paolo's reminder that his position will help win him his beloved Maria— she is imprisoned in her father's home as a result of her love affair and Fiesco's strong disapproval of the plebeian Boccanegra. From here to the end of the prologue the two versions largely correspond, although Verdi made numerous small revisions for 1881. First comes a chorus during which Paolo and Pietro convince the workers that they should vote for Boccanegra. The scene, remarkable for its restraint, centres on 'L'atra magion vedete?', in which Paolo describes the Fieschi's gloomy palace, where Maria is held prisoner.

As the crowd disperses, Fiesco emerges from his home, stricken with grief: his daughter has just died. After a stern recitative he sings the famous 'Il lacerato spirito', a minor-major Romanza notable for its extreme melodic simplicity but powerful emotional effect. Fiesco is then joined by Boccanegra for the first grand, multimovement duet of the opera. The first movement shows the usual violent alternation of moods: Fiesco accuses, Boccanegra tries to placate him, the old man agrees to pardon Boccanegra if he will give up the daughter Maria has borne him. But in a second movement, 'Del mar sul lido', again dominated by maritime figures in the orchestra, Boccanegra narrates how his daughter has mysteriously disappeared from the remote hiding place where she was lodged during his absence at sea. Fiesco, who contributes little to this movement, turns his back on Boccanegra, pretending to leave, but hides nearby. In a third movement, full of passionately anxious string figures, Boccanegra enters the palace in search of Maria. His cries of anguish at discovering her body are immediately countered by offstage cheers. To a jarring, festive theme—a kind of cabaletta substitute—the people enter to hail Boccanegra as their new leader.

ACT I Scene i *The gardens of the Grimaldi palace outside Genoa*   Twenty-five years have passed. An evocative orchestral prelude depicting the rising dawn introduces Amelia, whose French-style ternary-form aria, 'Come in quest'ora bruna', is notable for its delicately varied accompaniment and its injection of narrative mystery in the middle section. Gabriele's offstage voice is now heard in two stanzas of a *Trovatore*-like serenade, 'Cielo di stelle orbato'. In the 1857 version this leads to a cabaletta for Amelia, 'Il palpito deh frena', which in 1881 was replaced by a few bars of recitative. In the first movement of the lovers' ensuing duet, Gabriele tries to calm Amelia's fears for the future; in the second, the gentle Andantino 'Vieni a mirar la cerula', they pause to admire the sea around Genoa, although thinking too of enemies within the city walls. At the close of the Andantino the pair are joined by Pietro, who asks permission for the Doge to visit later that day. Amelia, sure that he is planning for her to marry Paolo, sends Gabriele away to prepare for their own wedding. In a cabaletta, 'Sì, sì, dell'ara il giubilo', much reduced in 1881, they swear to defy the whole world. Amelia hurries into the palace, but Gabriele is detained by Fiesco (who is posing under the name Andrea, and has long been watching over Amelia; he is very fond of her, although unaware of her real identity). Fiesco, informed of Amelia's and Gabriele's marriage plans, warns Gabriele that his intended bride is not of noble birth but an orphan who replaced the real Amelia Grimaldi, long since dead. In 1857 the episode was rounded off by a duet cursing Boccanegra, thought responsible for the death; in 1881 there is a *religioso* duet in which Fiesco gives a father's blessing to Gabriele.

Offstage trumpets herald Boccanegra. In a brief scena the Doge gives Amelia a paper showing that he has pardoned her presumed brothers (the Grimaldi, who have plotted against him). In the first movement of the ensuing duet, 'Dinne, perchè in quest'eremo', which is underpinned by a sinuous orchestral melody, Amelia admits her love for Gabriele and, feeling gratitude to Boccanegra, decides to tell him of her lowly birth. This she does in a second movement, the narration 'Orfanella il tetto umile', in the closing section of which Boccanegra joins her with a gathering sense of her true identity. The third movement, in which Boccanegra confirms that she is his long-lost daughter, quickly gives way to a cabaletta of mutual joy, 'Figlia! a tal nome io palpito', subtly varied in the 1881 version to increase the sense that both individuals have distinct musical personalities. Amelia leaves, and Boccanegra roughly tells Paolo to abandon hope of marrying her. When Boccanegra himself departs, Paolo tells Pietro of his plan to abduct Amelia.

Scene ii *The Council Chamber of the Doges' Palace* This scene was almost entirely recomposed for the 1881 version. The 1857 finale is set in a large square in Genoa and is a conventional four-movement concertato finale, a grand ceremonial scene in which the Doge appears amid festivities and is interrupted by Fiesco and Gabriele, who accuse him of abducting Amelia. As the scene reaches its climax Amelia herself appears, protesting the Doge's innocence and thus precipitating the central Andantino. Amelia then narrates her abduction and escape, but she refuses to reveal publicly who was responsible; all join in a stretta calling for the guilty one to be brought to justice.

In 1881 Verdi altered this traditional plan, vastly expanding the first movement, eliminating the last, and fashioning new music almost throughout. The scene begins with a stormy orchestral introduction, after which the Doge urges the Council to preserve peace between Genoa and Venice. A riot is heard outside as the plebeians demand death for the patricians and the Doge. Boccanegra orders the crowd to be brought in; a mass of people appears with Fiesco and Gabriele as captives, accused of killing Lorenzino, a leader of the plebeians. Gabriele in turn accuses the Doge of having Amelia abducted and is about to stab him when Amelia herself enters and interposes herself between them. She narrates her abduction and escape in 'Nell'ora soave', but refuses to reveal publicly who was responsible. A new argument develops between the opposing factions, this time violently quelled by the Doge, who launches the central Andante mosso, 'Plebe! Patrizi!', a magnificent ensemble movement in which the Doge's and Amelia's pleas for peace calm the crowd. The Andante over, the Doge pronounces a solemn curse on Amelia's abductor, forcing Paolo to repeat the words. As the chorus reiterate the curse, Paolo falls to the ground in horror.

ACT 2 *The Doges' room in the Ducal Palace at Genoa* In 1881, Verdi expanded Paolo's brief 1857 scena into a powerful recitative during which he meditates on the curse that has fallen on him and then puts poison in Boccanegra's drink. Fiesco and Gabriele are led in and, in spite of his hatred for Boccanegra, Fiesco refuses to be involved in Paolo's plot against the

Doge. Fiesco leaves, and Paolo informs Gabriele that the Doge wants Amelia for himself. Left alone, Gabriele breaks into a fit of jealous anger that culminates in the two-movement aria 'Sento avvampar nell'anima', the first movement driven by a furious orchestral figure, the second a lyrical Largo enhanced by delicate chromatic details in the vocal line.

There follows a highly condensed four-movement duet for Amelia and Gabriele. During the opening movement Gabriele accuses Amelia of betrayal; she denies this but will elaborate no further. In the second movement, the Andante 'Parla, in tuo cor virgineo', Gabriele begs her to explain herself while she continues to protest her innocence. A tiny connecting movement starts as Amelia hears the Doge approaching. Gabriele refuses to leave, but in a brief cabaletta she succeeds in making him hide on the balcony. The Doge enters and in a stormy recitative learns that she loves Gabriele, whom he now knows to be conspiring against him. Left alone, he drinks from the poisoned cup and lapses into sleep. Gabriele reappears and after some deliberation decides to murder the Doge; but he is stopped by the sudden appearance of Amelia. Boccanegra awakes and eventually reveals that Amelia is his daughter, the three principals cementing their newfound connection in the Andante 'Perdon, perdon, Amelia'. But a warlike chorus is heard in the distance: the people are in revolt against the Doge. Gabriele offers to sue for peace, and vows to fight at Boccanegra's side.

ACT 3 *Inside the Doges' Palace* An orchestral introduction and choral cries in praise of the Doge precede the appearance of Fiesco and Paolo. In an impassioned recitative, Paolo reveals that it was he who abducted Amelia and poisoned the Doge. He is led off to execution. A Captain orders that all the lights in the city be extinguished in honour of the dead. The Doge himself appears, a sluggish, chromatic string theme depicting the slow course of the poison through his body. In a shimmering arioso, he delights in his beloved Genoese sea, 'Oh refrigerio! . . . la marina brezza!', before being joined by Fiesco. In the first movement of their duet, 'Delle faci festanti al barlume', which contains the usual series of sharply contrasting episodes, Fiesco challenges the Doge and then admits his true identity. As the lights are gradually extinguished, Boccanegra reveals that 'Amelia' is really Fiesco's granddaughter. At this Fiesco breaks into tears, and the lyrical second movement, the Largo 'Piango, perchè mi parla', sees bass and baritone gradually reconciled. But ominous rhythmic figures in the orchestra warn us that Boccanegra is nearing death, and Fiesco tells him he has been poisoned. Amelia and Gabriele appear and Boccanegra blesses them in a final concertato, 'Gran Dio, li benedici'. With his dying breath he nominates Gabriele as his successor.

*   *   *

Simon Boccanegra is the mature Verdian opera most thoroughly revised by the composer, and the fact that these revisions were effected more than twenty years after the original version leaves the opera with some startling stylistic disjunctions. The 1857 drama was yet another radical departure, both from *Les Vêpres siciliennes* and from the last Italian opera, *La traviata*. There is little trace of the Gallic mode, whether the salon-like one of *La traviata* or the more grandiose explorations of *Les Vêpres*, but instead an exploration of the gloomy side of the Italian tradition. This is above all striking in the cast: there are no secondary female roles but a preponderance of low male voices. Most important, however, after the lyricism of *La traviata* and the extended 'musical prose' of *Les Vêpres*, *Simon Boccanegra* is characterized by an extreme economy of vocal writing, with the declamatory mode more prominent than ever before. This is most obvious in the music of the baritone protagonist: Boccanegra could be compared to Rigoletto in having no solo arias, instead expressing his inner thoughts through declamatory ariosos; but Rigoletto was depicted thus to emphasize his 'otherness', surrounded as he is by the lyricism of Gilda and the Duke. Boccanegra's spare language is, on the other hand, the standard discourse of the opera, to which the secondary male characters so important to the opera's atmosphere all tend.

However, this excitingly unusual vocal constellation is connected with, and in part causes, an important problem, one of which Verdi himself was well aware: the opera was too consistently dark in colour, too gloomy. The 1881 revisions do much to improve this aspect of the work. Although the distribution of voices remains the same, in retouching various scenes the mature Verdi invariably added new levels of harmonic and instrumental colour to the opera. And, perhaps most important, by adding the new Act 1 finale (the famous Council Chamber scene), he injected into the heart of the work an episode of vividness and power, enriching the character of Boccanegra in such a way that his subsequent death scene gains considerably in impressiveness.

It has been argued, though, that the revisions—especially the addition of the new Act 1 finale—create a further general problem, one of what we might call dramatic balance. The sheer weight of Boccanegra's new presence tends to overpower the other principals, Gabriele in particular, making their concerns seem unimportant or at least underarticulated. But perhaps critics tend to exaggerate the extent to which these essentially 'narrative' matters are crucial to the success of an opera. In recent years, and while the 1857 *Simon Boccanegra* has had some important outings, audiences have been in no doubt that the revised version contains some of the mature Verdi's greatest dramatic music. There seems little doubt now that the opera will retain its new status as one of the composer's most compelling creations.

Aroldo

Opera in four acts set to a libretto by Francesco Maria Piave after their earlier opera *Stiffelio*; first performed in Rimini, Teatro Nuovo, on 16 August 1857.

The cast at the première included Emilio Pancani (Aroldo), Marcellina Lotti (Mina), and Gaetano Ferri (Egberto).

Aroldo, *a Saxon knight*	tenor
Mina, *his wife*	soprano
Egberto, *her father, an old knight, vassal of Kent*	baritone
Briano, *a pious hermit*	bass
Godvino, *an adventurer knight, guest of Egberto*	tenor
Enrico, *Mina's cousin*	tenor
Elena, *also her cousin*	soprano
Jorg, *Aroldo's servant*	spoken

Crusader knights, ladies and gentlemen of Kent, squires, pages, heralds, huntsmen, Saxons, Scottish peasants

Setting In Egberto's castle in Kent, and on the shores of Loch Lomond in Scotland, in about 1200

The first performance of *Stiffelio*, at Trieste in November 1850, had met with severe problems from the local religious censors, particular objection being made to the final scene, which had to be changed radically and—Verdi thought—damagingly. The few subsequent revivals also tended to run into trouble, and in 1854 Verdi decided to collaborate with Piave on rescuing the opera by setting it to a different, less sensitive plot. In 1856 they started work, changing the tale of a nineteenth-century Protestant pastor into that of a thirteenth-century Saxon knight returned from the Crusades, Verdi taking the opportunity to make a number of further modifications. The brilliant young conductor Angelo Mariani directed the première at Rimini. The revised opera was a huge success; but revivals fared less well, and *Aroldo* soon disappeared from the general repertory, receiving only the occasional performance. In the discussion below, musical detail will be mentioned only if a passage differs substantially from *Stiffelio* or is new to *Aroldo*.

*   *   *

ACT I Scene i *A drawing room in Egberto's home*   The overture is substantially that of *Stiffelio*, but the opening of the act is new. A festive unaccompanied chorus, 'Tocchiamo! a gaudio insolito', welcomes Aroldo home from the Crusades. After an intense orchestral introduction, Mina enters to give voice to her remorse and offer a brief prayer, 'Salvami tu, gran Dio', an opening that immediately makes her a more forceful presence than was Lina in *Stiffelio*. Aroldo now arrives and introduces the hermit Briano, who saved his life in battle. His ensuing two-movement aria contains frequent anguished interpolations from Mina. The Andante, 'Sotto il sol di Siria', which describes how his thoughts on the battlefield were always for his wife, takes its theme from the overture; but (as in *Stiffelio*) the absence of Mina's ring arouses suspicions which he voices in the cabaletta 'Non sai che la sue perdita'. Mina, left alone, decides to write to her husband. She is interrupted by Egberto; the words and music of the following duet are, apart from a few details, identical with those in *Stiffelio*.

Scene ii *A suite of rooms illuminated for a grand celebration*   To a further theme borrowed from the overture, ladies and knights appear downstage as Godvino slips a letter to Mina into a book, observed—though only from behind—by Briano. In the interval between bursts of choral celebration, Enrico comes on, dressed like Godvino, and takes up the book. Briano is now convinced that Enrico placed the letter there, and warns Aroldo. Egberto enters and asks for a returning warrior to narrate the adventures of King Richard in Palestine. Aroldo obliges with 'Vi fu in Palestina', a largely declamatory episode that tells of a dishonourable man who betrayed his guests by writing a secret love letter to the lady of the house. He takes up the book to further illustrate the point, finds it locked, and tells a terrified Mina to open it. The ensuing concertato, 'Oh qual m'invade ed agita', is taken directly from *Stiffelio*, though with various expansions and musical changes, in particular to the main melodic line of the stretta.

ACT 2 *An old graveyard in the castle in Kent* The opening part of the scene, together with Mina's prayer 'Ah! dagli scanni eterei', is from *Stiffelio*. At the appearance of Godvino new music takes over in preparation for a new cabaletta, 'Ah dal sen di quella tomba', which—in line with the changes made to Mina's role in Act 1—requires an impressive musical and emotional range from the soprano. The remainder of the act follows *Stiffelio*: Egberto's duel with Godvino is interrupted by Aroldo; Egberto reveals to Aroldo that Godvino is Mina's seducer; and Briano narrowly prevents Aroldo from fighting a duel with Godvino.

ACT 3 *An antechamber in Egberto's home* The act is identical with Act 3 scene i of *Stiffelio*, although with occasional alterations to and expansions of Mina's role. Egberto contemplates suicide in his two-movement aria; Aroldo and Godvino have a brief scene; finally there is the long duet of confrontation between Aroldo and Mina, during which Egberto murders Godvino.

ACT 4 *A deep valley in Scotland* An opening chorus, 'Cade il giorno', offers generic local colour to mark the new geographical location. Aroldo and Briano, dressed as hermits, join the chorus in a prayer, 'Angiol di Dio', which makes prominent use of contrapuntal effects. A storm has been brewing and now breaks out to an orchestral accompaniment as elaborate in its instrumental virtuosity as anything Verdi had written to date. To the relief of the chorus, a boat seen approaching on the lake survives the storm; as the bad weather subsides the boat moors and from it disembark Mina and Egberto. They go to the hermit's cottage to seek shelter. The ensuing Quartetto finale divides into two large sections. First comes an Allegro, 'Ah da me fuggi', in which sharply differing emotional reactions are juxtaposed: Aroldo's violent rejection of his wife; Egberto's narration of his and Mina's painful exile after Godvino's death; and finally Mina's disjointed pleas for forgiveness. But Mina takes control and leads off the final Largo, 'Allora che gl'anni', in which she begs Aroldo to forgive her when she is old and near death. At last the conflicting voices join, and a sententious phrase about forgiveness from Briano eventually persuades Aroldo to pronounce the words 'Sei perdonata!' ('You are forgiven!').

*   *   *

As will be clear from the above, *Aroldo* differs from *Stiffelio* primarily in its first and last acts. However, there is surprisingly little stylistic disparity in the later opera, a fact that in part demonstrates the forward-looking nature of so much of *Stiffelio*. The relative merits of the operas are not such as to recommend one firmly over the other. *Aroldo* has a more forceful soprano presence, and its final act is remarkable, breaking new ground in its use of local colour and making a weightier close than the brief though effective choral finale of *Stiffelio*. On the other hand, Lina's reticence in the earlier opera is one of its most effective dramatic ploys, and *Stiffelio's* compelling sense of religious claustrophobia is somewhat diffused by the *Aroldo* story, which wavers uncertainly between the warlike and the religious. It is tempting to conclude that both operas deserve more performances than they at present receive; but *Aroldo* has of late fared markedly less well than *Stiffelio*, and would benefit from further attention.

Un ballo in maschera

('A Masked Ball')

Melodramma in three acts set to a libretto by Antonio Somma after Eugène Scribe's libretto *Gustave III, ou Le Bal masqué*; first performed in Rome, Teatro Apollo, 17 February 1859.

The cast at the première included Gaetano Fraschini (Riccardo), Leone Giraldoni (Renato), Eugénie Julienne-Dejean (Amelia), and Zelinda Sbriscia (Ulrica).

Riccardo, *Count of Warwick, Governor of Boston*	tenor
Renato, *a Creole, his secretary and husband of Amelia*	baritone
Amelia	soprano
Ulrica, *a negro fortune-teller*	contralto
Oscar, *a page*	soprano
Silvano, *a sailor*	bass
Samuel ⎫ *enemies of the Count*	bass
Tom ⎭	bass
A Judge	tenor
Amelia's Servant	tenor

Deputies, officers, sailors, guards, men, women, children, gentlemen, associates of Tom and Samuel, servants, masks, dancing couples

Setting In and around Boston, at the end of the seventeenth century

By February 1857 Verdi had agreed to write a new opera for the Teatro San Carlo in Naples, to be performed in the carnival season 1857–58. His first idea was *King Lear*, a setting of which he had planned with the playwright

Antonio Somma, but (not for the first time) the San Carlo singers were not to his liking and the project was postponed. By September 1857 the composer was becoming anxious about his approaching deadline, and eventually proposed to Somma and the San Carlo—albeit with some reservations about the libretto's conventionality—that he set a remodelled and translated version of an old Scribe libretto called *Gustave III, ou Le Bal masqué*, written for Auber in 1833. Somma and the theatre agreed; Verdi set to work advising his librettist, who had no experience writing for the musical theatre, on the necessary poetic proportions of the subject. The opera was at that time called *Gustavo III*.

As soon as a synopsis reached the Neapolitan censors, it became clear that the opera, which dealt with the assassination of the Swedish king Gustavus III, would have to be changed considerably if it were to be performed in Naples. Verdi agreed to change the king into a duke and to set the action back in time, and a new version of the story, now called *Una vendetta in dominò*, was patched together. This version made it into complete draft, though without orchestration. However, soon after the composer arrived in Naples in January 1858 the censor rejected this version, making a series of new, more stringent demands, notably that Amelia become a sister rather than a wife, that there be no drawing of lots by the conspirators, and that the murder take place offstage. The authorities of the San Carlo attempted to answer these objections by cobbling together a new version titled *Adelia degli Adimari*, but this Verdi angrily rejected. Eventually negotiations broke down, the planned performances fell through; Verdi undertook to satisfy his contract at a later date.

When it became clear that Naples would not stage the opera, Verdi decided to have it given at the Teatro Apollo, in Rome, even though it soon became clear that Roman censorship, though far less exigent than that at Naples, would require at least a change of locale and the demoting of the king to some lesser noble. Eventually, though, during the summer of 1858, Somma and Verdi agreed on a setting in the colonies of North America, with the king turned duke now Riccardo, Conte di Warwick, and the title *Un ballo in maschera*; as a protest Somma did not allow his name to appear on the printed libretto. The première was a great success, *Un ballo* becoming one of Verdi's most popular operas. Though not achieving the dissemination of *Rigoletto, Il trovatore,* or *La traviata*, it has never lost its place in the international repertory.

Some modern performances attempt to restore the opera to its original, eighteenth-century Swedish setting, even though such restoration seems not to have had Verdi's explicit approval. In the Swedish setting the names are as follows:

Riccardo	Gustavus III, *King of Sweden*
Renato	Captain Anckarstroem, *Gustavus's secretary*
Amelia	Amelia
Ulrica	Mademoiselle Arvidson
Oscar	Oscar
Silvano	Christian
Samuel	Count Ribbing
Tom	Count Horn
A Judge	Armfelt, *Minister of Justice*

There has also been an attempt at a 'hypothetical reconstruction' of *Gustavo III*, this using the (unorchestrated) draft of that version and of *Una vendetta in dominò*, onto which the editors have grafted either Verdi's orchestration for *Un ballo in maschera* or (when the versions differ too much) their own orchestration.

*   *   *

The brief prelude presents three of the main musical ideas of the opening scene: first a chorale-like chorus of loyal followers, then a fugato associated with the conspirators, and finally Riccardo's first aria; the whole argument is punctuated by a tiny rhythmic figure first heard in the second bar.

ACT I Scene i *A hall in the Governor's house*   The opening chorus, 'Posa in pace, a' bei sogni ristora', continues the prelude's musical juxtaposition of Riccardo's loyal followers with the conspirators (led by Samuel and Tom) who are planning to overthrow him. Riccardo appears and, in a style redolent of *opéra comique*, reviews with Oscar the guest list for the coming masked ball. At seeing the name of Amelia, however, he is visibly moved, and advances to the footlights to sing a brief aria privately expressing his guilty love for her, 'La rivedrà nell'estasi'. Its opening phrase, with expressive chromaticism and a rising 5th, will return later as a musical symbol of the love around which the story of the opera revolves. As the chorus disperses, the secretary Renato enters to warn Riccardo of plots against his life. His aria, 'Alla vita che t'arride', although formally more extended than Riccardo's, displays the same tendency towards condensation of traditional elements. Next to appear is a judge, requesting that Riccardo exile Ulrica, a fortune-teller suspected of supernatural practices. Oscar chooses to defend Ulrica in the ballata 'Volta la terrea', a French, two-stanza form studded with that light coloratura which will typify the page throughout. Riccardo decides that he and his followers will disguise themselves and pay a personal call on Ulrica. He leads off the final stretta, 'Ogni cura si doni al diletto', a number that continues the Gallic atmosphere in its celebration of the pleasures of life, despite continued mutterings from the conspirators in the musical background.

Scene ii *The fortune-teller's dwelling*   After an atmospheric orchestral introduction, full of low woodwind sonorities and sinister tritones, Ulrica sings the invocation 'Re dell'abisso', an aria that begins in the minor, is interrupted by Riccardo's entrance in disguise, and continues with a cabaletta substitute in the major. The atmosphere of foreboding is rudely interrupted by Silvano, a sailor who has seen no preferment and who—in the brief, sprightly solo 'Su, fatemi largo'—asks Ulrica to divine his future. Ulrica predicts wealth and a commission, something that Riccardo promptly brings to pass by secreting gold and the appropriate papers into Silvano's pocket. Silvano discovers his newfound wealth and all join in praise of Ulrica. They are interrupted by Amelia's servant, who requests an interview with Ulrica for her mistress. Ulrica dismisses the crowd; but Riccardo, who has recognized the servant, remains in his hiding place as Amelia comes in.

In an impassioned arioso, Amelia asks Ulrica to rid her of the love that torments her. Ulrica's reply is the sinuous, chromatic 'Della città all'occaso', which tells of a healing plant that grows in the gallows-field nearby. In the brief Terzetto that ensues, 'Consentimi, o Signore', Amelia prays that she may be healed, Ulrica tries to comfort her, and Riccardo, still hidden, vows to follow her on her quest. As Amelia departs, the stage is filled with Riccardo's entourage. Riccardo poses as a fisherman and sings the two-stanza Canzone 'Di' tu se fedele', replete with the characteristic signs of maritime musical language. He presents his hand to Ulrica who, in an imposing arioso, predicts that he will soon die by the hand of a friend. Riccardo attempts to disperse the tension by leading off the Quintet 'È scherzo od è follia', in which his breathless, 'laughing' line is accompanied by sinister chattering from Samuel and Tom, and by a sustained, high-lying melody for Oscar. Riccardo asks the identity of his murderer: Ulrica says it will be the first person who shakes his hand, a prophecy seemingly made absurd by Renato, who hurries on soon after and immediately clasps his master's hand. The act closes with a martial hymn, 'O figlio d'Inghilterra', in which the principals emerge from the vocal mass to re-state their differing positions.

ACT 2 *A lonely field on the outskirts of Boston* Amelia's grand Scena is preceded by a lengthy, impassioned orchestral prelude, which features her melody from the Act 1 Terzetto. Heavily veiled, she is terrified by her sur-roundings and in the aria 'Ma dall'arido stelo divulsa' prays for assistance in her ordeal. The aria, with its mournful English horn obbligato as a tra-ditional pointer of the isolated heroine, is interrupted by a terrifying vision as midnight sounds; but Amelia's final prayer reestablishes a kind of resigned calm. Riccardo appears, and so begins one of Verdi's greatest soprano-tenor duets, a number that, as was becoming common in middle-period Verdi, has a succession of contrasting 'dialogue' movements before its more conventional close with the cabaletta 'a 2'. In the opening Allegro agitato the pace of exchange is rapid: Riccardo declares his love and Amelia begs him to leave; the musical continuity comes for the most part from a driving string melody. In a second movement, 'Non sai tu che se l'anima mia', their individual attitudes are explored at greater length, with a particularly impressive modulation as the discourse turns from Riccardo to Amelia; but eventually Riccardo's pleas win the day and, to a passionate, soaring melody sustained by a pedal A-major chord, Amelia admits her love for him. A brief linking section leads to the cabaletta, 'Oh qual soave brivido', whose two stanzas and lively arpeggiated melody are separated by yet another impassioned declaration of mutual love.

The couple separate at the sound of footsteps: Riccardo recognizes Re-nato; Amelia, terrified, lowers her veil. In the first movement of the ensu-ing trio, 'Per salvarti da lor', Renato warns of approaching conspirators and lends his cloak to Riccardo in order to effect the latter's escape. Ric-cardo will leave only after muffled pleas from Amelia, and he solemnly charges Renato to escort his veiled companion to the gates of the city. Be-fore Riccardo rushes off, the three principals join in a furiously paced sec-ond trio, 'Odi tu come fremono cupi', in which the driving rhythm encloses a patterned alternation of solo statements. Riccardo is safely away when the conspirators appear, singing the contrapuntal music first heard in the prelude to the opera. They are challenged by Renato and, finding their prey has disappeared, decide to amuse themselves by seeing the face of his mysterious female companion. When it becomes clear that Renato, in his loyalty to the count, will fight rather than permit this, Amelia herself lets her veil fall. Renato is astounded: the conspirators cannot contain their mirth at the notion that Renato has had a nocturnal assignation with his own wife, and break into the nonchalant 'laughing' chorus, 'Ve' se di notte qui colla sposa'. In between statements of the main idea, Renato accuses Amelia; she begs for mercy. As a parting gesture, Renato arranges a meeting with Samuel and Tom later that morning; the conspirators stroll off together, still vastly amused, their laughter echoing as the curtain comes down.

ACT 3 Scene i *A study in Renato's house*   A stormy orchestral introduction ushers in Renato and Amelia. In an impassioned arioso, Renato insists that his wife must die. Although she admits her love for Riccardo, she insists that she has not betrayed her husband. But Renato is inflexible, and in the sorrowful aria 'Morrò ma prima in grazia', Amelia begs to see her child before dying, a cello obbligato adding to the pathos of the scene. Renato agrees to her request and once she has departed hurls furious insults at the portrait of Riccardo, which has a prominent place in his study. His anger coalesces into the famous aria 'Eri tu', a minor-major Romanza which, in the major section, turns from angry accusations to the pain of his lost love.

Yet again the contrapuntal theme introduces Samuel and Tom. Renato tells them that he knows of their conspiracy, but now offers to join in its execution, offering his son's life as proof of his good word. Samuel and Tom accept his word, and all three swear blood brotherhood in the martial hymn 'Dunque l'onta di tutti sol una'. They elect to draw lots over who will strike the fatal blow, and Renato takes advantage of Amelia's return to force her to draw the name from an urn. To dotted rhythms and tremolando strings, Amelia draws Renato's name; the conspirators again join in the martial hymn, this time with a terrified descant from Amelia.

In one of those abrupt changes of mood so characteristic of the opera, Oscar now appears, bringing with him once again the musical atmosphere of French *opéra comique*. He bears an invitation to the evening's masked ball, which Renato, Samuel, and Tom all accept. To close the scene, they join in a stretta led off by Oscar, 'Di che fulgor', in which the terror and exultation of the principals are subsumed under Oscar's delicate musical idiom.

Scene ii *The count's sumptuous study*   In an opening recitative, Riccardo decides to sign a paper sending Renato and Amelia back to England. He then muses on the loss of his love in the Romanza 'Ma se m'è forza perderti', which moves from minor to major but via an unusual intermediate section in which he feels a strange presentiment of death. Dance music is heard offstage, and Oscar brings an anonymous message warning

Riccardo that he risks assassination at the ball. The count, as ever heedless of the danger, concludes the scene with a passionate recollection of his Act 1 declaration of love for Amelia.

Scene iii *A vast, richly decorated ballroom*   The opening chorus, 'Fervono amori e danze', repeats the music heard offstage in scene ii. As Renato, Samuel, Tom, and their followers appear, a new, minor-mode theme emerges, over which the conspirators exchange passwords and search for the count. A third theme is heard as Oscar recognizes Renato. In spite of Renato's anxious questions, Oscar refuses to reveal Riccardo's costume, singing instead a lively French *couplets* form, 'Saper vorreste'. The opening chorus is heard again, and Renato renews his questions, pleading important business. Oscar finally discloses that the count is wearing a black cloak with red ribbon, after which he mingles with the crowd to yet more of the opening chorus. A new dance melody, this time a delicate mazurka, underpins a stifled conversation between Amelia and Riccardo: Amelia begs the count to escape; he reiterates his love but tells her that she is to return to England with her husband. They are bidding a last, tender farewell when Renato flings himself between them and stabs Riccardo. In the subsequent confusion, Oscar rips off Renato's mask and the chorus expresses its fury in a wild Prestissimo. But then the delicate mazurka briefly returns (the offstage dance orchestra as yet unaware of the events) as Riccardo bids his people release Renato. Leading off the final concertato, 'Ella è pura', Riccardo assures Renato that Amelia's honour is intact. He bids his subjects farewell, and a brief stretta of universal horror brings down the curtain.

*   *   *

If *Simon Boccanegra* is characterized by a single-mindedness of tone and purpose, *Un ballo in maschera*, as many have remarked, is a masterpiece of variety, of the blending of stylistic elements. Verdi's experiment with a 'pure' version of French grand opera in the mid-1850s, *Les Vêpres siciliennes*, was not entirely happy; here we see him instead gesturing to the lighter side of French opera (in particular the *opéra comique* idiom of Auber and his contemporaries), primarily with the character of Oscar, but also in aspects of Riccardo's musical personality. The juxtaposition of this style with the intense, interior version of Italian serious opera that Verdi had preferred in the early 1850s is extremely bold, particularly in sections such as Act 1 scene ii (where Riccardo confronts Ulrica) or in the finale to Act 2 (the so-called laughing chorus), in both of which the two styles meet head-on with little mediation. One of the reasons why the blend is so successful is that Verdi's treatment of the traditional forms at the backbone of his 'Italian' manner was itself changing, adapting towards the more elliptical manner of French models. *Un ballo* is, for example, notable for the brevity and intensity of many of its principal arias.

Another reason for the opera's success undoubtedly lies in its delicate balance of musical personalities. At the outer limits of the style, as it were, lie two musical extremes; Oscar, whose role throughout is cast in an unambiguously Gallic mould of light comedy; and Ulrica, whose musical personality is unrelievedly dark and austere. Within these two extremes lie Renato and Amelia, characters cast in the Italian style, fixed in their emotional range, but from time to time infected by the influence of their 'French' surroundings. And at the centre comes Riccardo, who freely partakes of both worlds, and who mediates between them so movingly and persuasively. In this sense the clash of styles in *Un ballo* is intimately written onto the key confrontations of the drama.

La forza del destino

('The Power of Fate')

Opera in four acts set to a libretto by Francesco Maria Piave after Angel de Saavedra, Duke of Rivas's play *Don Alvaro, o La fuerza del sino*, with a scene from Friedrich von Schiller's play *Wallensteins Lager*, translated by Andrea Maffei. *La forza del destino* was first performed in St Petersburg, Imperial Theatre, on 29 October/10 November 1862. The revised version, with additional text by Antonio Ghislanzoni, was first performed in Milan, Teatro alla Scala, on 27 February 1869.

The cast at the 1862 première included Caroline Barbot (Leonora), Francesco Graziani (Carlo), Enrico Tamberlik (Alvaro), and Constance Nantier-Didiée (Preziosilla). The cast for the 1869 revised version included Teresa Stolz (Leonora), Luigi Colonnese (Carlo), Mario Tiberini (Alvaro), and Ida Benza (Preziosilla).

The Marquis of Calatrava	bass
Donna Leonora, *his daughter*	soprano
Don Carlo di Vargas, *his son*	baritone
Don Alvaro	tenor
Preziosilla, *a young gypsy*	mezzo-soprano
Padre Guardiano	bass
Fra Melitone, *a Franciscan*	baritone
Curra, *Leonora's maid*	mezzo-soprano
An Alcalde	bass
Mastro Trabuco, *a muleteer, then pedlar*	tenor
A Surgeon *in the Spanish army*	bass

Muleteers, Spanish and Italian peasants, Spanish and Italian soldiers of various rank, their orderlies, Italian recruits, Franciscan friars, poor mendicants, vivandières

Dancers: Peasants, Spanish and Italian vivandières, Spanish and Italian soldiers

Walk-on parts: Innkeeper, innkeeper's wife, servants at the inn, muleteers, Spanish and Italian soldiers, drummers, buglers, peasants and children of both nations, a tumbler, pedlars

Setting Spain and Italy, around the middle of the eighteenth century

After *Un ballo in maschera* (finished in early 1858), Verdi experienced his most serious compositional hiatus to date, repeatedly telling friends that he had ceased to be a composer and that his farmlands at Sant'Agata now take up all his time. The breakthrough to fresh creativity came in late 1860 when the famous tenor Enrico Tamberlik wrote to Verdi offering him a commission from the Imperial Theatre at St Petersburg. Verdi first suggested Victor Hugo's *Ruy Blas*, which initially met with censorship problems and then apparently failed to hold the composer's interest. By the middle of 1861 he had decided on Rivas's *Don Alvaro, o La fuerza del sino*, a Spanish romantic melodrama, written under the influence of Hugo. The librettist was again to be Piave, although Verdi approached his friend and former collaborator Andrea Maffei about using material from Schiller's *Wallensteins Lager*—a move that immediately indicated his intention of writing an opera of wide-ranging dramatic ambience. Serious work began on the opera in August 1861 and by November it was more or less complete (except, as usual, for the orchestration, which Verdi still preferred to complete nearer the time of performance, when he had experienced the singers and the theatrical acoustics at first hand). Verdi left for Russia in late 1861, but the première was postponed owing to the illness of the prima donna. He undertook several lengthy European trips during the first half of 1862 and returned to supervise rehearsals at St Petersburg in September of that year. The first performance was praised in some journals, but was at best only a moderate success.

It is clear that Verdi was not entirely happy with this or subsequent performances, and by 1863 he was talking of making alterations to the score, notably to the endings of Acts 3 and 4. Various large-scale structural alterations were discussed during the next few years with a view to a Parisian première in the mid-1860s, but pressure of other work caused plans to be shelved. Then in 1868—after the première of *Don Carlos* at the Opéra—Verdi agreed to a new production of *La forza* at La Scala the following year. The librettist Antonio Ghislanzoni was drafted to help with modifications (the devoted Piave had in 1867 succumbed to a stroke, which incapacitated him for the rest of his life); Verdi eventually elected to replace the Preludio with a full-scale overture, to revise portions of Act 3, to make various minor alterations to other passages and, perhaps most important, to replace the bitter catastrophe of the denouement (in which all three principals die) with a scene of religious consolation. The performance, ably conducted by Angelo Mariani, was a considerable success, and *La forza* remained a popular element of the repertory during the later years of the nineteenth century. There is some evidence that Verdi was actively involved in a cut-down French version of the score, first heard in Antwerp in 1882; but this version seems to have survived only in vocal score and was never sanctioned by Verdi's publisher Ricordi.

∗ ∗ ∗

The overture (which, as mentioned above, belongs to the 1869 version, though deriving from the shorter Preludio of 1862) is a potpourri of the score's most memorable tunes, albeit with 'symphonic' aspirations. It begins with a solemn three-note unison (usually called the 'fate' motif) and then a driving string theme that proves to be the dominant idea. Subsequent melodies are taken, in order of appearance, from the final-act duet between Alvaro and Carlo, from Leonora's Act 2 aria 'Madre, pietosa Vergine', and from Leonora's Act 2 duet with Padre Guardiano (two themes, one associated with Leonora, one with the priest). The overture makes few concessions to classical ideas of balance, though it is given at least a surface impression of greater coherence by continual motivic references to the main theme.

ACT I *The Marquis of Calatrava's house in Seville* After twice sounding the three-note unison that began the overture, the scene begins with a restrained string theme, though one with syncopations and minor inflections that hint at troubled undercurrents. The Marquis of Calatrava bids goodnight to his daughter, concerned by her sadness. Leonora can offer only anguished asides. As the Marquis retires, the maid Curra begins preparations for Leonora's elopement with Alvaro, a Byronic figure whose father was a Viceroy in Peru and whose mother was the last descendant of Inca royalty. The heroine's indecision is intense, but Curra outlines the bloody consequences for her lover if he is now deserted. In the aria 'Me pellegrina ed orfana', which is in two contrasting sections and—as befits its dramatic position—involves no large-scale internal repetitions, Leonora bids a tender farewell to her homeland. The sound of approaching horses heralds Alvaro, who climbs in through a window. He immediately launches a four-movement duet, conventionally structured though economical throughout. The first movement, 'Ah, per sempre', is dominated by Alvaro's impetuosity, but when Leonora shows signs of reluctance he settles into a more lyrical second movement, 'Pronti destrieri', which begins as a typical 3/8 wooing piece for romantic tenor but develops unusual vocal power as Alvaro recalls the gods of his native land. The third movement (somewhat revised for 1869) as usual injects new action: Leonora begs that the elopement be postponed another day, protesting her love amid weeping that makes Alvaro suspicious; he accuses her of not loving him; she passionately affirms her feelings—and so to the cabaletta, 'Seguirti fino agl'ultimi', in which the lovers prepare to depart, and which is skilfully structured so that the final, curtailed reprise is preceded and precipitated by the sound of approaching footsteps. A brief recitative, in which Alvaro draws his pistol, is followed by the Scena-Finale, an action movement dominated by the pulsating main theme of the overture, modulating rapidly and purposefully to match events on stage. The Marquis of Calatrava enters. He insults Alvaro, goading him to a duel; Alvaro refuses and throws down his pistol. But the weapon accidentally discharges, fatally wounding the old man, who with his dying breath curses his daughter. Alvaro and Leonora make their escape, thus closing one of the most tightly constructed, economical acts in all Verdi.

ACT 2 Scene i *The village of Hornachuelos and its surroundings* This scene is as expansive and repetitious as the previous one was tight and economical. Eighteen months have passed. The opening chorus, 'Holà! Ben giungi, o mulattier', gives way to a peasant dance, both pieces richly imbued with Spanish local colour (the first more than a little reminiscent of passages in *Il trovatore*). Supper is announced and a 'student' (Don Carlo, in search of his sister and her 'seducer') says grace. The dance music continues. Leonora enters dressed as a young man, recognizes her brother, and immediately retreats. The stage is now taken by Preziosilla, who encourages the young men to join battle against the Germans; she sings a rousing Canzone, 'Al suon del tamburo', a French-influenced strophic song with refrain, which recalls Oscar's music in *Un ballo in maschera*. During the final stages of the song Preziosilla agrees to read Carlo's fortune; she predicts a miserable future.

A chorus of pilgrims is heard in the distance; their chant forms the basis of a large-scale concertato movement, 'Padre Eterno Signor', which is punctuated by Leonora's desperate cries for divine mercy. As the pilgrims depart, Carlo takes centre stage and treats the company to a narrative Ballata, 'Son Pereda, son ricco d'onore': his name is Pereda and he has been helping a friend track down the friend's sister and her lover. The predictable form and simple rhythm retain something of the comic opera atmosphere, although contrasting internal episodes give hints of tragic undercurrents. But Preziosilla and the others are happy enough, and the scene ends with elaborate exchanges of 'goodnight' and a lively reprise of the opening chorus and dance tune.

Scene ii *A small clearing on the slopes of a steep mountain* Leonora struggles towards the door of a monastery, and in a turbulent recitative recalls her horror at hearing her brother's story in the inn, especially his news that Alvaro, from whom she was separated in flight, has returned to his homeland in South America. She falls on her knees to beg divine forgiveness in 'Madre, pietosa Vergine', which is a minor-major Romanza, the first part underpinned by an obsessive string motif, the second based on the aspiring melody that had served as climax to the overture.

Leonora rings the monastery bell; it is answered by Melitone (a comic character), who departs to find Padre Guardiano (Father Superior). As she waits anxiously, the heroine sings a further arioso in which the overture's main theme is once again juxtaposed with the aspiring melody. The Padre appears and dismisses Melitone, so beginning one of the opera's grand duets. After a brief scena, the number falls into the conventional four movements, although with the basic difference that Leonora and Padre Guardiano have comparatively little vocal interaction: both remain enclosed within their very different views of the world. The first movement, 'Infelice, delusa', has as usual a series of sharply contrasting episodes, as Leonora tells her story and begs for refuge. The second movement, 'Chi può legger nel futuro', offers a brief respite as the two voices come together, but in the third contrast returns. Eventually Padre Guardiano agrees to help Leonora, and they join in a final cabaletta, 'Sull'alba il piede all'eremo'.

The great door of the church opens, and a long procession of monks files down the sides of the choir. In a solemn ritual, Padre Guardiano tells the monks that a hermit is to live in the holy cave, and that no one must invade his seclusion. All join in a curse on any violator, 'Il cielo fulmini, incenerisca'. The act closes with a quiet, simple hymn, 'La Vergine degli Angeli', before Leonora sets off to her hermitage.

ACT 3 Scene i *In Italy, near Velletri: a wood, at dead of night*   Both Alvaro and Carlo have become involved in the War of the Austrian Succession, which is raging about them. A robust orchestral introduction and
offstage chorus are hushed as Alvaro comes forward to the strains of a
long clarinet solo, which elaborates a theme first heard in the Act 1 love
duet. In an arioso punctuated by wisps of clarinet sound, Alvaro explains
his noble birth and unhappy childhood. Then, in 'Oh, tu che in seno agli
angeli', he asks Leonora (whom he believes dead) to look down on him
from heaven. The aria begins in conventionally patterned phrases but soon
takes on that 'progressive' form so typical of Verdi's later style. Offstage
noises disrupt Alvaro's pensive mood, and he departs to investigate. Moments later he returns with Carlo, having saved him from assassins. The
two exchange false names and then swear eternal allegiance in a brief,
sparsely accompanied duet. Further offstage cries alert them to a renewed
enemy attack; they rush off together to join the battle.

Scene ii *Morning: the quarters of a senior officer of the Spanish army*   As
the scene changes, the orchestra depicts a battle and a surgeon describes its
progress. Although victory is announced, Alvaro is carried on severely
wounded. Carlo tries to rally him, promising the Order of Calatrava; but
Alvaro reacts violently to the name. The wounded man requests a private
interview with Carlo, and in the famous duet 'Solenne in quest'ora' entrusts his new friend with the key to a case wherein lies a packet to be burnt
if Alvaro dies. The 'duet', dominated by Alvaro, is reminiscent of a traditional minor-major Romanza: the opening minor section as the tenor issues his solemn commands, the major emerging as he rejoices that he can
now die in peace. Alvaro is carried off. Left alone, Carlo recalls his new
companion's reaction at the name of Calatrava and begins to suspect that
he may be Leonora's seducer. He unlocks the case and is tempted to break
open the packet, but in 'Urna fatale', an Andante sostenuto within whose
early-nineteenth-century conventionality is buried powerful progressive
elements, he expostulates on how his honour forbids him from finding
the truth. He looks elsewhere in the case and soon finds a portrait of
Leonora. Just then the surgeon announces that Alvaro will live, and Carlo,
knowing he will now be able to exact his vengeance, breaks into a cabaletta
of savage joy, 'Egli è salvo!'

Scene iii *A military encampment near Velletri*   In the 1862 version the
scene progresses from a long choral episode to the quarrel between Alvaro
and Carlo, an offstage duel, and then to a closing two-movement aria for

Alvaro; the 1869 version—which defers the choral episode to the end of the act, has the duel onstage and omits Alvaro's aria—has much to commend it, not least that it clarifies the action and shortens one of Verdi's most demanding tenor roles. The scene opens with a comic-opera style chorus, 'Compagni, sostiamo' (new for 1869), in which a patrol makes a tour of inspection. Alvaro enters, accompanied by a minor-mode version of the clarinet theme that introduced him earlier in the act. Carlo joins him and, after innocently inquiring whether his wounds are healed (we must assume that several days have passed since the previous scene), calls Alvaro by his true name, so precipitating a grand, multimovement duet. The first movement is the traditional series of contrasting sections: Carlo reveals his own identity, Alvaro protests his innocence and finally Carlo informs Alvaro that Leonora is still alive. The second movement, 'No, d'un imene il vincolo', is a powerfully 'dissimilar' Andantino, in which Alvaro celebrates the news of his beloved's survival only to be confounded by Carlo's insistence on revenge. This leads swiftly to a closing cabaletta, 'Morte! Ov'io non cada', in which the two swear mutual defiance and begin to fight. But they are separated by a passing patrol; Carlo is dragged off, and Alvaro casts away his sword, swearing that he will seek refuge in the cloister.

Rolls on the side drum introduce the sequence of choruses and brief solos that will close the act. First comes 'Lorchè pifferi e tamburi', a lively chorus that leads directly into Preziosilla's two-strophe, French-influenced song 'Venite all'indovina', in which she offers to tell the soldiers' fortunes. A further brief round of choral celebrations precedes Trabuco's 'A buon mercato', a Jewish pedlar song in which the chorus again joins. The mood darkens with the next episode, in which a group of beggars, their lands destroyed by the war, are followed by a group of miserable conscripts. But some vivandières and Preziosilla soon brighten the atmosphere, leading the conscripts in a tarantella. Melitone enters as the dance is at full tilt and treats the company to an elaborate comic sermon (the passage is taken almost word for word from Maffei's translation of Schiller's *Wallensteins Lager*). The soldiers eventually tire of Melitone and chase him away, leaving Preziosilla to round off the act with a 'Rataplan' chorus.

ACT 4 Scene i *Inside the monastery of Our Lady of the Angels, near Hornachuelos* Five years have passed. A crowd of beggars appears, quickly followed by Melitone carrying a cauldron of soup. In a comic-opera *parlante*, Melitone chides the beggars for requesting too much, continuing even when Padre Guardiano advises kindness to the suffering poor. Eventually

Melitone's patience runs out: he kicks the pot over and orders the beggars away in the comic cabaletta 'Il resto, a voi prendetevi'. In the subsequent recitative, Melitone mentions to Padre Guardiano the strange behaviour of 'Father Raffaele' (we soon guess that this must be Alvaro). The Padre counsels patience in a brief closing duet, 'Del mondo i disinganni', which contrasts his solemn ecclesiastical style with Melitone's frankly comic idiom.

The monastery bell rings; Melitone answers it to find Carlo, who dispatches him to seek 'Father Raffaele'. In the ensuing recitative Carlo reiterates his desire to avenge the family honour. Alvaro enters, thus initiating a grand duet in which the traditional four movements are still present, albeit radically altered in light of the dramatic situation. The first movement, 'Col sangue sol cancellasi', offers the usual stark contrasts: Carlo's calls for a duel are underpinned by a martial theme in the orchestra; Alvaro's offers of peace are more lyrical and subdued. The central Andante, 'Le minaccie, i fieri accenti', based on the second theme of the overture, is of the 'dissimilar' type, with Alvaro's opening melody repeated by Carlo with agitated orchestral accompaniment. The movement breaks down as Carlo taunts Alvaro as a half-breed: this is too much, and Alvaro takes up the challenge. Before rushing off to fight, the two offer mutual defiance in a very brief, coda-like cabaletta, 'Ah, segnasti la tua sorte!'

Scene ii *A valley amid inaccessible rocks*   Strains of the overture's main theme introduce Leonora, pale, worn and in great agitation. Her famous aria, 'Pace, pace, mio Dio!', in which she restates her love for Alvaro and begs God for peace, is like a distant homage to Bellini, whose 'long, long, long melodies' Verdi so admired. Length indeed is here, as is the simple arpeggiated accompaniment typical of Bellini, but Verdi's line is injected with declamatory asides and harmonic shifts, a perfect expression of the new aesthetic that had overtaken Italian opera. As the aria comes to a close, Leonora takes up food left by Padre Guardiano but retreats hurriedly as others approach.

In the 1862 version, the final scene reaches a bloody conclusion. Alvaro and Carlo enter duelling; Carlo falls mortally wounded; Alvaro summons Leonora. On recognizing each other they sing a brief duettino before Carlo calls Leonora to him as he dies, and, vengeful to the last, stabs her fatally. The heroine has a final, intense arioso, 'Vedi destino! io muoio!', before dying in Alvaro's arms. Sounds are heard below, and the monks appear. Padre Guardiano calls out to Alvaro, but he retreats to the highest point of the mountain and hurls himself into the abyss. For the 1869 version, Verdi decided on a radical change. The opening arioso, which includes the offstage duel up to Alvaro and Leonora's meeting, is largely the same, but there is no duettino for the lovers, merely a continuation of the declamation until Leonora departs to help her brother. Alvaro has time for a brief soliloquy before an offstage scream interrupts him. Leonora, mortally wounded, is led on by Padre Guardiano: furious, dissonant 'death figures' in the orchestra cause a breakdown in the musical flow. But from this arises the final, lyrical trio, 'Non imprecare, umiliati', led off in the minor by Padre Guardiano. At first the two lovers can offer only fragmentary comments, but then the music turns to the major, and a new, transfiguring melody arises from the orchestra, over which Alvaro declaims that he is 'redeemed'. Leonora leads off the final section, which concludes the opera with a sense of resolution and lyrical space.

*   *   *

La for₂a del destino reached something of a low point in the early years of the twentieth century, its sprawling action and mixture of comic, tragic, and picturesque finding no resonance in a climate dominated by the Wagnerian model. But times have changed, and since the 1930s the opera has become one of the more popular of Verdi's works. This swing of fortune suggests an important shift in our expectations of what constitutes satisfying musical drama, because *La for₂a* is undoubtedly Verdi's most daring attempt at creating a 'patchwork' drama—or, as he once called it, an 'opera of ideas'. As in *Un ballo in maschera*, there are attempts boldly to incorporate a variety of styles, but the mixture is far less controlled, with little of the earlier opera's balance. The famously episodic plot and extended geographical and temporal span is matched by an extraordinary range of operatic manners: frankly post-Rossinian *buffa* with Fra Melitone; frankly *opéra comique* with Preziosilla; Meyerbeerian scenes of religious grandeur; and at the centre a classic love-triangle in the best Italian tradition. We look in vain for the kind of unifying colours found in *Rigoletto* or *Il trovatore*, and it is surely no accident that Verdi's 1869 revision could so radically change certain sequences in the action, even—as in Act 3—transferring passages from one part of a scene to another. The revision's radical alteration of the dénouement, replacing the *fatalità* of the original melodramatic ending with a trio of religious consolation, is, rather than a clarification of the drama, merely the replacing of one possible stylistic strand with another. The opera is, in other words, only loosely linear: a significant precursor of 'native' Russian operas such as *Prince Igor* and *Boris Godunov*.

The presence of certain recurring themes, in particular the main theme of the overture (frequently dubbed a 'destiny' or 'fate' motif) has often been mentioned by commentators and is sometimes advanced as exemplifying the score's 'musical unity'. Perhaps that is so, but one could equally well see these recurring elements as an attempt to give some semblance of musical connectedness to a score that conspicuously lacks the cohesion Verdi so effortlessly achieved in his middle-period works. Nor are the themes used in anything like a consistent manner. An opera such as this, whose time gaps and scope make necessary a steady sequence of narratives (all the major characters are obliged to explain their past actions to each other), might easily have used a system of recurring motifs on a large scale. Nothing like that is attempted; indeed, in one sense the recurring motifs by their very literalness alert us to the extravagant gaps that are constantly and excitingly thrown up by this most challenging of works.

Don Carlos

Opéra in five acts set to a libretto by Joseph Méry and Camille Du Locle after Friedrich von Schiller's dramatic poem *Don Carlos, Infant von Spanien*; first performed in Paris, Opéra, on 11 March 1867. The revised *Don Carlos*, in four acts (the French text was revised by Du Locle, and an Italian translation was supplied by Achille de Lauzières and Angelo Zanardini), was first performed in Milan, Teatro alla Scala, on 10 January 1884.

The cast at the 1867 première included Louis-Henri Obin (Philippe), Paul Morère (Don Carlos), Jean-Baptiste Faure (Posa), Marie Sasse (Elisabeth), and Pauline Guéymard-Lauters (Eboli). The cast for the 1884 revised version included Alessandro Silvestri (Filippo), Francesco Tamagno (Don Carlo), Paul Lhérie (Rodrigo), Abigaille Bruschi-Chiatti (Elisabetta), and Giuseppina Pasqua (Eboli).

Philippe II, *King of Spain*	bass
Don Carlos, *Infante of Spain*	tenor
Rodrigue, *Marquis of Posa*	baritone
The Grand Inquisitor	bass
Elisabeth de Valois, *Philippe's queen*	soprano
Princess Eboli	mezzo-soprano
Thibault, *Elisabeth de Valois' page*	soprano
The Countess of Aremberg	silent
The Count of Lerma	tenor
An Old Monk	bass
A Voice from Heaven	soprano
A Royal Herald	tenor

| Flemish Deputies | basses |
| Inquisitors | basses |

Lords and ladies of the French and Spanish court, woodcutters, populace, pages, guards of Henry II and Philippe II, monks, officers of the Inquisition, soldiers

Setting France and Spain, about 1560

Schiller's *Don Carlos* had been suggested to Verdi—and rejected by him— as a possible subject for the Paris Opéra in the early 1850s, when negotiations were beginning for the work that would become *Les Vêpres siciliennes*. In 1865, with another full-scale Verdi grand opera being planned for Paris's foremost theatre, the composer clearly saw new potential in the subject. Emile Perrin, the new director of the Opéra, had discussed various topics with Verdi, for the most part via the composer's French publisher and friend Léon Escudier. Verdi pronounced *King Lear*, ever near to his heart at this period, too lacking in spectacle for the Opéra; *Cleopatra* was better, but the lovers would not arouse sufficient sympathy. *Don Carlos*, however, was now 'a magnificent drama', even though Verdi immediately saw the need to add two new scenes to the scenario offered him: one between the Inquisitor and Philippe, the other between Philippe and Posa. As the libretto took shape, the composer took his usual active part in advising on everything from large structural matters to minute details of phrasing and vocabulary.

Verdi worked steadily on the opera during the first half of 1866 and arrived in Paris in July of that year with most of the score completed. Then came the notoriously long, arduous rehearsal period at the Opéra, during which Verdi made several important changes, including the addition of a scene for Elisabeth at the start of Act 5. As rehearsals neared completion in February 1867 it became clear that the opera was too long, and Verdi made substantial cuts, among which were the lengthy and impressive Prelude and Introduction to Act 1, part of the Philippe-Posa duet in Act 2, and both the Elisabeth-Eboli and the Carlos-Philippe duets in Act 4. The première was not a great success, and *Don Carlos* disappeared from the Opéra repertory after 1869.

Early Italian revivals, in a translation by Achille de Lauzières, were sometimes successful; but the opera's length continued to present problems, and it was frequently given in severely cut versions. In 1872 Verdi himself made further revisions, restoring and rewriting passages of the

Philippe-Posa duet and cutting a portion of the final duet between Carlos and Elisabeth. Then, in 1882–83, he made a thoroughgoing revision, in part to reduce the opera to more manageable proportions, in part to replace pieces he now found unsatisfactory. The most important cuts were the whole of Act 1 (although Carlos's aria was inserted into the following act), the ballet and its preceding scene in Act 3, and the Act 5 Inquisitors' chorus. Many other passages were revised, recomposed, or reordered. The La Scala première of this new, four-act version, was given in Italian translation. Some two years later a further Italian version, which restored the original Act 1, began to be performed and was published (we must assume with Verdi's approval).

It is important to bear in mind that, although the 1884 version was first given in Italian, the revisions Verdi made were to a French text: in other words, there is no 'Italian version' of *Don Carlos*, merely an 'Italian translation'. The following discussion will move through the opera by act, marking in italics the version to which various passages belong: *1867* means the version eventually performed at the Parisian première, *1884* the substantially revised four-act version. Where appropriate, French incipits are followed by their Italian equivalents.

✦   ✦   ✳

ACT I *(1867) The forest at Fontainebleau*   An impressive introductory chorus, in which a band of woodcutters laments the hardships of war, was cut during rehearsals, although it is often restored in modern revivals. At the 1867 première the opera started with a brief Allegro brillante; offstage fanfares and huntsmen's calls introduce the princess Elisabeth, who (observed by Carlos) gives alms to the woodcutters and then departs. Carlos, who has arrived incognito from Spain, has now seen for the first time his betrothed; in the brief, Italianate aria, 'Je l'ai vue' ('Io la vidi'), he declares love at first sight. He is about to follow Elisabeth when a horn-call warns him that night is falling. Thibault and Elisabeth become lost in the wood, and Carlos offers help, introducing himself simply as 'a Spaniard'. Thibault goes off for assistance, so making way for the duet that will dominate this brief act. The opening movement, 'Que faites-vous donc?' ('Che mai fate voi?'), is formed from a series of contrasting episodes, the tension rising as Elisabeth eagerly questions this stranger about the Infante Carlos whom she is to marry. Carlos presents her with a portrait of her betrothed, which she immediately recognizes as the man before her. This precipitates the second movement, 'De quels transports' ('Di qual amor'), a cabaletta-like celebration of their good fortune, based on a melody that recurs through the opera as a symbol of their first love.

Their joy is short-lived. Thibault returns to announce that Henri II has decided to give Elisabeth to the widowed Philippe instead of to his son, so decisively putting an end to the war between Spain and France. The couple express their horror in the restrained, minor-mode 'L'heure fatale est sonnée!' ('L'ora fatale è suonata!'), which is immediately juxtaposed with the major-mode offstage chorus of celebration, 'O chants de fête' ('Inni di festa'). The Count of Lerma arrives to request Elisabeth's formal approval of the match, a female chorus adding their pleas for peace. Elisabeth reluctantly accepts, and the stage clears to a triumphant reprise of 'O chants de fête'. Carlos is left alone to bemoan his fate.

ACT 2 (*1867*)/1 (*1884*) Scene i   *The cloister of the St Yuste monastery*
Both versions   A solemn introduction for four horns precedes the offstage chorus 'Charles-Quint, l'auguste Empereur' ('Carlo, il sommo Imperatore'), a funeral dirge for Charles V. A solitary Old Monk adds his prayer to theirs but admits that Charles was guilty of folly and pride.

1867   Carlos enters: he has come to the monastery to forget the past. In a solemnly intoned, sequential passage, 'Mon fils, les douleurs de la terre', the Monk tells him that the sorrows of the world also invade this holy place. The Monk's voice reminds a terrified Carlos of the late emperor himself.

1884   Carlos's extended scena explores his anguish at losing Elisabeth; it culminates in a revised version of 'Je l'ai vue' ('Io la vidi') from the original Act 1 (the act entirely omitted from this version). There follows a curtailed exchange with the Monk.

1867   Rodrigue, Marquis of Posa, appears and is greeted by Carlos. Posa launches into a description of the battles in Flanders (a first portion of this part of the duet, beginning 'J'étais en Flandre', was cut from the 1867 version during rehearsals), and Carlos responds with a lyrical declaration of friendship, 'Mon compagnon, mon ami'. Carlos then admits his secret love for Elisabeth, now the wife of his father Philippe. Posa reiterates his friendship in a reprise of 'Mon compagnon', advising Carlos to forget his sorrows in the battle for Flanders.

1884   The above-described portion of the duet was further condensed and enriched, with a skilful link from the scene with the Monk, and with 'Mon compagnon' becoming 'Mon sauveur, mon ami' ('Mio salvator, mio fratel').

Both versions   The final section of the duet, the cabaletta 'Dieu tu semas dans nos âmes' ('Dio, che nell'alma infondere'), is a 'shoulder-to-shoulder' number reminiscent of Verdi's earliest manner, the tenor and baritone vowing eternal friendship in parallel 3rds. In an impressively scored coda, Philippe, Elisabeth, and a procession of monks cross the stage and enter the monastery. Carlos and Posa join the chanting monks before a thrilling reprise of their cabaletta brings the scene to a close.

Scene ii   *A pleasant spot outside the St Yuste monastery gates*   Eboli and the other ladies-in-waiting are not allowed in the monastery, so they amuse themselves outside. The female chorus sets the scene with 'Sous ces bois au feuillage immense' ('Sotto ai folti, immensi abeti'), and then Eboli sings her famous 'Chanson du voile' (Veil Song), 'Au palais des fées' ('Nel giardin del bello'): the two-stanza song with refrain, packed with both harmonic and instrumental local colour, tells the story of Achmet, a Moorish king who one evening mistakenly wooed his own wife in the garden. A disconsolate Elisabeth appears, soon followed by Posa, who hands the queen a letter from her mother in which is hidden a note from Carlos. As Elisabeth reads, Posa makes courtly conversation with Eboli; but in the background of their dalliance we hear from Elisabeth that Carlos's letter asks her to trust Posa. At a word from Elisabeth, Posa begins his two-stanza Romance, 'L'Infant Carlos, notre espérance' ('Carlo, ch'è sol il nostro amore'), in which he tells how Carlos, rejected by his father, requests an interview with his new 'mother'. In between stanzas, Eboli wonders whether Carlos's dejection has been caused by love for her; Elisabeth trembles with confusion. With the completion of the second stanza, however, Elisabeth agrees to the interview; Posa and Eboli walk off together, and the ladies-in-waiting leave.

The ensuing duet between Carlos and Elisabeth, 'Je viens solliciter' ('Io vengo a domandar'), is one of Verdi's boldest attempts to match musical progress to the rapid alternations of spoken dialogue: there is little sense of a conventional four-movement form (except perhaps for a cabaletta-style ending), the duet instead passing through a rapid series of contrasting episodes, a sense of musical connection coming from repeated motifs. In a controlled opening, Carlos asks Elisabeth to intercede on his behalf with Philippe, who will not allow him to leave for the Spanish possession of Flanders; there is trouble there stemming from religious persecution, and Carlos, who is in sympathy with the dissidents, feels strongly that he can calm the situation. Elisabeth agrees, but Carlos can restrain himself no further and pours out his love. Elisabeth at first attempts to deflect him, but eventually admits her feelings; Carlos falls into a swoon, and Elisabeth fears he is dying. As he awakens he begins a final, passionate declaration, 'Que sous mes pieds' ('Sotto al mio piè'); but when he attempts to embrace his beloved, she recovers herself and angrily rejects him, telling him sarcastically that to claim her he must kill his father. Carlos rushes off in despair, just as Philippe himself appears, angry that Elisabeth has been left alone. He orders her lady-in-waiting, the Countess of Aremberg, back to France; Elisabeth bids the Countess a tender farewell in the two-stanza, minor-major Romance, 'O ma chère compagne' ('Non pianger, mia compagna'). Philippe, left alone, gestures for Posa to remain with him.

1867 After a brief recitative, Posa begins the first movement of a duet by describing his soldierly life ('Pour mon pays') and narrating his journeys in war-torn Flanders ('O Roi! j'arrive de Flandre'). Philippe stresses the need for political control and sternly curbs Posa's idealism. The impasse produces a lyrical second movement, 'Un souffle ardent', in which the two men are placed in patterned opposition before joining voice in a final section. Posa throws himself at Philippe's feet: Philippe forgives his rashness but bids him beware the Inquisitor. The king then confides in Posa, beginning the closing cabaletta, 'Enfant! à mon coeur éperdu', with an admission of his troubled personal feelings.

1884 In this radical revision, virtually all trace of the conventional four-movement form disappears from the duet, being replaced by the kind of fluid dialogue we find in *Otello*. Posa's 'O Roi! j'arrive de Flandre' ('O signor, di Fiandra arrivo') is retained, but most of the remaining music is new. Particularly impressive is Philippe's advice to beware the Inquisitor, in which solemn chords serve momentarily to halt the musical flow. Philippe is more explicit about his fears, going so far as to mention Carlos and Elisabeth; but he closes the duet with yet another sinister reference to the power of the Inquisitor.

ACT 3 (*1867*)/2 (*1884*) Scene i *The queen's gardens*
1867 Festivities are in progress; Philippe is to be crowned the next day. In a further essay in local colour, an offstage chorus sings 'Que de fleurs et que d'étoiles' to the accompaniment of castanets. Elisabeth appears with Eboli: the queen is already weary of the celebrations and changes masks with Eboli so that she can retire to seek religious consolation. When Elisabeth leaves, Eboli has a brief solo, 'Me voilà reine pour une nuit', which recalls the central section of the Veil Song. She writes a letter of assignation to Carlos, hoping to entice him.

The ensuing ballet, called 'La Pérégrina', tells of a fisherman who happens on a magic cave containing the most marvellous pearls in the ocean. He dances with the White Pearl; gradually the other pearls join in. Philippe's page enters to the strains of a Spanish hymn played by the brass; he has come to find for his master the most beautiful pearl in the world. At the climax of the ballet, Eboli (posing as Elisabeth) appears as La Pérégrina: the page's search is at an end. Verdi's music for the ballet, some fifteen minutes long, is the traditional mixture of orchestral sophistication and relative musical simplicity.

1884 The short, understated prelude is based on the first phrase of Carlos's 'Je l'ai vue' ('Io la vidi'); it clearly belongs to Verdi's late manner, particularly in the overt use of thematic transformation and the ease with which it moves between distantly related keys.

Both versions Carlos enters, reading the letter of assignation; this briefly sets the scene for the ensuing ensemble, which follows the common Italian four-movement pattern, led off by a condensed series of contrasting lyrical episodes, each punctuated by some dramatic revelation. As Eboli appears, Carlos breaks into a passionate declaration of love, thinking she is Elisabeth. Eboli responds with matching phrases, but the lyrical development abruptly breaks down as she removes her mask. Eboli at first misconstrues Carlos's confusion, and attempts to reassure him: but she soon guesses the truth, and accuses him of loving the queen. At this point Posa arrives, and a brief transitional passage leads to the second main movement, 'Redoubtez tout de ma furie!' ('Al mio furor sfuggite invano'), in which the baritone's and mezzo's agitated rhythms are set against the tenor's long, impassioned melody. A brief transition movement during which Carlos restrains Posa from killing Eboli leads to the final stretta, 'Malheur sur toi, fils adultère' ('Trema per te, falso figliuolo'), in which Eboli brings down furious curses on the man who has rejected her and threatens to denounce him. She rushes off, leaving Carlos and Posa alone; in a brief coda, Carlos—after some hesitation—entrusts his friend with some secret papers. The scene concludes with a brash orchestral reprise of their earlier cabaletta, 'Dieu tu semas dans nos âmes' ('Dio, che nell'alma infondere').

Scene ii *A large square in front of Valladolid Cathedral* This central finale, the grand sonic and scenic climax of *Don Carlos*, is formally laid out along traditional Italian lines but, in response to the added resources of the Opéra, is on a scale Verdi had never before attempted. The opening chorus,

'Ce jour heureux' ('Spuntato ecco il dì'), is a kind of rondò: the main theme alternates with a funereal passage in which monks escort heretics to the stake, and with a more lyrical idea in which the monks promise salvation to those who repent. A solemn procession fills the stage; a herald announces Philippe, who appears on the steps of the cathedral. He is confronted by six Flemish deputies, escorted by Carlos. They kneel before him and, with a solemn prayer for their country, 'Sire, la dernière heure' ('Sire, no, l'ora estrema'), lead off a grand concertato movement in which all the principals join: Elisabeth, Carlos, and Posa add their pleas to those of the deputies; Philippe and the monks stubbornly resist. A transitional movement begins as Carlos steps forward, asking to be sent to Flanders. When Philippe refuses, Carlos threateningly draws his sword. No one dares intervene until Posa steps forward and demands Carlos's surrender. To a soft, veiled reprise of their friendship cabaletta, Carlos relinquishes his weapon, upon which Philippe pronounces Posa promoted to a dukedom. The scene closes with a grand reprise of the opening choral sequence. As the heretics go to their death, a voice from heaven assures them of future bliss.

ACT 4 (*1867*)/3 (*1884*) Scene i *The king's study*   The king, alone with his official papers, sings the famous soliloquy 'Elle ne m'aime pas!' ('Ella giammai m'amò!'). As a complex psychological portrait, the aria has few rivals in Verdi. The king's mood swings from self-pity at his emotional isolation (an arioso accompanied by obsessive string figures and culminating in the passionate outburst of 'Elle ne m'aime pas!'), to a sombre meditation on his mortality (mock-medieval horns accompany his picture of the stone vault in which he will lie), to a recognition of his power (a triplet bass melody hinting at the musical grandeur of the preceding concertato). But the aria closes with a reprise of its opening outburst: Philippe's tragedy, at this point in the drama, is primarily a personal one.

The subsequent duet with the old and blind Grand Inquisitor, 'Suis-je devant le Roi?' ('Sono io dinanzi al Re?'), continues the aria's relative formal freedom, the sense that the musical flow reacts immediately and flexibly to the shifting emotions of the dialogue. The opening orchestral idea, with its concentration on low strings, ostinato rhythms, and restricted pitches, sets the scene for a mighty power struggle between two basses. Philippe seems in command as he asks the Inquisitor how to deal with Carlos and his support for the religious reforms in Flanders; but, as the controlled opening gives way to freer declamation, the Inquisitor takes over, stating that Posa, with his liberal idealism, is the more serious threat and demanding that he be turned over to the Inquisition. Philippe resists, but in an imposing declamatory climax the Inquisitor warns him that even kings can be brought before the tribunal. As the opening orchestral idea returns, Philippe attempts to restore peace; but the Inquisitor is indifferent and leaves Philippe in no doubt as to how the struggle will be resolved.

The Scène et Quatour that follows (much revised for the 1884 version) is more conventionally structured. To the kind of lyrically enriched recitative that was now the Verdian norm, Elisabeth rushes in to announce the theft of her jewel case. Philippe produces it—Eboli had purloined it—and invites her to reveal its contents; when she refuses he breaks the lock and finds inside a picture of Carlos. Deaf to her protestations, Philippe accuses her of adultery; the queen faints, and Philippe summons Posa and Eboli, who arrive to precipitate the formal quartet, 'Maudit soit le soupçon infâme' ('Ah! sii maledetto, sospetto fatale'). The ensemble is at first dominated by Philippe, whose opening statements—fragmentary expressions of remorse—gradually form into a lyrical idea that interweaves with Posa's decision to take action and Eboli's cries of remorse. But towards the end Elisabeth's sorrowful lament takes on increasing urgency and focus.

Philippe and Posa leave. Originally the scene continued with a duet for Elisabeth and Eboli, but this was omitted during rehearsals for the 1867 première, when the cut extended some way into Eboli's confession; however, Verdi recomposed and expanded this for the 1884 version, in which Eboli first admits her love for Carlos and then, over a bare, almost motifless rhythmic idea in the strings, reveals that she has been the king's mistress. Elisabeth orders Eboli to quit the court, and then departs. Eboli's ensuing aria, 'O don fatal' ('O don fatale'), in which she laments her fatal beauty, is cast in a conventional minor-major form, with the major section (in which she bids farewell to the queen) strongly reminiscent in its chromaticism and wide-spaced orchestral sonority of Verdi's last style. In a cabaletta-like coda, Eboli resolves to spend her final hours at court in an attempt to save Carlos.

Scene ii *Carlos's prison* A string introduction of unusual depth and density introduces Posa to the waiting Carlos. Posa bids farewell to his friend in a touching Romance, 'C'est mon jour suprême' ('Per me giunto è il dì supremo'), and then explains that he has made sure that he, and not Carlos, is implicated in the secret papers Carlos gave him. A shot rings out; Posa falls mortally wounded. After telling Carlos that Elisabeth awaits him at the monastery of St Yuste, he delivers a second Romance, 'Ah! je meurs' ('Io morrò'), happy that he can die for the sake of his dear friend. A duet for Philippe and Carlos that followed this episode was cut before the 1867 première, although Verdi drew on its material for the 'Lacrymosa' of the *Messa da Requiem*. There follows a riot scene (subsequently pruned for the 1884 version) in which Eboli appears at the head of a group intent on liberating Carlos. Philippe also appears, but the crowd is silenced by the entry of the Inquisitor, who orders all to their knees before the king.

ACT 5 (*1867*)/4 (*1884*) *The monastery at St Yuste*   An extended orchestral prelude introduces Elisabeth at the tomb of Charles V. Her aria, 'Toi qui sus le néant' ('Tu, che le vanità'), is in French ternary form: the outer sections are a powerful invocation of the dead emperor, and their firm, periodic structure stabilizes the number, allowing for remarkable variety and musical contrast during the long central section in which the queen's thoughts stray to memories of the past. Carlos appears for their final duet (from here to the end of the opera, Verdi made a number of important revisions in 1884). The sequence begins with the conventional series of contrasting sections, in the most prominent of which, 'J'avais fait un beau rêve' ('Sogno dorato io feci!'), Carlos announces that he has done with dreaming and will now try to save Flanders. The final movement, 'Au revoir dans un monde' ('Ma lassù ci vedremo'), a kind of ethereal cabaletta in which the couple bid each other a tender farewell, is similar to the closing duet of *Aida* in its restraint and delicate orchestral fabric. As they bid each other 'Adieu! et pour toujours', Philippe bursts in with the Inquisitor and various officials. The king tries to deliver his son to the priests, but Carlos retreats towards the tomb of Charles V. The tomb opens and the Old Monk appears, wearing the emperor's crown and mantle. He gathers Carlos to him and, with a few sententious words, draws him into the cloister.

*   *   *

Don Carlos was Verdi's second and final attempt to write a French grand opera, and after the experiences of the previous three Italian operas he was clearly more secure in his handling of the large French canvas, particularly in matching his lyrical gifts to the French language. However, soon after the 1867 première the composer voiced doubts about the entire grand opera tradition. While he was always ready to praise the care with which productions were mounted—particularly in comparison with much of Italy, where he often judged standards to be unacceptably low—he was also aware that the sheer size of the undertaking, the number of different demands that had to be catered for, could take their toll on a work's balance and coherence of effect. He might well have had *Don Carlos* in mind. As we have seen, the opera in rehearsal proved impracticably long; the subsequent cuts were made for practical rather than dramatic reasons, leaving the 1867 version with many inconsistencies and imbalances. Clearly some of the outstanding problems were put right by the revisions of the 1870s and 1880s; but even the final versions of the opera pose uncomfortable dramatic questions.

Possibly the most serious difficulty comes in the comparative weight assumed by various characters. Philippe and Eboli are the most successful and well-rounded portraits, and arguably Elisabeth achieves her proper sense of importance only by means of her magnificent fifth-act aria and final duet with Carlos. Posa's musical physiognomy is strangely old-fashioned: his music almost all dates from the earliest layers of the score, and even then recalls the Verdi of the early 1850s (or even 1840s). On the other hand, it can be argued that this sense of anachronism is in keeping with Posa's dramatic position—as a nostalgic look at youthful days of action within the context of sterner political realities. With Carlos, however, few would deny an unsolved problem: his musical portrait never seems to find a centre, a true nexus of expression such as each of the other principals eventually achieves.

It is perhaps an indication of our changing views and tastes that, in spite of these difficulties, *Don Carlos* has of late become one of the best-loved and most respected of Verdi's operas. The simple fact is, of course, that Verdi dedicated to the work some of his greatest dramatic music. One need think only of the magnificent series of confrontational duets that form such a large part of the drama. As has been noted earlier, several of these break decisively with traditional models, forging for themselves a vital new relationship between musical and dramatic progress. It is for such moments that *Don Carlos* will be remembered and treasured, and they will surely continue to prove more powerful than any large-scale dramatic obstacles the work might present. What is more, even the opera's famously unstable text has proved a stimulus to modern performers, encouraging them to choose creatively among the versions Verdi left us, and so renewing their and their audiences' interpretive energies.

Aida

Opera in four acts set to a libretto by Antonio Ghislanzoni after a scenario by Auguste Mariette; first performed in Cairo, Opera House, on 24 December 1871.

The cast at the première included Eleonora Grossi (Amneris), Antonietta Pozzoni-Anastasi (Aida), Pietro Mongini (Radames), and Francesco Steller (Amonasro).

The King of Egypt	bass
Amneris, *his daughter*	mezzo-soprano
Aida, *an Ethiopian slave*	soprano
Radames, *Captain of the Guards*	tenor
Ramfis, *Chief Priest*	bass
Amonasro, *King of Ethiopia, Aida's father*	baritone
The High Priestess	soprano
A Messenger	tenor

Priests, priestesses, ministers, captains, soldiers, functionaries, Ethiopian slaves and prisoners, Egyptian populace, etc.

Setting Memphis and Thebes, during the reign of the Pharaohs

During the late 1860s the search for suitable librettos began to cause Verdi increasing problems. One of his most active helpers was the French librettist and impresario Camille Du Locle, with whom Verdi had collaborated in the making of *Don Carlos*. Du Locle sent Verdi a stream of possible subjects covering a wide variety of genres: from comic plots that might have continued the manner of *Un ballo in maschera* to large-scale dramas suitable for conversion into grand opera. But Verdi became more and more difficult to please, finding the comic subjects structurally or temperamentally unsuitable, while often complaining of the 'patchwork' quality of grand opera and its inherent lack of coherence. The breakthrough came in the early months of 1870, when Du Locle sent Verdi a scenario by the archaeologist and Egyptologist Auguste Mariette, based on an invented story set in Egyptian antiquity. Verdi had the previous year declined to supply an inaugural hymn as part of the celebrations to open the Suez Canal; but he accepted this new Egyptian idea—which was to open the new Cairo Opera House—almost immediately, appointing as librettist Antonio Ghislanzoni, his collaborator in the revised *La forza del destino*. Work on the opera, whose scenario was adapted and enlarged by both Du Locle and Verdi, proceeded through 1870, Verdi as usual taking a considerable hand in the libretto's formation, even in minor details of line length and wording. The stage sets for the Cairo première were, as was often the case in an increasingly international operatic world, constructed in Paris.

As the composer decided not to attend the première, he proceeded to complete the orchestration of his score in Italy; but by that stage it was clear that production of the opera would be delayed by the Franco-Prussian War, the siege of Paris having trapped the sets and costumes there. There was in addition a series of intense struggles over the première cast, in which as usual Verdi took a close interest. Eventually *Aida* was premièred in Cairo—with predictable success—in late 1871, directed by the famous double bass player Giovanni Bottesini. Verdi also devoted great attention to the Italian première at La Scala, making various slight changes to the score and minutely rehearsing a carefully chosen group of principals. This second performance, conduced by Franco Faccio, took place on 8 February 1872 and included Maria Waldmann (Amneris), Teresa Stolz (Aida), Giuseppe Fancelli (Radames), and Francesco Pandolfini (Amonasro). It was again hugely successful with the public, although some of the more sophisticated critics voiced reservations about passages they found conventional or old-fashioned. Verdi was reluctant to allow further performances in Italy without assurances of a sensitive staging, but by the mid-1870s the opera had entered the general repertory, where it has remained to the present day. Some time before the Milanese première, Verdi wrote a full-scale overture; but after hearing it rehearsed he decided to withdraw it and reinstate the prelude.

*　　　*　　　*

The prelude juxtaposes and combines two themes: the first, chromatic and presented on high strings, will be associated with Aida through most of the opera; the second, contrapuntally developed scalar idea will be associated with the priests.

ACT I Scene i *A hall in the King's palace in Memphis*   To the accompaniment of a restrained development of motifs from the prelude, Ramfis and Radames are in conversation: Ramfis advises that the Ethiopian enemy is again on the attack, and that Isis has named the commander of the Egyptian troops. As Ramfis departs, Radames eagerly anticipates becoming that leader, and then muses on his beloved Aida in the Romanza 'Celeste Aida', a ternary-form piece shot through with atmospheric instrumental effects. Radames is then joined by Amneris, who has fallen in love with the young warrior, but who harbours suspicions about the direction of his affections. Their agitated duet, 'Quale inchiesta!', is interrupted by the appearance of Aida (and her characteristic theme); Radames's longing glances confirm Amneris's jealousy. The duet turns into a trio as Amneris relentlessly questions the confused lovers.

   A series of fanfares heralds the King of Egypt accompanied by Ramfis and a large group of followers. A messenger announces that Amonasro, King of the Ethiopians, is leading an army against them; the King of Egypt reveals that Isis has named Radames as their commander. All join in the martial hymn, 'Su! del Nilo', Aida's syncopated countermelody underlining her distress at the forthcoming battle. After a final unison cry of 'Ritorna vincitor!' ('Return victor!') the crowd disperses, leaving Aida alone. Her long, multisectioned arioso, which begins with an anguished verbal echo of the chorus's 'Ritorna vincitor!', explores in depth her predicament: Amonasro is her father, but the victory of her family would see the defeat of her beloved Radames. The soliloquy ends with a delicate but intense prayer, 'Numi, pietà', in which Aida begs the gods to have pity on her suffering.

Scene ii *Inside the temple of Vulcan in Memphis*   The scene is an old-fashioned tableau, so beloved of French grand opera. The opening chorus, 'Possente Fthà', has many gestures to local colour, notably in its use of the melodic diminished 3rd. There follows a priestesses' dance during which Radames is conducted to the altar. In solemn tones, Ramfis bids Radames protect the homeland and then leads off the concertato 'Nume, custode e vindice', which gradually gains in power, mingles with the opening strains of the scene, and culminates in a triumphant cry of 'Immenso Fthà!'.

ACT 2 Scene i *A room in Amneris's apartments*   A chorus of female slaves, singing in praise of Radames's recent victories, is followed by a dance of

Moorish slaves, Amneris punctuating the choral song with a languorous appeal for her warrior to return. Aida is seen approaching, and Amneris dismisses her slaves, to begin one of the great confrontational duets of Verdi's later operas, a number that has echoes of the traditional four-movement form though with equally significant divergences. First comes a succession of contrasting episodes, 'Fu la sorte dell'armi', in which Amneris, with her characteristic sinuous chromaticism, attempts to trap Aida into admitting her love for Radames. Aida's confusion crystallizes into an anguished statement of her identifying theme, but Amneris continues the interrogation by announcing Radames's death, and then by contradicting the news. The intensity of Aida's reactions leaves no doubt of her feelings and, in an Adagio second movement, 'Pietà ti prenda del mio dolore', she begs in vain for Amneris to show mercy. They are interrupted by fanfares and an offstage chorus singing 'Su! del Nilo' from Act 1 (Verdi revised this final section after the first performance in Cairo). Superimposed over the choral background, Amneris and Aida sing a cabaletta-like closing movement, 'Alla pompa che s'appresta', Amneris's line matching the martial atmosphere of the chorus, Aida's minor-mode answer—with syncopated accompaniment—in sharp contrast. Amneris storms out, to leave Aida alone for a last, desperate reprise of 'Numi, pietà'.

Scene ii *One of the city gates of Thebes* The grand concertato finale—one of Verdi's most spacious—begins with a celebratory chorus, 'Gloria all'Egitto', which features interludes for a female group and for the priests, the latter with a version of their characteristic contrapuntal theme. The stage gradually fills to strains of the famous march for 'Egyptian' trumpets; then comes a ballet sequence, full of harmonic and instrumental local colour; then a reprise of 'Gloria all'Egitto' during which the victorious Radames finally appears. Amneris places a laurel wreath on the warrior's head, and the king grants him any wish he may desire. Radames asks that the prisoners be brought forth, and Aida sees among them Amonasro. She inadvertently reveals to all that he is her father, but Amonasro quickly stops her from disclosing his regal identity. The Ethiopian king now takes centre stage to lead off the central slow movement, which begins with his account of the battle and then shades into the main lyrical passage, a prayer for clemency, 'Ma tu, Re, tu signore possente'. The prayer is taken up by Aida and the prisoners, is angrily countered by the priests (who demand death for the defeated), and develops into a broad and lengthy tutti. The set piece over, Radames asks the Egyptian king to show clemency towards the prisoners; Ramfis objects, but Radames carries the day. In a final gesture the king gives him a last reward: Amneris's hand in marriage. The scene concludes with a reprise of 'Gloria all'Egitto', varied and expanded to allow the principals to express their reactions to the new situation.

ACT 3 *The banks of the Nile*   A single note, G, is sustained by a complex blend of orchestral sonorities to invoke moonlight on the banks of the Nile. An offstage chorus adds to the effect by chanting a hymn to Isis, 'O tu che sei d'Osiride'. Amneris and Ramfis disembark from a boat and enter the temple to pray on the eve of Amneris's marriage. Aida's theme sounds as she cautiously enters for a clandestine meeting with Radames. In a Romanza that Verdi added to the opera only at the last minute, 'Oh, patria mia', Aida invokes her long-lost homeland, the restless accompaniment and harmonies combining with a formal layout of remarkable freedom, even for the later Verdi.

Amonasro now appears; the ensuing duet between him and Aida is best seen as the first half of a conventional four-movement number. After a brief scena in which Amonasro shows that he knows of her love for Radames, the first movement, 'Rivedrai le foreste imbalsamate', is the usual juxtaposition of contrasting sections: Amonasro invokes their beautiful homeland and reminds Aida of the cruelty of their enemies, but when she refuses to ask Radames about the route his troops will take, and so help the Ethiopians ambush the Egyptians, he angrily reproaches her in 'Su, dunque, sorgete'. Aida is by now broken down, and in the Andante assai sostenuto second movement, 'Padre! . . . a costoro', painfully accepts her duty to the homeland: her fragmented line is 'healed' by Amonasro and finally flowers into a lyrical acceptance of her fate. As Amonasro hides, Radames appears and a second, more conventional four-movement duet ensues. In a hectic first movement, Radames assures Aida of his love but warns that he must again lead his troops in battle. The Andantino second movement, 'Fuggiam gli ardori inospiti', sees Aida recall the musical idiom of 'Oh, patria mia' in an effort to persuade Radames to run away with her. A brief transition movement, in which Aida accuses the still-reluctant Radames of not loving her, leads to the duet cabaletta, 'Sì: fuggiam da queste mura', in which Radames emphatically agrees to join her in flight. The cabaletta halts abruptly before its final cadences as Aida asks Radames about the route his army will take. As soon as Radames discloses the information, Amonasro emerges from the shadows, triumphantly announcing that his troops will be there to meet the Egyptians. In a closing trio, 'Tu! . . . Amonasro!', Radames rails at his lost honour. Aida and Amonasro try to comfort him, but they delay too long: Amneris and Ramfis appear;

Amonasro tries to kill Amneris but is prevented by Radames; and, as father and daughter rush off, Radames gives himself up to justice at the hands of the priests.

ACT 4 Scene i *A hall in the King's palace*   After an orchestral prelude based on the main theme of the trio in Act 1 scene i, Amneris sings an extended arioso in which she determines to save Radames. He is led on by the guards, and yet another multimovement duet ensues. In the first movement, 'Già i sacerdoti adunansi'. Amneris begs Radames to defend himself; but Radames refuses, having lost all interest in life. The slow movement, 'Ah! tu dei vivere', allows Amneris to declare her love, although Radames still wishes only for death. The main melody of the opening movement returns in the third as Amneris reveals that Aida, whom Radames believed dead along with Amonasro, is still alive. This revelation precipitates a brief cabaletta, 'Chi ti salva', in which Amneris explodes with renewed jealousy and Radames rejoices that he can now die to protect his beloved.

Radames is led back to the dungeon, and a restrained version of the priests' theme, punctuated by anguished cries from Amneris, sounds as the priests and Ramfis follow him in. They chant a solemn prayer, 'Spirto del Nume', before beginning the trial. Radames is accused by Ramfis three times: each time he refuses to answer, the priests brand him traitor ('Traditor!'), and Amneris begs the gods for mercy. The priests then pronounce the horrible sentence: he will be entombed alive below the altar of the god he has outraged. In an unrestrained arioso, Amneris begs for mercy; but the priests are inflexible. As they depart, she hurls after them a bitter curse, 'Empia razza! Anatema su voi!'.

Scene ii *The scene is on two levels: the upper represents the interior of the temple of Vulcan, gleaming with gold and light; the lower is a vault*   Priests are closing the stone over Radames's head as he sings his opening recitative, full of thoughts of Aida. But he hears a groan and quickly finds his beloved: she has stolen into the vault to die in his arms. Their duet has none of the usual contrasting movements, but is rather a sustained piece of delicate lyricism with three main ideas. First comes Radames's 'Morir! sì pura e bella!', in which he laments her death; Aida counters with 'Vedi? . . . di morte l'angelo', whose scoring and vocal style suggest that the heroine is already speeding to a celestial haven. And finally, with the addition of chanting from above, comes the most substantial lyrical idea, 'O terra addio', whose extreme simplicity of formal outline is matched, perhaps permitted, by the unusually angular melodic arch. In the final moments, with the lovers singing 'O terra addio' in unison, Amneris kneels above the vault and implores peace for the soul that lies beneath.

*   *   *

Although *Aida* is still one of Verdi's most popular operas, its reputation has perhaps declined slightly of late, overtaken for the first time by works such as *Don Carlos* and *Simon Boccanegra*. The reasons for this reverse are doubtless complex, but the comparative conservatism of *Aida* must surely have played a part. If any rough division of Verdi's mature output were made according to 'experimental' versus 'conservative' works (with, say, *Rigoletto, La traviata,* and *La forza del destino* in the first category, and *Il trovatore* and *Un ballo in maschera* in the second), then *Aida* would undoubtedly figure with the latter group. In formal terms it shows a consistent attempt to renew (rather than discard) the standard forms of Ottocento opera, with very few essays into the 'musical prose' found in the operas of the previous decade. Above all, it concentrates on the conventional set pieces of grand opera: the grand ceremonial scene and— most of all—the large-scale multisectional duet, of which there are several magnificent examples. True, there is a considerable array of variants within these duets, but both contemporary critics and more recent commentators have nevertheless seen certain elements of their formal structures as throwbacks to an earlier aesthetic. The level of musical characterization is also indicative of this conservative stance. In common with the characters of *Il trovatore* and *Un ballo in maschera*, the principal roles in *Aida*—with the partial exception of Amneris—hardly develop during the opera, tending to remain within their initial vocal personalities as the plot moves their emotions hither and thither.

But to regard the restricted focus of *Aida* purely in these terms is to take a one-sided view of Verdi's capacities as a musical dramatist, and to emphasize unduly the radical aspect of his personality. Indeed, *Aida*'s greatest artistic successes are born of this 'conservatism': in magnificently controlled ceremonial scenes such as Act 2 scene ii—in which a kind of flexible variation technique allows episodes such as the opening chorus to reappear as the culmination of the scene; or in the telling effects gained when various multimovement duets dovetail into each other, as in the sequence that closes Act 3.

There is, moreover, one important aspect in which *Aida* remains the most radical and 'modern' of Verdi's scores: its use of local colour. *Aida*, constantly alluding to its ambience in harmony and instrumentation, is the one Verdi opera that could not conceivably be transported to another geographical location. In this respect it was an important precursor of the influence local colour would come to have over *fin-de-siècle* opera, and an object lesson on the delicacy and control with which this colour could be applied to the standard forms and expressive conventions of Italian opera.

Otello

('Othello')

Dramma lirico in four acts set to a libretto by Arrigo Boito after William Shakespeare's play *Othello, or The Moor of Venice*; first performed in Milan, Teatro alla Scala, on 5 February 1887.

The cast at the première included Francesco Tamagno (Otello), Victor Maurel (Iago), and Romilda Pantaleoni (Desdemona).

Otello, *a Moor, general of the Venetian army*	tenor
Iago, *an ensign*	baritone
Cassio, *a platoon leader*	tenor
Roderigo, *a Venetian gentleman*	tenor
Lodovico, *an ambassador of the Venetian Republic*	bass
Montano, *Otello's predecessor as Governor of Cyprus*	bass
A Herald	bass
Desdemona, *Otello's wife*	soprano
Emilia, *Iago's wife*	mezzo-soprano

Soldiers and sailors of the Venetian Republic, Venetian ladies and gentlemen, Cypriot populace of both sexes, Greek, Dalmatian, and Albanian men-at-arms, island children, an innkeeper, four servants at the inn, common sailors

Setting A maritime city on the island of Cyprus, at the end of the fifteenth century

As the 1870s progressed, Verdi seemed increasingly isolated from current trends in Italian music, in particular by the tendency of both public and composers to look outside Italy (to France and, later, to Germany) for new ideas and aesthetic attitudes. It is against this background that we should examine his reluctance to write new works after the *Messa da Requiem* of 1874: Verdi was a composer who, after being at the forefront of Italian musical taste for more than two decades, found himself accused of being old-fashioned, out of touch with the times; the fact that he probably felt so himself only exacerbated the situation. Those who sought to lure him out of self-imposed retirement, among whom the prime mover was the new young director of the Ricordi publishing house, Giulio Ricordi, had to tread carefully. Ricordi eventually teamed up with Arrigo Boito, the librettist and composer, who in the 1860s had been one of the most visible of the Italian avant-garde, but whose respect for the old maestro grew with the years and with Boito's own gradual conservatism. In June 1879 Ricordi and Boito raised with Verdi the possibility of an *Otello*. Verdi betrayed cautious enthusiasm, and by the end of the year Boito had produced a draft libretto, full of ingenious new rhythmic devices but with an extremely firm dramatic thread.

Although Verdi agreed—with a characteristic show of reluctance—to collaborate with Boito on *Otello*, the project was long in the making. First came the revisions to *Simon Boccanegra* (1881, effected with Boito's help) and to *Don Carlos* (1884). Verdi also bombarded Boito with alterations to the libretto draft of *Otello*, especially to the Act 3 finale, which he felt must furnish occasion for a grand concertato finale in the traditional manner. The opera was then composed in a series of intensive bursts, the comparative speed suggesting that Verdi had previously sketched the music rather thoroughly. The cast was carefully selected and intensively coached by Verdi himself, and the première (conducted by Franco Faccio) was a predictable, indeed a well-nigh inevitable success, even though some critics of course lamented the sophistication and lack of immediacy they found in Verdi's new manner. The opera was soon given in the major European capitals and became an important element of the operatic repertory. Although it has never reached the level of popularity of some of the operas of the 1850s and 1860s—hardly surprising considering the severe vocal and orchestral demands made by the score—*Otello* remains one of the most universally respected of Verdi's operas, often admired even by those who find almost all his earlier works unappealing.

For the Paris première at the Théâtre de l'Opéra in 1894, Verdi added a ballet score to the third act and also made some significant revisions to that act's concertato finale, reducing the musical detail in an effort to bring out the embedded conversations. These revisions were not incorporated into the Italian version and are rarely heard today.

*   *   *

ACT 1 *Outside the castle*   A sudden burst of orchestral dissonance begins the opera with an immediacy Verdi had never before attempted: it was a clear sign that this work would engage with a more realistic notion of musical drama. A violent storm is raging, and the onlookers from the shore, among them Iago, Cassio, and Montano, comment on the fortunes of their leader Otello's ship. The crowd's reaction momentarily coalesces into 'Dio, fulgor della bufera', a desperate prayer to save the ship; but then all is again confusion until, to cries of 'È salvo!', Otello safely arrives. He greets his followers with a ringing salute, 'Esultate!', proudly announcing that the Turks have been beaten. The crowd then closes this opening 'storm' scene with a triumphant victory chorus, 'Vittoria! Sterminio!'.

As the crowd goes about its work, Iago and Roderigo come to the fore. In a texture alternating simple recitative with arioso, Iago assures his friend that Desdemona will soon tire of her new husband, Otello, and thus become available to the besotted Roderigo. Iago then reveals his hatred for Cassio, whom he thinks has unjustly overtaken him in rank. Their conversation is followed by the fireside chorus 'Fuoco di gioia!', a series of contrasting ideas tied together by brilliant orchestral effects imitating the crackling flames. As the fire dies down, Iago encourages Cassio to drink, eventually breaking into the brindisi 'Inaffia l'ugola', a three-stanza song with choral refrain, by the end of which Cassio is far the worse for wine. Roderigo provokes him to a fight, which is interrupted by Montano, who himself becomes embroiled with Cassio. Iago skilfully stage-manages the confusion by ordering Roderigo to call the alarm; soon there is general panic. At the height of the disturbance, Otello enters, sword in hand, and with an imperious gesture, 'Abbasso le spade!' ('Lower your swords!'), restores calm. His inquiry finds Cassio guilty, and he dismisses him from service (to a stifled cry of triumph from Iago).

Desdemona has by now appeared, and Otello tells the crowd to disperse, so that he can be left alone with his new bride. The ensuing love duet, although it bears a certain distant relationship to earlier nineteenth-century practices, is really *sui generis*, the form's tendency towards a series of short, contrasting sections all but obliterating vestiges of any larger, multimovement structure. After a brief orchestral transition as the stage clears, a choir of solo cellos heralds the opening exchange, 'Già nella notte densa'; Otello evokes the nocturnal ambience before Desdemona turns to reminiscences, and in the largest lyrical section, 'Quando narravi l'esule tua vita', recalls with Otello the way in which his stories of past exploits first won her over. At the close of this episode the lovers exchange symmetrical phrases, 'E tu m'amavi per le mie sventure', a paraphrase of Shakespeare's 'She lov'd me for the dangers I had passed, And I lov'd her that she did pity them'. In a Poco più mosso, Otello wishes for death at this moment of ecstasy, but soon their mutual feelings spread forth into a final gesture of intimacy: a thrice-repeated kiss ('Un bacio . . . ancora un bacio') whose intensity is reflected in the *appoggiatura*-laden violin melody and elliptical cadence that underpin the stage action. With a final gesture towards the night, 'Vien . . . Venere splende', Otello leads Desdemona back into the castle. The solo cellos return to effect a tender close.

ACT 2 *A room on the ground floor of the castle* After an orchestral introduction suggesting Iago's busy energy, the villain assures Cassio that with help from Desdemona he will regain his place in Otello's estimation. Iago sends Cassio off to attend her and comes forward to deliver his famous soliloquy, 'Credo in un Dio crudel', a kind of evil credo in which he plays to the hilt his demonic character. As befits Iago's slippery energy, this dynamic outburst hovers between arioso and aria, its devious harmonic and formal twists continuing to the last. Iago now notices Desdemona and Emilia in the garden and offers a *sotto voce* commentary as Cassio approaches them with his suit. Then, seeing Otello approach, he positions himself for the crucial confrontation.

The Otello-Iago duet that ensues continues to the end of the act, although interrupted by a series of set pieces and dialogues that become increasingly caught up in the central action. The first phase of the duet, and its most fragmentary, involves the initial testing of Otello: Iago's teasing questions and repetitions, Otello's angry confusion, and then Iago's first mention of 'jealousy', to a sliding chromatic figure of great harmonic audacity. The first set-piece interruption is a jarring one: Desdemona is seen again in the garden, and distant voices serenade her in a simple chorus, 'Dove guardi splendono raggi', a piece whose musical atmosphere recalls the choral evocations of Act 1 in both style and tonality. As the chorus ends, Desdemona approaches Otello and asks him to intercede on Cassio's behalf. But Otello's response is disjointed and distracted: so much so that Desdemona gently asks for pardon in a second set piece, the quartet 'Dammi la dolce e lieta parola', in which Otello bemoans his imagined loss while Iago extracts from Emilia a handkerchief of Desdemona's that has been cast aside in the preceding dialogue. As the quartet comes to a close, Otello dismisses Desdemona and Emilia, and is again left alone with Iago. This time the emotional temperature is near boiling point, and a few comments from Iago are enough to precipitate the aria 'Ora e per sempre addio', in which Otello bids farewell to his past life in a closed form that, appropriately given the dramatic situation, has strong hints of the younger Verdi's lyrical style. The aria disintegrates into furious orchestral figures as Otello demands proof of his wife's infidelity, eventually grabbing Iago by the throat and hurling him to the ground. Iago now takes over and gradually calms the atmosphere. He then launches a gentle, seductively chromatic narrative, 'Era la notte', in which—to a musical structure as complex and surprising as Otello's was simple and direct—he offers as 'proof' some words he has overheard Cassio mumble in his sleep. From there to the end of the act, all is gathering dramatic energy. Iago produces Desdemona's handkerchief—which he claims to have seen in Cassio's hands—as a final, visible proof, and Otello unleashes the cabaletta, 'Sì, pel ciel', in which he and then Iago swear to exact a terrible vengeance.

ACT 3 *The great hall of the castle*   An orchestral introduction derived from Iago's Act 2 description of jealousy shows that his machinations are still working. A herald announces the imminent arrival of Venetian ambassadors; Iago directs Otello to conceal himself and await the arrival of Cassio and further 'proof'. As Iago retires, Desdemona appears for the second of her extended duets with Otello; like the first, it is loosely structured around contrasting sections, with a prominent thematic reminiscence to aid the sense of closure. First comes 'Dio ti giocondi, o sposo', in which the semblance of lyrical normality (a patterned exchange in the voices, and periodic phrasing) soon gives way to agitated, fragmentary music as Desdemona mentions the plight of Cassio. Otello describes with repressed intensity the magical properties of the handkerchief Desdemona has mislaid, his anger rising further as she again attempts to deflect him into talk of Cassio. Finally he hurls at her a brutal accusation of infidelity. Desdemona is crushed and at first can only murmur confusedly; but then, with 'Io prego il cielo per te', her melody flows into the lyrical centre of the duet as she prays for Otello and bids him look at the first tears she has shed through grief. Otello at first seems calmed by this outburst, but soon his accusations return with added fury. As a cruel parting gesture, he recalls the calmer opening music of the duet, only to break it off with a gross insult and push Desdemona from the room.

Otello returns to centre stage for his most extended solo of the opera, the self-pitying soliloquy 'Dio! mi potevi scagliar', which begins in barely coherent fragments, rises gradually to a controlled lyricism, and again collapses, this time into furious invective. Iago appears and quickly takes charge, leading Otello aside to where he can observe Cassio; he then engages Cassio in discussion of his dalliance with the courtesan Bianca (Otello believes that Desdemona is the subject of their conversation). The Terzetto 'Essa t'avvince coi vaghi rai', set in the form of a scherzo and trio, skilfully counterposes Iago's and Cassio's comic exchange with Otello's anguished commentary. Cassio even produces Desdemona's handkerchief (hidden in his lodgings by Iago); Iago's elaborate description of this item forms a hectic stretta to the Terzetto.

Offstage trumpets announce the arrival of Venetian ambassadors. As the ceremonial sounds approach, Otello hurriedly discusses with Iago the method by which Desdemona should die; they agree that she should be strangled in her bed. As Iago slips off to fetch Desdemona the dignitaries appear, welcomed by a choral salute. Lodovico gives Otello a letter from the Doge, but is disturbed in his ensuing conversation with Desdemona by Otello's violent interruptions, especially when she voices the hope that Cassio will be reinstated. Otello reports that the letter calls him back to Venice, with Cassio left in his place. During this speech, Otello directs a series of angry asides to Desdemona and at its close he seizes his wife with such violence that she falls to the ground. The general amazement precipitates the Largo concertato, 'A terra! . . . sì . . . nel livido fango', led off by an unusually long and thematically developed solo from Desdemona, much of it later repeated by the ensemble. As the Largo unfolds, Iago works furiously in the background, assuring Otello that he will deal with Cassio and delegating Roderigo for the task. As the movement comes to a close, Otello wildly dismisses everyone, unleashing on Desdemona a final, terrible curse. Left alone with Iago, he can only mutter incoherently before fainting away. Iago gestures triumphantly at the body and, with offstage voices still hailing Otello as the 'Lion of Venice', brings down the curtain with a derisive shout of 'Ecco il Leone!' ('Here is the Lion!').

ACT 4 *Desdemona's bedroom* A mournful English horn solo with fragmentary phrases sets the tone of this final act. Desdemona discusses with Emilia the present state of her husband and then, with presentiments of death upon her, sings the famous Willow Song, 'Piangea cantando', whose three stanzas with refrain poignantly tell of a young girl abandoned by her lover. After a final, heartfelt farewell to Emilia, Desdemona kneels to offer an 'Ave Maria', softly intoned over a gentle string accompaniment before flowering into 'Prega per chi adorando', Desdemona's personal entreaty for divine assistance. To music for high strings of the utmost delicacy, Desdemona settles in her bed.

A mysterious, recitative-like double bass solo introduces Otello to the bedchamber. Miming to an instrumental recitative punctuated by motivic fragments, he lays down his sword, puts out the torch that illuminates the room, approaches the bed, and to a repetition of the 'bacio' music from the end of Act 1, kisses the sleeping Desdemona. On the third kiss she awakens, so beginning the final and in many ways the freest of the Otello-Desdemona duets, a confrontation that even dispenses with the clear sectional form of earlier examples, reflecting through the proliferation and intensification of motivic repetitions an inexorable progress towards Desdemona's death. At the brutal climax of the scene, deaf to Desdemona's protestations of innocence and to her final pleas, Otello suffocates his wife with a terrible cry of 'È tardi!' ('It is too late!'). Only then does the orchestral surge finally flow back and attain some stasis. To a succession of weighty chords, Otello admits Emilia, who tells him that Cassio has killed Roderigo and has himself survived. She discovers the dying Desdemona, who with her final gasps desperately attempts to protect Otello. But Emilia guesses the truth and raises the alarm. Soon the room is filled with Lodovico, Cassio, Iago, and armed men. Again the free, arioso musical texture takes over as Iago's plot is unravelled, first by Emilia's admission that Iago had obtained the handkerchief from her, then by the appearance of Lodovico, who reports that the dying Roderigo revealed his part in the conspiracy. Otello, finally understanding his tragic error, grabs his sword and, to slow, solemn chords, begins his final oration, 'Niun mi tema'. He reflects on his past glory, apostrophizes Desdemona in an unaccompanied passage that briefly flowers into lyricism, and then, to general horror, stabs himself. His dying utterance as he drags himself towards Desdemona's body is yet another repetition of the 'bacio' music from Act 1.

*   *   *

The chronological position of *Otello* in Verdi's long list of tragic operas—it is the last work, separated from all the others by a considerable time gap—has inevitably made it seem a special case; indeed, for many earlier in the century, perhaps even for some today, it is his only serious opera to merit sustained critical attention. Recent critics have sometimes reacted against this by stressing the many traditional aspects of the score: its reliance, especially in Act 1, on 'characteristic' numbers such as the storm scene, victory chorus, and brindisi; the clear remnants of traditional forms in the 'cabaletta substitutes' such as 'Sì, pel ciel'; and of course its most un-equivocal gesture to traditional form, the great concertato finale that closes Act 3. Some have gone even further, and suggested for example that passages such as the Act 1 love duet should be regarded as additional manipulations of the standard four-movement duet, and that there is in effect an unbroken tradition with Verdi's earlier works.

This last position may swing too far towards the claims of tradition. It is probably more profitable to think of *Otello* as an opera that attempts a break with the past in an effort to produce a new, more modern conception of musical drama. There may well be gestures towards the traditional, normative structures of earlier in the century—it would be difficult to imagine how any opera could completely avoid them. But for the most part the opera strives for a different, more fluid type of musical drama: one that is closer to prose drama in its willingness to admit a swift succession of emotional attitudes during a series of dramatic confrontations. Of course, no value judgments should be attached to this greater fluidity: musical drama is endlessly protean in the manner and the forms in which it may be expressed, and there is nothing intrinsically superior in a type of opera that approaches the rhythms of the spoken theatre. We should, however, preserve a sense of distance between *Otello* and Verdi's earlier operas.

This sense of distance should not, though, shade into another common view, one that sees Verdi's last works as divorced from everyday concerns, a trope often used in discussing an artist's final creative stage. The image of course chimes well with those famous pictures of Verdi in the 1880s and '90s: the felt hat, the simple frock coat, the all-knowing, gentle smile. There is much evidence, however, to suggest that the composer was far from serene about the political and artistic direction his country was taking, and that the last operas in some ways reflect this dissatisfaction. Perhaps a key to *Otello* in this regard is offered in one of the composer's late letters:

> Desdemona is a part in which the thread, the melodic line, never ceases from the first note to the last. Just as Jago has only to declaim and laugh mockingly, and just as Otello, now the warrior, now the passionate lover, now crushed to the point of baseness, now ferocious like a savage, must sing and shout, so Desdemona must always, always sing.

If we follow the terms of this interpretation, it suggests that Verdi managed to channel Boito's very modern tendency towards the symbolic and the interior to his own ends, making the conflicts between the main characters in *Otello* into a story about the violent upheavals of Italian *fin-de-siècle* musical drama. The opera's principals vocally embody the violently conflicting demands of the lyrical and the declamatory, the old style and the new. Iago, the modern man, is constantly in the declamatory mode—when he sings beautifully, it is merely to deceive; and Desdemona is a symbol of that lost time when bel canto was at the centre of theatrical communication. Otello, like Verdi himself, is caught between the new and the old. But, despite or even because of this, the composer managed to renew himself, perhaps in part by symbolically recreating his creative struggle within the very fabric of the opera's central concerns.

Falstaff

Commedia lirica in three acts set to a libretto by Arrigo Boito after William Shakespeare's plays *The Merry Wives of Windsor* and *King Henry IV*; first performed in Milan, Teatro alla Scala, on 9 February 1893.

At the première the cast included Victor Maurel (Falstaff), Antonio Pini-Corsi (Ford), Edoardo Garbin (Fenton), Adelina Stehle (Nannetta), and Giuseppina Pasqua (Mistress Quickly).

Sir John Falstaff	baritone
Fenton	tenor
Dr Caius	tenor
Bardolfo [Bardolph], *follower of Falstaff*	tenor
Pistola [Pistol], *follower of Falstaff*	bass
Mrs Alice Ford	soprano
Ford, *Alice's husband*	baritone
Nannetta, *their daughter*	soprano
Mistress Quickly	mezzo-soprano
Mrs Meg Page	mezzo-soprano
Mine Host at the Garter	silent
Robin, *Falstaff's page*	silent
Ford's Page	silent

Bourgeoisie and populace, Ford's servants, masquerade of imps, fairies, witches, etc.

Setting Windsor, during the reign of Henry IV of England

Verdi, who by the time he came to write his last operas was a national monument, talked intermittently of writing a comic opera during the latter part of his career, but never found a libretto to his taste until some two years after the success of *Otello* in 1887. His librettist for that opera, Arrigo Boito, suggested a work largely based on Shakespeare's *The Merry Wives of Windsor*. Verdi was immediately enthusiastic about Boito's draft scenario, made relatively few structural suggestions, and by August 1889 even announced that he was writing a fugue (quite possibly the comic fugue that ends the opera). Composer and librettist worked closely together during the winter of 1889–90, and by the spring of 1890 the libretto was complete.

The composing of the opera took a considerable time, or rather was carried out in short bursts of activity interspersed with long fallow periods. Act 1 was completed—at least in short score—not long after the libretto was finished, but then Verdi fell into a depression, the deaths of various close friends making him fear he would not live to finish the project. However, the remaining two acts were gradually completed. It seems that, unusually for Verdi, certain scenes were finished out of chronological order (perhaps an indication of the relative independence of individual scenes). By September 1891 the opera was largely complete in short score, and a year later Verdi had finished the orchestration. The première at La Scala, which was conducted by Edoardo Mascheroni, took place almost to the day six years after that of *Otello*. It was, perhaps inevitably at this stage of Verdi's career, a huge triumph and was soon seen in the major international opera houses. Verdi made various minor changes to the score (notably recomposing and shortening the final minutes of Act 3 scene i) during these early revivals. *Falstaff* has always retained its place in the international repertory, though it is less frequently heard than many of the works of the 1850 and 1860s.

*   *   *

ACT 1   Scene i   *Inside the Garter Inn*   An offbeat C-major chord and descending arpeggio set in immediate motion a scene (indeed an opera) that is remarkable for its sense of rapid change and relentless forward movement. Falstaff, busy sealing two letters as the curtain rises, is upbraided by Dr Caius, who accuses him of causing drunken confusion in Caius's house. Falstaff calmly accepts the charge. Caius then accuses Pistol and Bardolph of getting him drunk and stealing his money. Pistol challenges the doctor to a mock duel and exchanges a furious round of insults with him. But Caius has had enough, and storms out after making a solemn promise never to get drunk with such scoundrels again. This hectic first episode is dominated by two main themes: the arpeggiated idea that opened the opera, and a contrasting second theme of more regular tread, appearing as Falstaff replies to Caius's first accusation. The two themes are played out in an overtly developmental manner, with various comic allusions to sonata form, not least in the ineptly contrapuntal 'Amen' intoned by Pistol and Bardolph as Caius leaves and the 'sonata' comes to a close.

After some vain searching for funds, Falstaff lambasts his companions before celebrating his enormous belly in a suitably grandiose climax. Then, in a relatively stable musical episode, the central thread of the drama is first put forward: Falstaff has amorous designs on both Alice Ford and Meg Page, the wives of rich townsfolk. Pistol and Bardolph refuse to deliver his love letters, saying it is beneath their 'honour' to do so. Falstaff sends off his page with the letters and then, in the famous 'Onore' monologue, excoriates the traitors and their high-flown ideals. The solo is typical of the opera as a whole, rapidly shifting in mood, full of ironic references, a veritable index of startling orchestral combinations and textures. As C major makes a late, triumphant return, Falstaff takes up a broom and drives his followers from the room.

Scene ii *The garden outside Ford's house*   A scherzo-like introduction leads in Meg and Mistress Quickly, who meet Alice and Nannetta on the threshold of Alice's house. Meg and Alice discover that Falstaff has sent them identical letters, extracts from which they quote first to the mournful accompaniment of an English horn, later to a passionately lyrical phrase, undermined at the final cadence by mocking vocal trills. In an elaborate unaccompanied quartet, they pour scorn on the amorous knight and vow to revenge themselves on him. From the other side of the stage appears a male quintet (Fenton, Caius, Bardolph, Pistol, and Ford) who, unaware of the women, superimpose their own ensemble. As the women fade into the background, Bardolph and Pistol warn Ford of Falstaff's designs; Ford vows to keep a close watch. The women return and, at the sight of each other, the two groups disperse, leaving Fenton and Nannetta together for the first of their brief love duets, 'Labbra di foco'. One of Boito's early ideas for the drama was to present the young lovers 'as one sprinkles sugar on a tart, to sprinkle the whole comedy with [their] love', and Verdi responded by weaving round them a musical world quite separate from the main body of the score: relaxed and lyrical, shot through with delicate chromaticism and soft orchestral textures. But the spell is soon broken: the women return and resolve to send Quickly to Falstaff as their go-between. Nannetta and Fenton snatch a few further moments; then the men reappear,

Ford announcing that he will visit Falstaff in disguise to ascertain his intentions. The finale of the scene involves a masterly superimposition of
the women's and men's ensembles. The ladies have the last word: a triumphantly derisive reprise of Falstaff's most passionate epistolary style.

ACT 2 Scene i *The Garter Inn* The opening of the act is extraordinary—
even in the context of *Falstaff*—for the extravagant manner in which musical ideas match verbal tags: first as Pistol and Bardolph make elaborate,
chest-beating penance before Falstaff; then as Mistress Quickly introduces
herself with a low 'Reverenza!'; then as she expresses the amorous states of
Alice and Meg with the phrase 'Povera donna!'; and finally as she makes an
appointment for Falstaff with the former, 'dalle due alle tre' ('between two
and three'). Quickly leaves, and Falstaff has time for a gleeful episode of
self-congratulation, 'Va, vecchio John', before 'Mastro Fontana' (Ford in
disguise) is shown in. In the ensuing duet, Fontana offers Falstaff money
to seduce one Alice Ford (who will thus be made easier for Fontana himself
to conquer); Falstaff gleefully agrees, saying that he has already arranged
an appointment 'between two and three'. The passage carries vague echoes
of earlier nineteenth-century formal practice—perhaps particularly in the
cabaletta-like close—but is more usefully seen as a kind of musical prose,
in constant flux as the moods of the principals swing to and fro. Highlights
include the magnificent orchestral depiction of the money Ford offers Falstaff; Ford's passionate declaration of his feelings for Alice (a hint of the
serious tone that will soon break through in this character's discourse); and
Falstaff's rousing conclusion in 'Te lo cornifico' ('I'll cuckold him for
you'). As the knight goes off to pretty himself, Ford is left alone to brood
on what he has heard (the impassioned arioso 'È sogno?'). For the first and
only time, the opera swings for an extended period into the language of serious opera: to the accompaniment of insistent horn-calls (a pun on cuck-
oldry) and tortured fragments of the preceding duet (in particular 'dalle
due alle tre'), Ford contemplates what he believes is his wife's deception.
However, no sooner has Verdi sealed the monologue with a stunning orchestral climax than there is yet another stylistic volte-face: to a delicate,
trilling violin melody, Falstaff appears, tricked out in his finest clothes; the
two men show exaggerated politeness before leaving the scene together to
an orchestral reprise of 'Va, vecchio John'. Our knight, the orchestra seems
to tell us, is winning the day.

Scene ii *A room in Ford's house* A bustling string introduction brings in -
Alice and Meg. They are soon joined by Quickly, who entertains them with

a detailed narrative of her interview with Falstaff, replete with mocking repetitions of 'Reverenza!' and 'dalle due alle tre'. Realizing that the hour of assignation is almost upon them, the women hurry about their preparations; a large laundry basket is carried in; but the busy mood is interrupted by Nannetta, who tearfully reveals that Ford has ordered her to marry old Dr Caius. Alice will have none of this, and assures Nannetta of her support. Preparations then continue, with Alice directing operations and briefly coming to the fore with 'Gaie comari di Windsor!', one of the few, brief moments (at least before the final scene) in which Verdi even hints at a conventional solo aria.

Alice then settles down to strum her lute and is soon joined by Falstaff, who offers elaborate courtship with an ornamented song of Beckmesser-like awkwardness before celebrating his younger, nimbler self in the delightful vignette, 'Quand'ero paggio del Duca di Norfolk'. However, just as the courtship is about to reach an intimate stage, Quickly rushes in to announce the imminent arrival of Meg Page. The music dives into a furious Allegro agitato, so beginning the first movement of a conventionally structured but highly complex concertato finale. This first movement is in a near-constant state of manic energy: Falstaff hides behind a screen as Meg enters to announce the arrival of an insanely jealous Ford; Ford appears at the head of a band of followers, searches the laundry basket, then rushes off to search elsewhere; Falstaff is then wedged painfully into the basket and covered with dirty clothes. A brief moment of calm ensues as Nannetta and Fenton meet and slip behind the screen for a few moments together, but very soon the energy is again released as the men reappear to continue their search. The music grinds to a halt as a loud kiss is heard behind the screen: the men are sure they have trapped their quarry, and the realization precipitates the second movement of the concertato, the Andante 'Se t'agguanto!'. In the traditional way, this movement forms a still centre during which all can reflect on their contrasting positions: the men cautiously prepare to pounce; the women vow to keep the game alive; Falstaff emits muffled cries from his suffocating confinement; Nannetta and Fenton, oblivious to all, rise above the ensemble in lyrically expansive phrases. Eventually the spell is broken. The men overturn the screen, only to find Nannetta and Fenton, the latter angrily rebuked by Ford. But Bardolph seems to see Falstaff outside, and the men rush off again, allowing the women to summon their pages who—with a huge effort—hoist the basket up to the window. The men return just in time to see Falstaff tipped into the river below, and the act closes with a riotous fanfare of triumph.

ACT 3 Scene i *Outside the Garter Inn*   As Boito remarked in a letter to
Verdi, the problem in finding dramatic form for comic subjects was one of
predictability: how to convince the audience that they should stay for the
third act when the unravelling of the plot is already clear. In the case of
Falstaff this problem is acute, as the protagonist's most clamorous punishment has already been inflicted by the close of Act 2. The startlingly original solution Boito and Verdi chose to overcome the difficulty will be
revealed in the second half of this act; but this first scene was troublesome
and was the last to be composed. Perhaps for this reason, its musical discourse is as radical as any in Verdi. Falstaff's opening monologue is certainly the most fragmented passage in the opera, occasional reminiscences
jostling with a series of violent changes as the knight bemoans his disgrace, calls for wine, and finally revives as the liquor tingles through his
body to the accompaniment of a magnificent orchestral trill. The ensuing
duet with Quickly repeats some of the motifs of their earlier encounter as
Falstaff is again convinced, at first with some difficulty, of Alice's affec-
tion. A new assignation is made: Falstaff is to await his intended paramour
at midnight under Herne's Oak in the Royal Park, disguised as the Black
Huntsman. Quickly paints an evocative picture of the supernatural ambience and, as she leads Falstaff into the inn, the evocation is taken up by
Alice, who has been observing the scene with Ford, Meg, Nannetta, Fenton, and Caius. The scene then plays itself out in a relaxed, French-
influenced musical setting, as the plotters decide on their disguises.
Quickly overhears Ford and Caius, who are planning Caius's marriage to
Nannetta that very night, and privately vows to stop them.

Scene ii *Windsor forest*   Distant horn-calls introduce Fenton, whose
lengthy aria immediately marks the departure taken in this final scene,
which for the most part is structured in discrete units, without the rapid
changes that characterize the rest of the opera. And the delicate, nocturnal
ambience serves further to make this final scene self-contained, separate in
both formal and timbral terms from the main drama, thus sidestepping the
danger of anticlimax that Boito had feared. That the scene begins with
Fenton's extended sonnet, 'Dal labbro il canto', is also significant: the delicate atmosphere established in intervals by the young lovers through the
opera now becomes the dominant strain in the music.

   Fenton is rudely interrupted by Alice, who provides him with a disguise
before they rush off to take their positions. Falstaff appears and solemnly
counts the twelve bells of midnight. He is joined by Alice, and a fleeting
repetition of their earlier meeting takes place before Meg enters to warn of

an approaching pack of witches. As Falstaff throws himself to the ground, fearing death if he sees these supernatural beings, Nannetta begins a delicate invocation that eventually flowers into 'Sul fil d'un soffio etesio', yet another aria suffused with the soft orchestral colours that characterize this scene. A sudden Prestissimo ushers in the rest of the cast, who begin tormenting Falstaff in earnest. Their gleeful chorus, 'Pizzica, pizzica', later adorned with mock religious chanting, is halted only when Bardolph gets carried away and allows his hood to slip. Falstaff immediately recognizes him and subjects him a generous torrent of abuse. Soon the entire deception is revealed, Falstaff assuming new stature in his philosophical acceptance of what has befallen him.

A gentle minuet introduces Caius and 'The Queen of the Fairies' (whom Caius thinks is Nannetta). They are joined by another couple, and both pairs receive Ford's blessing. But with Ford's final words, a further deception is uncovered: 'The Queen of the Fairies' turns out to be Bardolph in disguise, and the other couple are—of course—Fenton and Nannetta. This time it is Ford's turn to admit defeat and (the minuet returning) he agrees to accept his daughter's marriage. Falstaff leads off the final ensemble, a comic fugue to the words 'Tutto nel mondo è burla' ('All the world's a joke'). The ironic reference to an academic form, the polyphony and confusion of voices, and most of all, the constant, driving energy of the piece form a fitting end to Verdi's final opera.

$$*\qquad*\qquad*$$

Perhaps the most immediately obvious level of difference between *Falstaff* and all Verdi's previous operas lies in the music's tendency to respond in unprecedented detail to the verbal element of the drama. In much of the score, but especially in the great duets and monologues, the listener is bombarded by a stunning diversity of rhythms, orchestral textures, melodic motifs, and harmonic devices. Passages that in earlier times would have furnished material for an entire number here crowd in on each other, shouldering themselves unceremoniously to the fore in bewildering succession. And a large number of these fresh ideas spring in a direct and literal way from the words. Such exaggerated literalism would be obtrusive in a tragic opera, in which the need for underlying emotional communication often overrides responses to individual words. But here, in the comic context, it furnishes an important means of filling the musical space with an endless variety of colours. And this is by no means the only level of diversification in the score, for it is clear that Verdi was fully aware of the opera's 'polyphonic' texture and was—on occasion—even prepared to interrupt the drama in order to enhance it. As he said in a letter to Boito discussing Fenton's sonnet in Act 3, 'as far as the drama goes we could do without it; but . . . the whole piece provides me with a new colour for the musical palette'.

These new aspects, possible only through the medium of comedy, served to stimulate Verdi's creative imagination to new levels of fecundity. In the midst of an increasingly fragmented aesthetic world, he seemed to be able to follow the whim of the moment, gazing back on past achievements. Verdi himself certainly encouraged such interpretations of his last work, frequently reiterating in letters and interviews that 'in writing *Falstaff* I haven't thought about either theatres or singers. I have written for myself and my own pleasure'. It may be comforting to nurture this picture of serene old age. The opera can, if we follow this line interpretation, leave us with a musical image that exactly reflects those famous photographs of Verdi in his last years: an old man, in black hat, with eyes that have lived through a lifetime of struggle, smiling out wisely at the world.

Falstaff, however, is more complicated than that. An opera that begins with a mock sonata form and ends with a comic fugue also gestures to the darker side of Verdi's later career, to his sense that time had passed him by and that the younger generation of Italian composers were losing their way. In this sense, the fugue and the sonata chime well with a constant stream of admonitions that Verdi sent out via the press in later life: that young Italians should study counterpoint and avoid the 'symphonic' at all costs. Perhaps the parallels even go further. *Falstaff* is, for example, more highly chromatic than any other Verdi opera, but equally it is obsessed by cadence, forever punctuated by unequivocal gestures of closure. Related to this, but on a larger level, is the contrast between the work's enormous variety of expression and looseness of form on the one hand, and on the other its many gestures of massive closure, its huge orchestral climaxes that seem to overwhelm and even overdetermine what precedes them. Perhaps these matters can also be related to Verdi's complex reaction to musical modernity, to his desire to progress from his own past, harmonically and formally, but also his need aggressively to counter what he saw as the disastrously international and cosmopolitan tendencies of his younger contemporaries. One thing is sure: that *Falstaff* will, like all of Verdi's operas, remain patient of interpretation, constantly stimulating us to find new ways in which it responded to its own time and can now respond to ours.

Plate 1. Wolfgang Gussmann's stark but dramatic set for the Netherlands Opera's production of *Don Carlos*, 2004.

Plate 2. Title-page of the first edition of the vocal score *Rigoletto* (Milan: Ricordi, 1851), with a vignette showing the opening scene of Act 3; the costumes are identical to Ricordi's published *figurini* for the opera.

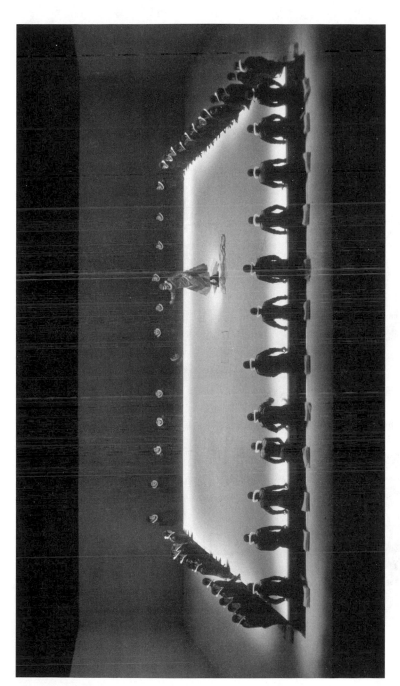

Plate 3. Michael Levine's strikingly modern set for the Netherlands Opera's production of *Rigoletto*, 2004.

Plate 4. Franco Zeffirelli's opulent set and Raimonda Gaetani's costumes for the Metropolitan Opera's production of *La traviata*, 2006. (Jonas Kaufmann as Alfredo and Angela Gheorghiu as Violetta)

Act II, Scene 2, of Verdi's "Aida."   Photo: Marty Sohl/Metropolitan Opera

Plate 5. Gianni Quaranta's large-scale set for the Metropolitan Opera's production of *Aida*, 2005.

Plate 6. A photograph of Act 2 scene iii of an early-twentieth-century production of *Aida*.

Plate 7. This engraving of the opening scene of *Otello*, first performed 1887, depicts a set that follows Verdi's set directions almost exactly.

Plate 8. This 1994 production of *Otello* at the Verona Arena, Italy, also closely follows Verdi's original set directions and uses the space of an outdoor set.

Plate 9. This 2005 production of *Otello* at the Glyndebourne Festival, with sets designed by Peter Hall, breaks with Verdi's set directions for a more modern look.

Plate 10. Photograph of Giuseppe Verdi by Nadar, 1860s.

Glossary

Act One of the main divisions of an opera, usually completing a part of the action and often having a climax of its own. The classical five-act division was adopted in some early operas and common in serious French opera of the seventeenth to the mid-nineteenth centuries; in Italian opera a three-act scheme was soon standard, later modified to two in *opera buffa*.

Appoggiatura (It.) A 'leaning note', normally one step above the note it precedes. *Appoggiature* were often introduced by performers in nineteenth-century Italian opera, both in recitatives and arias, to make the musical line conform to the natural inflection of the words or (in arias) to increase the expressiveness.

Aria (It.) A closed, lyrical piece for solo voice, the major vehicle for vocal expression on the part of an operatic character. Arias appear in the earliest operas; by the early eighteenth century they usually follow a da capo pattern (*ABA*); later in the century they took various forms, among them the slow-fast type, sometimes called rondò. In Italian opera during most of the nineteenth century the multimovement type (typically a slow movement, *tempo di mezzo* and cabaletta) became the norm, although more complex forms, sometimes in four sections with interruptions to reflect changes of mood, appear in the operas of Donizetti and Verdi. The aria as a detachable unit became less popular later in the century.

Arioso (It.: 'like an aria') A short passage in regular tempo in the middle or at the end of a recitative.

Ballabile (It.: 'suitable for dancing') A movement intended for dancing; Verdi used the term in Act 3 of *Macbeth* for the chorus and dance of the witches.

Ballata (It.) A dance-song or ballad; Verdi used the term for the Duke's 'Questa o quella' in *Rigoletto*.

Barcarolle A piece with a lilting rhythm, suggesting the songs of Venetian gondoliers.

Baritone A male voice of moderately low pitch, normally in the range $A-g'$. The voice became important in opera in the late eighteenth century, particularly in Mozart's works, although the word 'baritone' was little used at this time. Verdi used the baritone for a great variety of roles.

Bass The lowest male voice, normally in the range *F–f'*. The voice is used in operas of all periods, often for gods, figures of authority (a king, a priest, a father) and for villains and sinister characters. There are several subclasses of bass: the *basso buffo* (in Italian comic opera), the *basso cantante* or French *basse-chantante* (for a more lyrical role), and the *basso profundo* (a heavy, deep voice).

Brindisi A song inviting the company to raise glasses and drink. There are examples in Verdi's *Macbeth, La traviata,* and *Otello.*

Cabaletta (It.) A term for the concluding movement, generally in a fairly rapid tempo, of a multimovement aria or duet, sometimes dramatically motivated by an interruption. One of the most famous Verdian examples is Violetta's 'Sempre libera degg'io' in Act ı of *La traviata.*

Cadenza A passage of florid, rhythmically free writing inserted in an aria, usually near the end, either improvised by the singer or, as in Verdi's later operas, written out by the composer.

Canzone (It.) A term used for items presented as songs, sung outside the dramatic action. Verdi used the term several times, notably for Desdemona's Willow Song in *Otello.*

Cavatina (It.) In eighteenth-century opera a short aria, without da capo. In the nineteenth century often used to refer to a multimovement entrance aria.

Coloratura (It.) Florid figuration or ornamentation. The term is usually applied to high-pitched florid writing, exemplified by such roles as Violetta in *La traviata.* The term 'coloratura soprano' signifies a singer of high pitch, lightness, and agility, appropriate to such roles.

Comic opera A musico-dramatic work of a light or amusing nature. The term may be applied equally to an Italian *opera buffa,* a French *opéra comique,* a German *Singspiel,* or a Spanish *zarzuela.*

Contralto (It.) A voice normally written for the range *G–f''*. In modern English the term denotes the lowest female voice. In opera, true contralto (as distinct from mezzo-soprano) roles are unusual: Ulrica is a famous Verdian example.

Duet (It.) A piece for two singers. It was used in opera almost from the outset, often at the end of an act or when the principal lovers were united (or parted). In nineteenth-century Italian opera the grandest examples were often in four movements, sometimes with stage action of some kind marking the shift from one movement to another.

Finale (It.) The concluding, continuously composed, section of an act of an opera. The ensemble finale developed at the beginning of the second half of the eighteenth century. In nineteenth-century Italian opera the grandest examples were often in four movements, sometimes with stage action of some kind marking the shift from one movement to another.

Grand opéra A term used to signify a series of monumental works performed at the Paris Opéra during its period of greatest magnificence, including Rossini's *Guillaume Tell* and several operas composed to librettos by Eugène Scribe, by Meyerbeer and others during the 1830s. Verdi's operas in the genre are *Les Vêpres siciliennes* and *Don Carlos*.

Leitmotif (Ger.: 'leading motif') A theme, or other musical idea, that represents or symbolizes a person, object, place, idea, state of mind, supernatural force, or some other ingredient in a dramatic work. It may recur unaltered, or it may be changed in rhythm, intervallic structure, tempo, harmony, orchestration, or accompaniment, to signify dramatic development, and may be combined with other Leitmotifs. The concept is particularly associated with Wagner, who used it extensively in his later operas, but it can also be found in Verdi, notably in *I due Foscari* and *Aida*.

Libretto (It.: 'small book') A printed book containing the words of an opera; by extension, the text itself.

Melisma A passage of florid writing in which several notes are sung to the same syllable.

Melodrama A kind of drama, or a technique used within a drama, in which the action is carried forward by the character speaking in the pauses of, or during, orchestral passages, similar in style to those in operatic accompanied recitative. Its invention is usually dated to Rousseau's *Pygmalion* (ca. 1762). Most nineteenth-century opera composers used it as a dramatic device; Verdian examples include the letter scenes in *Macbeth* (Act 1) and *La traviata* (Act 3).

Melodramma (It.) A term for a dramatic text written to be set to music, or the resultant opera. It should not be confused with Melodrama. Among Verdi's operas the term appeared in *I masnadieri*, *Rigoletto*, and *Un ballo in maschera*; *Un giorno di regno* was called a *melodramma giocoso*; *Luisa Miller* was a *melodramma tragico*. However, it is hard to attach any special significance to the word, as terms such as *Dramma lirico* and *Tragedia lirica* seemed to be used interchangeably with it.

Mezzo-soprano A term for a voice, usually female, normally written for within the range $a–a''$. The distinction between the florid soprano and the weightier mezzo-soprano became common only towards the mid-eighteenth century; it was more keenly sensed in the nineteenth century, although the mezzo-soprano range was often extended as high as b''. Mezzo-sopranos with an extended upper range tackled the lower of two soprano roles in such operas as Bellini's *Norma* (Adalgisa) and Donizetti's *Anna Bolena* (Jane Seymour). A prominent example in Verdi is Amneris *(Aida)*.

Modulation The movement out of one key into another as a continuous musical process. It is particularly used in opera as a device to suggest a change of mood.

Motif A short musical idea, melodic, rhythmic, or harmonic (or any combination of those).

Number opera An opera consisting of individual sections or 'numbers' that can be detached from the whole, as distinct from an opera consisting of continuous music. It applies to the various forms of eighteenth-century opera and to many nineteenth-century operas. During the later nineteenth century the number opera became unfashionable, although vestiges of it remain even in Verdi's last operas.

Opera buffa (It.: 'comic opera') A term commonly used to signify Italian comic opera, principally of the eighteenth and early nineteenth centuries, with recitative rather than spoken dialogue.

Ostinato (It.) A term used to refer to the repetition of a musical pattern many times over.

Overture A piece of orchestral music designed to precede a dramatic work (in Italian the word is 'Sinfonia'). For Bellini, Donizetti, and Verdi the short prelude ('Preludio') was an alternative, one that became normal in Italian opera after the mid-nineteenth century.

Parlando, Parlante (It.: 'speaking') A direction requiring a singer to use a manner approximating speech.

Pezzo concertato (It.) A section within a finale in Italian nineteenth-century opera in which several characters express divergent emotions simultaneously, as it were, in a 'multiple soliloquy'. It is usually in slow tempo and is sometimes called 'Largo concertato'.

Preghiera (It.: 'prayer') A number common in nineteenth-century opera, in which a character prays for divine assistance in her or (rarely) his plight. Prominent Verdian Preghiere appear in Act 4 of *Nabucco* and Act 1 of *I Lombardi*; Desdemona's 'Ave Maria' in Verdi's *Otello* is a famous late example.

Preludio (It.: 'prelude') *see* Overture.

Prima donna (It.: 'first lady') The principal female singer in an opera or on the roster of an opera company; almost always a soprano. In Verdi's operas, many of the leading singers (men as well as women) shaped in important ways the librettos and scores written with them in mind; in this sense the fact that they are sometimes called 'creators' of their roles is apt and revealing.

Prologue The introductory part of a dramatic work, in which the author explains, either directly or indirectly, the context and meaning of the drama to follow. In Italian nineteenth-century opera, it was often used to denote a first act that took place long before the action of the other acts: *Simon Boccanegra* is the most famous example.

Quartet A composition for four singers. Verdi's best-known example is from *Rigoletto*, Act 3.

Rataplan A term used onomatopoeically for a type of chorus based on the martial life, with flourishes of drums, fanfare-like figures, etc.

Recitative A type of vocal writing that follows closely the natural rhythm and accentuation of speech, not necessarily governed by a regular tempo or organized in a specific form. Simple recitative with keyboard accompaniment fell out of use in the mid-nineteenth century. Recitative-like declamation, however, remained an essential means of expression, not least in Verdi.

Romance A term used in eighteenth- and nineteenth-century opera for a single-movement aria, often in French. Posa has some fine examples in Verdi's *Don Carlos*.

Scena (It.), **Scène** (Fr.) A term used to mean (1) the stage, e.g., 'sulla scena' (on the stage), 'derrière la scène' (behind the stage); (2) the scene represented on the stage; (3) a division of an act (*see* Scene). In Italian opera it also means an episode with no formal construction, usually consisting of an orchestral prelude and recitative. The 'Scena ed Aria' and 'Scena e Duetto' are typical units in Italian opera of the Verdian period.

Scene (1) The location of an opera, or an act or part of an act of an opera; by extension, any part of an opera in one location. (2) In earlier usage, a scene was a section of an act culminating in an aria (or occasionally an ensemble); any substantial (in some operas, any) change in the characters on the stage was reckoned a change of scene, and the scenes were numbered accordingly.

Set piece An aria or other number clearly demarcated from its context.

Soprano (It.) The highest female voice, normally written for within the range $c'-a''$. Italian sopranos of the nineteenth century typically developed a coloratura style and the ability to sustain a long lyrical line; later, with larger opera houses and orchestras, the more dramatic 'spinto' and 'lirico spinto' types began to be distinguished.

Spinto (It.: 'pushed') Term for a lyric voice, usually soprano or tenor, that is able to sound powerful and incisive at dramatic climaxes. The full expression is 'lirico spinto'. The term is also used to describe roles that require voices of this character, for example Mimì in Puccini's *La bohème* and Alfredo in Verdi's *La traviata*.

Stretta (It.) A term used to indicate a faster tempo at the concluding section of a multimovement ensemble.

Strophic A term for a song or an aria in which all stanzas of the text are set to the same music.

Tempo d'attacco (It.) A term used in Italian nineteenth-century opera for the first movement of a multimovement duet.

Tempo di mezzo (It.: 'middle movement') A term used in Italian nineteenth-century opera for a transitional passage following the slow movement, and preceding the cabaletta.

Tenor The highest natural male voice, normally written for within the range *c–b'*. Although the tenor voice was sometimes valued in early opera, it came to prominence in the mid-nineteenth century. Several of Verdi's operas are named after their tenor protagonists.

Trio An ensemble for three singers. Trios have been used throughout the history of opera, but the form occasionally came to prominence in operas by Verdi. There are three examples in *Un ballo in maschera*, but perhaps the most famous is the one that closes *Ernani*.

Tonal A term used for music in a particular key, or a pitch centre to which the music naturally gravitates. The use of tonalities, or the interplay of keys, can be an important dramatic device.

Index of Role Names

Abdallo (tenor)	*Nabucco*
Abigaille (soprano)	*Nabucco*
Acciano (bass)	*I Lombardi*
Adhemar de Monteil (bass)	*Jérusalem*
Aida (soprano)	*Aida*
Alfredo Germont (tenor)	*La traviata*
Alice Ford (soprano)	*Falstaff*
Alvaro (bass)	*Alzira*
Alvaro, Don (tenor)	*La forza del destino*
Alzira (soprano)	*Alzira*
Amalia (soprano)	*I masnadieri*
Amelia (soprano)	*Un ballo in maschera*
Amelia Grimaldi (soprano)	*Simon Boccanegra*
Amneris (mezzo-soprano)	*Aida*
Amonasro (baritone)	*Aida*
Anna (soprano)	*Nabucco*
Annina (soprano)	*La traviata*
Aremberg, Countess of (silent role)	*Don Carlos*
Arminio (tenor)	*I masnadieri*
Aroldo (tenor)	*Aroldo*
Arrigo (tenor)	*La battaglia di Legnano*
Arvino (tenor)	*I Lombardi*
Araliba (bass)	*Alzira*
Attila (bass)	*Attila*
Azucena (mezzo-soprano)	*Il trovatore*
Banquo/Banco (bass)	*Macbeth*
Barbarigo (tenor)	*I due Foscari*
Barbarossa (bass)	*La battaglia di Legnano*
Bardolph/Bardolfo (tenor)	*Falstaff*
Belfiore (baritone)	*Un giorno di regno*
Béthune, Sire de (bass)	*Les Vêpres siciliennes*
Boccanegra, Simon (baritone)	*Simon Boccanegra*
Borsa (tenor)	*Rigoletto*
Briano (bass)	*Aroldo*
Caius, Dr (tenor)	*Falstaff*
Calatrava, Marquis of (bass)	*La forza del destino*
Carlo (tenor)	*I masnadieri*

Carlo, Don (baritone)	*Ernani*
Carlo di Vargas, Don (baritone)	*La forza del destino*
Carlos/Carlo, Don (tenor)	*Don Carlos*
Cassio (tenor)	*Otello*
Ceprano, Count (bass)	*Rigoletto*
Ceprano, Countess (mezzo-soprano)	*Rigoletto*
Carlo VII (tenor)	*Giovanna d'Arco*
Corrado (tenor)	*Il corsaro*
Cuniza (mezzo-soprano)	*Oberto*
Curra (mezzo-soprano)	*La forza del destino*
Daniéli (tenor)	*Les Vêpres siciliennes*
Delil (tenor)	*Giovanna d'Arco*
Desdemona (soprano)	*Otello*
D'Obigny, Marchese (bass)	*La traviata*
Dorotea (mezzo-soprano)	*Stiffelio*
Douphol, Baron (baritone)	*La traviata*
Duncan/Duncano (silent role)	*Macbeth*
Eboli, Princess (mezzo-soprano)	*Don Carlos*
Edoardo (tenor)	*Un giorno di regno*
Egberto (baritone)	*Aroldo*
Egypt, King of (bass)	*Aida*
Elena (soprano)	*Aroldo*
Elisabeth de/Elisabetta di Valois (soprano)	*Don Carlos*
Elvira (soprano)	*Ernani*
Emilia (mezzo-soprano)	*Otello*
Enrico (tenor)	*Aroldo*
Ernani (tenor)	*Ernani*
Ezio (baritone)	*Attila*
Falstaff (baritone)	*Falstaff*
Federica, Duchess (contralto)	*Luisa Miller*
Federico di Frengel (tenor)	*Stiffelio*
Fenena (soprano)	*Nabucco*
Fenton (tenor)	*Falstaff*
Ferrando (bass)	*Il trovatore*
Fiesco, Jacopo (Andrea) (bass)	*Simon Boccanegra*
Fleance/Fleanzio (silent role)	*Macbeth*
Flora Bervoix (mezzo-soprano)	*La traviata*
Ford (baritone)	*Falstaff*
Foresto (tenor)	*Attila*
Francesco (baritone)	*I masnadieri*
Francesco Foscari/Doge (baritone)	*I due Foscari*
Gabriele Adorno (tenor)	*Simon Boccanegra*
Gaston (tenor)	*Jérusalem*
Gastone, Vicomte de Letorières (tenor)	*La traviata*
Germont, Giorgio (baritone)	*La traviata*

Giacomo (baritone)	*Giovanna d'Arco*
Gilda (soprano)	*Rigoletto*
Giovanna (soprano)	*Ernani*
Giovanna (soprano)	*Giovanna d'Arco*
Giovanna (soprano)	*Rigoletto*
Giovanni (bass)	*Il corsaro*
Giselda (soprano)	*I Lombardi*
Giulietta di Kelbar (soprano)	*Un giorno di regno*
Godvino (tenor)	*Aroldo*
Grand Inquisitor (bass)	*Don Carlos*
Gulnara (soprano)	*Il corsaro*
Gusmano (baritone)	*Alzira*
Hélène (soprano)	*Jérusalem*
Hélène/Elena, Duchess (soprano)	*Les Vêpres siciliennes*
Henri/Arrigo (tenor)	*Les Vêpres siciliennes*
Iago (baritone)	*Otello*
Imelda (mezzo-soprano)	*La battaglia di Legnano*
Imelda (soprano)	*Oberto*
Ines (soprano)	*Il trovatore*
Isaure (soprano)	*Jérusalem*
Ismaele (tenor)	*Nabucco*
Jacopo Foscari (tenor)	*I due Foscari*
Jacopo Loredano (bass)	*I due Foscari*
Jago (bass)	*Ernani*
Jorg (bass)	*Stiffelio*
Judge (tenor)	*Un ballo in maschera*
Kelbar, Baron (bass)	*Un giorno di regno*
La Rocca (bass)	*Un giorno di regno*
Laura (mezzo-soprano)	*Luisa Miller*
Leone (bass)	*Attila*
Leonora (soprano)	*Il trovatore*
Leonora (soprano)	*La forza del destino*
Leonora (soprano)	*Oberto*
Lerma, Count of (tenor)	*Don Carlos*
Lida (soprano)	*La battaglia di Legnano*
Lina (soprano)	*Stiffelio*
Lodovico (bass)	*Otello*
Lucrezia Contarini (soprano)	*I due Foscari*
Luisa (soprano)	*Luisa Miller*
Luna, Count di (baritone)	*Il trovatore*
Macbeth (baritone)	*Macbeth*
Macbeth, Lady (soprano)	*Macbeth*
Macduff (tenor)	*Macbeth*
Maddalena (contralto)	*Rigoletto*
Mainfroid/Manfredo (tenor)	*Les Vêpres siciliennes*

Malcolm (tenor)	*Macbeth*
Manrico (tenor)	*Il trovatore*
Mantua, Duke of (tenor)	*Rigoletto*
Marchesa del Poggio (mezzo-soprano)	*Un giorno di regno*
Marcovaldo (baritone)	*La battaglia di Legnano*
Marullo (baritone)	*Rigoletto*
Massimiliano, Count Moor (bass)	*I masnadieri*
Medora (baritone)	*Il corsaro*
Meg Page (mezzo-soprano)	*Falstaff*
Melitone, Fra (bass)	*La forza del destino*
Miller (baritone)	*Luisa Miller*
Mina (soprano)	*Aroldo*
Monk (bass)	*Don Carlos*
Montano (bass)	*Otello*
Monterone, Count (bass)	*Rigoletto*
Montfort, Guy de/Montforte (baritone)	*Les Vêpres siciliennes*
Moser (bass)	*I masnadieri*
Nabucco (baritone)	*Nabucco*
Nannetta (soprano)	*Falstaff*
Ninetta (contralto)	*Les Vêpres siciliennes*
Oberto (bass)	*Oberto*
Odabella (soprano)	*Attila*
Oronte (tenor)	*I Lombardi*
Oscar (soprano)	*Un ballo in maschera*
Otello (tenor)	*Otello*
Otumbo (tenor)	*Alzira*
Ovando (tenor)	*Alzira*
Padre Guardiano (bass)	*La forza del destino*
Pagano (bass)	*I Lombardi*
Paolo Albiani (bass)	*Simon Boccanegra*
Philippe II (bass)	*Don Carlos*
Pietro (baritone)	*Simon Boccanegra*
Pirro (bass)	*I Lombardi*
Pistol/Pistola (bass)	*Falstaff*
Posa, Marquis of/Rodrigo/Rodrigue (baritone)	*Don Carlos*
Preziosilla (mezzo-soprano)	*La forza del destino*
Prior of Milan (tenor)	*I Lombardi*
Procida, Jean (bass)	*Les Vêpres siciliennes*
Quickly, Mistress (mezzo-soprano)	*Falstaff*
Radames (tenor)	*Aida*
Raffaele von Leuthold (tenor)	*Stiffelio*
Ramfis (bass)	*Aida*
Ramla, Emir of (bass)	*Jérusalem*
Raymond (tenor)	*Jérusalem*
Renato (baritone)	*Un ballo in maschera*

Riccardo (tenor)	*Oberto*
Riccardo, Don (tenor)	*Ernani*
Riccardo (tenor)	*Un ballo in maschera*
Rigoletto (baritone)	*Rigoletto*
Robert/Roberto (baritone)	*Les Vêpres siciliennes*
Roderigo (tenor)	*Otello*
Rodolfo (tenor)	*Luisa Miller*
Roger (bass)	*Jérusalem*
Rolando (baritone)	*La battaglia di Legnano*
Rolla (tenor)	*I masnadieri*
Ruiz (tenor)	*Il trovatore*
Samuel (bass)	*Un ballo in maschera*
Seid, Pasha (baritone)	*Il corsaro*
Selimo (tenor)	*Il corsaro*
Silva, Don Ruy Gomez de (bass)	*Ernani*
Silvano (bass)	*Un ballo in maschera*
Sofia (soprano)	*I Lombardi*
Sparafucile (bass)	*Rigoletto*
Stankar (baritone)	*Stiffelio*
Stiffelio (tenor)	*Stiffelio*
Talbot (bass)	*Giovanna d'Arco*
Thibault/Tebaldo (soprano)	*Don Carlos*
Thibault/Tebaldo (tenor)	*Les Vêpres siciliennes*
Tom (bass)	*Un ballo in maschera*
Toulouse, Count of (baritone)	*Jérusalem*
Trabuco, Mastro (tenor)	*La forza del destino*
Uldino (tenor)	*Attila*
Ulrica (contralto)	*Un ballo in maschera*
Vaudemont, Comte de (bass)	*Les Vêpres siciliennes*
Viclinda (soprano)	*I Lombardi*
Violetta Valéry (soprano)	*La traviata*
Voice from Heaven (soprano)	*Don Carlos*
Walter, Count (bass)	*Luisa Miller*
Wurm (bass)	*Luisa Miller*
Zaccaria (bass)	*Nabucco*
Zamoro (tenor)	*Alzira*
Zuma (mezzo-soprano)	*Alzira*

Suggested Listening Guide

What follows is a highly selective (and also highly personal) list. It nominates just one recording of each of Verdi's operas. As might be imagined, making this choice has been rather easy with many of the earlier operas but a matter of great difficulty with most of the later ones, where literally dozens of recordings vie with each other, all having some particular point of interest or excellence. However, these recordings are the ones that I turn to (and return to) with greatest frequency. I have placed asterisks (*) by a few of the selections: ones that are, in my view, exceptional by any standards.

OBERTO, CONTE DI SAN BONIFACIO

Cuniza	Ruza Baldani
Riccardo	Carlo Bergonzi
Oberto	Rolando Panerai
Leonora	Ghena Dimitrova

Bavarian Radio Chorus and Orchestra, cond. Lamberto Gardelli
Label: Orfeo 105 842 (2CDs)
Date: 1983

UN GIORNO DI REGNO

Belfiore	Ingvar Wixell
Kelbar	Wladimiro Ganzarolli
Marchesa	Fiorenza Cossotto
Giulietta	Jessye Norman
Edoardo	José Carreras

Ambrosian Singers, Royal Philharmonic Orchestra, cond. Lamberto Gardelli
Label: Philips 422 429-2 (2CDs)
Date: 1974

NABUCCO

Nabucco	Tito Gobbi
Ismaele	Bruno Prevedi
Zaccaria	Carlo Cava
Abigaille	Elena Suliotis
Fenena	Dora Carral

Chorus of the Wiener Staatsoper, Wiener Opernorchester, cond. Lamberto Gardelli
Label: Decca 417 407-2 (2CDs)
Date: 1965

I LOMBARDI ALLA PRIMA CROCIATA

Arvino	Jerome Lo Monaco
Pagano	Ruggero Raimondi
Giselda	Cristina Deutekom
Oronte	Plácido Domingo

Ambrosian Singers, Royal Philharmonic Orchestra, cond. Lamberto Gardelli
Label: Philips 422 420-2 (2CDs)
Date: 1972

*ERNANI

Ernani	Carlo Bergonzi
Don Carlo	Mario Sereni
Silva	Ezio Flagello
Elvira	Leontyne Price

Chorus and Orchestra of the RCA Italiana, cond. Thomas Schippers
Label: BMG RCA GD 86 503 QR (2CDs)
Date: 1967

I DUE FOSCARI

Francesco	Piero Cappuccilli
Jacopo	José Carreras
Lucrezia	Katia Ricciarelli
Loredano	Samuel Ramey

Chorus and Symphony Orchestra of the Österreichischer Rundfunk, cond. Lamberto Gardelli
Label: Philips 422 426-2 (2CDs)
Date: 1976

GIOVANNA D'ARCO

Carlo VII	Plácido Domingo
Giacomo	Sherrill Milnes
Giovanna	Montserrat Caballé
Talbot	Robert Lloyd

Ambrosian Opera Chorus, London Symphony Orchestra, cond. James Levine
Label: EMI 653763226-2 (2CDs)
Date: 1972

ALZIRA

Alvaro	Jan Hendrik Rootering
Gusmano	Renato Bruson
Zamoro	Francisco Araiza
Alzira	Ileana Cotrubas

Chorus of the Bayerischer Rundfunk, Münchener Radio-Orchester, cond. Lamberto Gardelli

Label: Orfeo 057 832-2 (2CDs)

Date: 1983

ATTILA

Attila	Ruggero Raimondi
Ezio	Sherrill Milnes
Odabella	Cristina Deutekom
Foresto	Carlo Bergonzi

Ambrosian Singers, Royal Philharmonic Orchestra, cond. Lamberto Gardelli

Label: Philips 426 115-2 (2CDs)

Date: 1972

MACBETH

Macbeth	Piero Cappuccilli
Banquo	Nicolai Ghiaurov
Lady Macbeth	Shirley Verrett
Macduff	Plácido Domingo

Chorus and Orchestra of the Teatro alla Scala, cond. Claudio Abbado

Label: DG 449 732-2 (2CDs)

Date: 1976

I MASNADIERI

Massimiliano	Ruggero Raimondi
Carlo	Carlo Bergonzi
Francesco	Piero Cappuccilli
Amalia	Montserrat Caballé

Ambrosian Singers, New Philharmonia Orchestra, cond. Lamberto Gardelli

Label: Philips 422 423-2 (2CDs)

Date: 1974

JÉRUSALEM

Gaston	José Carreras
Roger	Siegmund Nimsgern
Hélène	Katia Ricciarelli

Chorus and Orchestra of the RAI di Torino, cond. Gianandrea Gavazzeni
Label: Bella Voce 107 213-2 (2CDs)
Date: 1975

IL CORSARO

Corrado	José Carreras
Medora	Jessye Norman
Gulnara	Montserrat Caballé
Seid	Giampiero Mastromei

Ambrosian Singers, New Philharmonia Orchestra, cond. Lamberto Gardelli
Label: Philips 426 118-2 (2CDs)
Date: 1975

LA BATTAGLIA DI LEGNANO

Federico	Nicola Ghiuselev
Rolando	Matteo Manuguerra
Lida	Katia Ricciarelli
Arrigo	José Carreras

Chorus and Orchestra of the Österreichischer Rundfunk, cond. Lamberto Gardelli
Label: Philips 422 435-2 (2CDs)
Date: 1977

LUISA MILLER

Walter	Gwynne Howell
Rodolfo	Plácido Domingo
Federica	Elena Obraztsova
Wurm	Wladimiro Ganzarolli
Miller	Renato Bruson
Luisa	Katia Ricciarelli

Chorus and Orchestra of the Royal Opera House, Covent Garden, cond. Lorin Maazel
Label: DG 459 481-2 (2CDs)
Date: 1979

STIFFELIO

Stiffelio	José Carreras
Lina	Sylvia Sass
Stankar	Matteo Manuguerra
Jorg	Wladimiro Ganzarolli

Chorus and Orchestra of the Österreichischer Rundfunk, cond. Lamberto Gardelli

Label: Philips 422 432-2 (2CDs)
Date: 1979

*RIGOLETTO

Duke	Giuseppe Di Stefano
Rigoletto	Tito Gobbi
Gilda	Maria Callas
Sparafucile	Nicola Zaccaria

Chorus and Orchestra of the Teatro alla Scala, cond. Tullio Serafin
Label: EMI CDS 556 327-2 (2CDs)
Date: 1955

*IL TROVATORE

Di Luna	Rolando Panerai
Leonora	Maria Callas
Azucena	Fedora Barbieri
Manrico	Giuseppe Di Stefano

Chorus and Orchestra of the Teatro alla Scala, cond. Herbert von Karajan
Label: EMI 556 333-2 (2CDs)
Date: 1956

*LA TRAVIATA

Violetta	Ileana Cotrubas
Flora	Stefania Malagù
Alfredo	Plácido Domingo
Germont	Sherrill Milnes

Chorus and Orchestra of the Bayerische Staatsoper, Munich, cond. Carlos Kleiber
Label: DG 459039-2 (2CDs)
Date: 1976

LES VÊPRES SICILIENNES (Here as *I vespri siciliani*)

Monforte	Sherrill Milnes
Elena	Martina Arroyo
Procida	Ruggero Raimondi
Arrigo	Plácido Domingo

John Alldis Choir, New Philharmonia Orchestra, cond. James Levine
Label: RCA 9026 634922 S (3CDs)
Date: 1973

*SIMON BOCCANEGRA (1881 Version)

Boccanegra	Piero Cappuccilli
Amelia	Mirella Freni
Fiesco	Nicolai Ghiaurov
Adorno	José Carreras
Paolo	José van Dam

Chorus and Orchestra of the Teatro alla Scala, cond. Claudio Abbado
Label: DG 449 752-2 (2CDs)
Date: 1976

AROLDO

Aroldo	Gianfranco Cecchele
Mina	Montserrat Caballé
Egberto	Juan Pons

New York Oratorio Society, Westchester Choral Society, Opera Orchestra of New York, cond. Eve Queler
Label: Sony CD 79 328 (2CDs)
Date: 1979

UN BALLO IN MASCHERA

Riccardo	Plácido Domingo
Renato	Piero Cappuccilli
Amelia	Martina Arroyo
Ulrica	Fiorenza Cossotto
Oscar	Reri Grist

Chorus of the Royal Opera House, Covent Garden, New Philharmonia Orchestra, cond. Riccardo Muti
Label: EMI 56651029 (2CDs)
Date: 1975

*LA FORZA DEL DESTINO (1869 version)

Marquis	Giorgio Surian
Leonora	Mirella Freni
Carlo	Giorgio Zancanaro
Alvaro	Plácido Domingo
Preziosilla	Dolora Zajick
Padre Guardiano	Paul Plishka
Melitone	Sesto Bruscantini

Chorus and Orchestra of the Teatro alla Scala, cond. Riccardo Muti
Label: EMI 7474858 (3CDs)
Date: 1987

DON CARLOS (Five-act French version)

Philippe II	José van Dam
Don Carlos	Roberto Alagna
Posa	Thomas Hampson
Grand Inquisitor	Eric Halfvarsson
Elisabeth	Karita Mattila
Eboli	Waltraud Meier

Choir of the Théâtre du Châtelet, Orchestre de Paris, cond. Antonio Pappano
Label: EMI 556152-2 0 (3CDs)
Date: 1996

*AIDA

Amneris	Fedora Barbieri
Aida	Zinka Milanov
Radames	Jussi Björling
Ramfis	Boris Christoff
Amonasro	Leonard Warren

Chorus and Orchestra of the Teatro dell'Opera di Roma, cond. Jonel Perlea
Label: BMG RCA 8665-2 (3CDs)
Date: 1955

*OTELLO

Otello	Plácido Domingo
Iago	Sherrill Milnes
Desdemona	Renata Scotto
Emilia	Jean Kraft

Ambrosian Opera Chorus, National Philharmonic Orchestra, cond. James Levine
Label: RCA 74321 39501-2 (2CDs)
Date: 1978

*FALSTAFF

Falstaff	Tito Gobbi
Ford	Rolando Panerai
Fenton	Luigi Alva
Alice	Elisabeth Schwarzkopf
Nannetta	Anna Moffo
Quickly	Fedora Barbieri

Philharmonia Chorus and Orchestra, cond. Herbert von Karajan
Label: EMI Classics 567083-2 (2CDs)
Date: 1956

Suggested Further Reading

During Verdi's lifetime there were many important assessments of his work, almost all initially appearing in periodicals. The most influential has been Abramo Basevi's *Studio sulle opere di Giuseppe Verdi* (1859), which deals in technical detail that, although unusual for the period, chimed well with the analytical concerns of our recent past. Nineteenth-century biographies of Verdi were all of the 'anecdotal' kind. The most influential was Arthur Pougin's, which in its Italian translation contained annotations by 'Folchetto' (the journalist Jacopo Caponi) and included a highly unreliable 'autobiographical sketch' supposedly dictated by the composer himself. The annotations by 'Folchetto' also put in place several of the most long-standing myths about the composer's 'patriotic' effect on the masses.

The first sixty years of the twentieth century saw an indispensable series of epistolary and biographical publications. Since the 1960s an important stimulus has come from the Istituto Nazionale di Studi Verdiani in Parma, which has assembled a considerable archive and has published a vast amount of biographical and critical writing. Much of this activity was brought to a larger audience, and magnificently synthesized, in Julian Budden's three-volume commentary on the operas. The most recent full-scale biography is by Mary Jane Phillips-Matz; Frank Walker's biography nevertheless remains a classic of the genre; and John Rosselli's shorter treatment of the life and works has much to offer.

*   *   *

CATALOGUES
Cecil Hopkinson: *A Bibliography of the Works of Giuseppe Verdi, 1813–1901*, i (New York, 1973) [vocal and instrumental works excluding operas]; ii (New York, 1978) [operas]
Martin Chusid: *A Catalog of Verdi's Operas* (Hackensack, NJ, 1974)

LETTERS AND DOCUMENTS
Charles Osborne: *Letters of Giuseppe Verdi* (London, 1971)
Marcello Conati: *Interviews and Encounters with Verdi* (London, 1984)
Marcello Conati and Mario Medici, eds.: *The Verdi-Boito Correspondence* (Chicago, 1994)

BIOGRAPHY, LIFE, AND WORKS
Frank Walker: *The Man Verdi* (London, 1962)
William Weaver: *Verdi: A Documentary Study* (London, 1977)
William Weaver and Martin Chusid, eds.: *The Verdi Companion* (New York, 1979)
David R. B. Kimbell: *Verdi in the Age of Italian Romanticism* (Cambridge, 1981)
Julian Budden: *Verdi* (London, 1985)
Mary Jane Phillips-Matz: *Verdi: A Biography* (Oxford, 1993)
John Rosselli: *Verdi* (Cambridge, 2000)
Barbara Meier: *Verdi* (London, 2003)

ANNALS
Thomas Kaufman: *Verdi and His Major Contemporaries: A Selected Chronology of Performances with Casts* (New York, 1990)

MUSICAL STUDIES
Charles Osborne: *The Complete Operas of Verdi* (London, 1969)
Julian Budden: *The Operas of Verdi*, i: *From* Oberto *to* Rigoletto (London, 1973); ii: *From* Il trovatore *to* La forza del destino (London, 1978); iii: *From* Don Carlos *to* Falstaff (London, 1981)
Pierluigi Petrobelli: *Music in the Theater: Essays on Verdi and Other Composers* (Princeton, NJ, 1994)
Martin Chusid, ed.: *Verdi's Middle Period, 1849–1859: Source Studies, Analysis, and Performance Practice* (Chicago, 1997)
Gilles de Van: *Verdi's Theatre: Creating Drama Through Music* (Chicago, 1998)
Scott Balthazar, ed.: *The Verdi Companion* (Cambridge, 2004)

OPERAS
David Rosen and Andrew Porter, eds.: *Verdi's 'Macbeth': A Sourcebook* (New York, 1984)
Nicholas John, ed.: *Macbeth* (London, 1990); *Rigoletto* (London, 1982); *Il trovatore* (London, 1983); *La traviata* (London, 1981); *Simon Boccanegra* (London, 1985); *Un ballo in maschera* (London, 1990); *The Force of Destiny* (London, 1983); *Don Carlos* (London, 1992); *Aida* (London, 1980); *Otello* (London, 1981); *Falstaff* (London, 1982) [ENO opera guides]
Hans Busch: *Verdi's 'Aida': The History of an Opera in Letters and Documents* (Minneapolis, 1978)
James A. Hepokoski: *Giuseppe Verdi: Otello* (Cambridge, 1987)
Hans Busch: *Verdi's 'Otello' and 'Simon Boccanegra' (revised version) in Letters and Documents* (Oxford, 1988)
James A. Hepokoski: *Giuseppe Verdi: Falstaff* (Cambridge, 1983)
Hans Busch: *Verdi's 'Falstaff' in Letters and Contemporary Reviews* (Bloomington, 1997)